MW01297318

White Gold Laborers

The Spanish Colony of Greeley, Colorado

Left to Right: Domingo Duran, Augustine "Gus" Lopez, unknown child, Moses Espinosa, Ernest Espinosa, standing in truck bed David Lopez, sitting on bumper Tim Garcia, standing next to him Elfego Duran, squatting Edward "Lalo" Lopez, and Frank Torrez.. Courtesy of Robert Duran.

Jody L. Lopez and Gabriel A. Lopez

with Peggy A. Ford

AuthorHouse™
1663 Liberty Drive, Suite 200
Bloomington, IN 47403
www.authorhouse.com
Phone: 1-800-839-8640

AuthorHouse™ UK Ltd.
500 Avebury Boulevard
Central Milton Keynes, MK9 2BE
www.authorhouse.co.uk
Phone: 08001974150

© 2007 Jody L. Lopez & Gabriel A. Lopez with Peggy A.Ford. All rights reserved.

No part of this book may be reproduced, stored in a retrieval system, or transmitted by any means without the written permission of the author.

First published by AuthorHouse 3/29/2007

ISBN: 978-1-4259-9562-1 (sc)

Library of Congress Control Number: 2007901285

Printed in the United States of America
Bloomington, Indiana

This book is printed on acid-free paper.

Dedication

White Gold Laborers is dedicated to our children (Kimberly Dee Barnhill and husband Kevin David Barnhill, Mario Anthony Lopez and wife Diana Alvarado Lopez), and our grandchildren (Angelika Maria, Marivel Augustina, Benicio Gabriel Lopez, and Jacoby Anthony Barnhill).

This book is also dedicated to the remarkable individuals of Greeley's Spanish Colony, so that present and future generations can appreciate their perseverance and achievements.

We offer a special dedication to Peggy Ford for her tireless help and encouragement and for her unflagging belief in the book and in us.

Acknowledgements

Sincerest appreciation to all Spanish Colony residents and their descendents, whose insightful interviews and inspiring memories provided the foundation for this project.

Thanks to the City of Greeley Museums and Municipal Archives for allowing us to access files and research data.

Thank you to Gilbert "Gil" Carbajal for translating material from English to Spanish and for providing Vato and Proverbs sayings.

Thanks to Peggy Ford for her research and interview expertise.

Thank you to JoAnna Stull for her assistance in locating photographs and historic records.

Thank you to Nancy "Nan" Reed for doing a great job of editing this book, her patience, and dedication in making this book easy to read.

Preface

In 1920, a recruiting agent from the Great Western Sugar Company arrived in Hurley, New Mexico, to recruit permanent *stoop laborers* to cultivate and harvest sugar beets in Colorado. Growing sugar beets, known as *White Gold*, was a highly successful and profitable enterprise.

Employing permanent workers was a new concept in the agricultural industry for farmers and workers alike. This raised concerns for the New Mexican Hispanics. If they worked in another state, how long would they be gone? Would it be necessary and possible for the entire family to relocate?

The recruiting agent assured the people there were homes and work for those who permanently moved to Northern Colorado. The agent's proposition was carefully considered; the workers were eager to accept the opportunity to be employed and live in such a prosperous area, because the well being of their families was a priority.

Of necessity, the Great Western Sugar Company entered the housing market by developing *colonias* where the elite of the Hispanic stoop laborers had permanent homes. This arrangement saved the Great Western Sugar Company the high cost of round-trip train fares for migrant workers' transportation. The communities also profited by this arrangement, as it kept the earnings of the stoop laborers in the area's economy. The Great Western Sugar Company built colonies in Colorado, Wyoming, Nebraska, and Montana.

One of the thirteen *colonias* established in Northern Colorado in1924, known as the Spanish Colony, is five miles northwest of Greeley, Colorado. This is the story of that Colony and its remarkable residents.

Introduction

When asked by my son to compile our genealogy, I started with my father's family. I asked relatives about their lives and the lives of my grandparents and great grandparents. My wife, Jody, and I investigated the story of their lives working in the sugar beet fields, on farms, and living in the Spanish Colony. Through research and family input, we began to appreciate the work ethics and cultural teachings handed down to our generation, e.g. my father taught us to say yes or no and mean it, to offer help without being asked. My parents, grandparents, and great grandparents endured hard labor and prejudice, so that we and our children could lead successful, fulfilled lives.

Mexican Americans became a minority in the United States not by immigrating but by being conquered during the Mexican War. At the war's termination, the 1848 Treaty of Guadalupe-Hidalgo guaranteed the rights of these new American citizens, but the treaty was not enforced or maintained. (Moore, Joan W. 1976 *Mexican Americans*. New Jersey: Prentice Hall.)

By 1853, the United States acquired the present states of Texas, New Mexico, Arizona, Utah, Nevada, and parts of Colorado and California. Mexican people living in these areas became Mexican Americans but did not enjoy the full rights and privileges of American citizens.

In 1919, the Great Western Sugar Company, producer of a quarter of the nation's sugar, began recruiting the descendents of the original Mexican-Americans as beet field laborers in Weld County, Colorado. The Hispanics left their homes in New Mexico, Southern Colorado, Texas, Arizona, and Mexico for the promise of work and homes. They encountered harsh realities as *stoop laborers*, and were often treated as outcasts, not equals. Despite hardships they stayed, because their survival depended on it. "We worked hard; we had to, or we starved," relates Moses Espinosa.

The Hispanic beet workers learned to be content with giving the best they had to offer. "When I was ten, I used to cry every time we had to work in the field. But once there we did our best to finish the day," recalls Kate Espinosa Lopez Cassel. Their hard work in agriculture helped Greeley's economy grow, although, as Tito

Garcia, Jr. remembers, "We were poor, but we didn't know that. We were happy."

Contrary to the 1920 stereotype of Hispanics, they were not dumb. They improved their lives by taking advantage of the education available to them. According to Tito Garcia, Jr., when a child didn't want to go to school, the parents would say, "When the Lord left the world, he said, 'May the smart ones live off the dumb ones.' In other words, go to school and become one of the smart ones."

"It was not cultural differences but a language barrier which separated us from the rest of the Greeley community," said Tito Garcia, Jr. "The [Anglos] thought we were stupid, because our English was bad." The Hispanics learned and improved their English, becoming bilingual.

Being *stoop laborers* in the field was not the workers' ultimate dream, and through sacrifice and determination, many overcame racial discrimination, inequities in wages, deplorable housing conditions, and personal disappointments to excel in a variety of professions. It has truly been our privilege to preserve the Spanish Colony residents' legacy, their memories, and their stories compiled from recorded audio and video interviews and printed resources.

Notes

- To clearly reflect the events and temper of the times, information was gleaned from *Through the Leaves*, a monthly publication of the Great Western Sugar Company.

- Interviews with Spanish Colony residents have been paraphrased with permission from interviewees.

- Multiple terms have been used in the research to describe the ethnic and cultural groups which were part of this period of history. (See Appendix A.) The terms, as used in this book, are listed and defined below, followed by a generalized time line of terms.

> Alien - A person born in another country; a foreigner
> American - A citizen of the United States
> Anglo - A non-Hispanic, white inhabitant of the United States
> Chicano - An American of Mexican descent living in the U.S.
> Citizen - A person born in a country or one who has passed a test to become a member of that country
> Deport - To force a person to leave a place or country; to send an alien home
> Hispanic/Hispano - Relating to or being a person of Latin American descent living in the U.S.
> Immigrant - A person who comes to live in a different country from the country where he was born
> Latino - A native or inhabitant of Latin American origin living in the U.S.
> Legal Alien - Someone who is not a citizen of a country, but who has papers from the government allowing residence in that country
> Mexican - A native or naturalized resident of Mexico
> Mexican-American - An American citizen originally from Mexico or of Mexican descent
> Migrant - A person who moves his home often within the same country, usually to find a new job

Spanish-American - U.S. citizens whose first language is Spanish

Wetback - (*Mojado* in Spanish) - Often used in a negative way to refer to a Mexican worker who comes to the U. S. illegally by swimming the Rio Grande River at the U.S.-Mexican border; wetback has come to mean any illegal Mexican worker in the United States

TIME LINE OF COMMONLY USED TERMS
1920s and 1930s - Mexicans
1940s - Latinos
1950s - Mexican Americans
1960s and 1970s - Chicanos
1980s onward - Hispanics

Contents

Chapter 1

We Were Promised Jobs and Homes

Taken from *Through The Leaves,* November 1929, cover page. The topped sugar beets were placed in the center of six rows and the crew loaded these beets onto a trailer pulled by horses, later by trucks. Courtesy of City of Greeley Museums.

The Spanish-speaking worker was an important factor in the development of American agriculture. His toil built her railroads, cultivated and harvested her crops, and developed her resources. His labor was considered necessary, but his reward was small; profits were large for all but him.[1]

From the early history of the development of agriculture in Northern Colorado, the Spanish-American sugar beet *(white gold)* laborer played a vital role in making Northern Colorado the "Sugar Bowl," one of the most productive and profitable agricultural areas in the United States.

Sugar beets were first cultivated in the 17th through 19th centuries in Europe. Before World War I, Germany was a world agriculture leader, in part due to her sugar industry.[2] In 1830, sugar beets were introduced into the United States. An 1838 report by the United States Committee of Agriculture indicated that no country in the world was better adapted to sugar beet growing than the United States because of its ideal soil and climate.[3]

In 1859, a Swedish farmer living southwest of Denver on the South Platte River planted the first known sugar beets in Colorado. Colorado proved to be an ideal place to produce sugar. Sugar beets were first planted in Weld County in 1872.[4] Colorado sugar beets were superior to those grown in Germany, averaging more tons per acre with greater sugar content. When Congress passed the 1897 Dingly Tariff Act, which placed a duty of 78.87 percent on imported sugar, it became cheaper to process sugar locally than to import cane sugar.[5]

Former Colorado Governor Benjamin H. Eaton was a pioneer resident of Weld County, a member of the Union Colony, and an early advocate of the sugar beet industry. He proposed that if sugar beet promoters would offer $8.00 per ton instead of $4.00 per ton, more farmers would stop raising potatoes at 50 cents per 100 ctw (100 lbs. weight). Potatoes had been the first viable cash crop in the Greeley district.

Charles E. Mitchell, a druggist in Grand Junction, Colorado, built the first Colorado sugar factory in 1899. The first sugar factory built in Northern Colorado was in Loveland in Larimer County in

1901. By 1901/1902, the first factories in Weld County were built in Eaton and Greeley.

At first, Greeley resisted the sugar beet industry. The local citizens did not want their 30-year utopian town invaded by field and factory workers who were sometimes illiterate and, frequently, were immigrants or migrants; however, progress and profits promised by the new *white gold* crop prevailed over all protests.[6] By 1902, Greeley's first sugar beet crop was ready to harvest.

Raising sugar beets was a labor-intensive operation. The first laborers were the farmers and their families; however, they soon learned more hands were needed. One sugar beet seed produced multiple sprouts. Farmers realized that the thinning, hoeing, blocking, and topping of sugar beets was a back-breaking job from the planting through the harvest.

Migrant laborers were the obvious answer to this dilemma. For a few seasons, laborers were recruited from neighboring states. By 1901/1902 German-Russian immigrants and their large families came to Colorado to work the fields. The 1902 *The Greeley Tribune* reported that seventy German-Russian families had arrived by train to work the sugar beets.[7] By 1910, many of the German-Russians who had worked in Northern Colorado as migrant workers had settled there permanently, purchasing farms and growing sugar beets as owners and growers.

The next immigrant wave was the Japanese who, like the German-Russians, first worked as migrant laborers beginning in 1904. They also saved their money and bought their own farms. The new German-Russian and Japanese landowners now found themselves in need of field workers. Spanish-Americans from southwestern United States and later Mexican Nationals were recruited to fill this void.[8] Spanish-American migrant workers became known as the proven laborers, reliable regardless of weather, living conditions, and prejudicial treatment.

Beginning in 1913, the Great Western Sugar Company began publishing *Through The Leaves*. This monthly magazine contained articles relevant to sugar beet production, all aspects of sugar beet planting, and innovative ideas and techniques for sugar beet farmers. There were articles covering a variety of subjects, e.g. "The Ideal Hired Man", "The Beet Labor Question", "Irrigation Water and the

Spread of Weed Seed", "Official Investigation Shows Value of Tractor", "Meteorological Report", "What is Good Farming", "Common Faults in the Treatment of Labor by Farmers", "Why Fall Plow", "Pulling and Topping and What Can Be Done to Increase the Tons Per Acre".

United States farm production accelerated during World War I. A *Through the Leaves,* January 1918, article noted [Article title unknown]

> The nation as a whole is being urged to increase farm products… Colorado being in the front rank in domestic sugar production naturally is expected to do the most. A subsequent article in the same issue, "Labor Question for 1918" noted, We believe few realize the important part this beet labor has taken every year in the general labor supply, and the serious shortage that might exist if the beet acreage should be curtailed to any considerable extent.

Increased production required more laborers not only for beets, but also for other farm produce such as onions, potatoes, and hay. Laborers were also needed for general farm work. Many *Through The Leaves* articles were published to instruct farmers in training farm laborers. *Through The Leaves* continually noted the prejudicial treatment of Spanish-American and Mexican workers and advised farmers on the importance of treating this premium work force with respect and dignity.

> A June 1918, p.274, *Through The Leaves* editorial reported, A number of our farmers are taking a little time and trouble to teach some of their Mexican and Russian beet workers to help them with their farm work. The Mexicans are making very good teamsters, and as there are a great many of these people available, the labor problem can be largely solved by the farmers themselves if they will be willing to take a little time for the coaching of this untrained help.

Through The Leaves repeatedly noted that many farmers were disrespectful to Hispanics and routinely treated them inhumanely. The farmers' treatment of laborers directly affected the amount of beet tonnage produced. Farmers who mistreated their laborers produced less tonnage, and it was hard to hire laborers for the next year.

The *Through The Leaves*, April 1919, p.187, article, "News from Factory and Field," stated that,

> The supply of Russian help is limited, but there is plenty of Mexicans. In this connection we are finding that this year, more than ever before, the farmer with good house for his beet help is getting the better quality. Just one instance occurred recently three different families (all good workers), who had worked at different times for a beet grower, each refused to consider this contract this year because of poor housing conditions... This matter of living quarters is uppermost in the minds of most of these laborers, and must be given consideration if you expect the better class of workers.

On investigation, the Great Western Sugar Company found that labor housing was often farm shacks as small as 8' x 8' with a single door and sometimes a tiny window. If, however, laborers had good houses to live in while doing the farming work, they were more content and willing to sign a contract for the next season.

> The solution of the problem is plain and easy, and is being solved by advanced farmers today. It is simply this: Arrange to employ your labor the year round and reduce the amount of extra labor during harvest to the minimum. This is entirely practicable, but involves the reconstruction of our system of farming, a reconstruction which we will be forced by circumstances to do. (*Through The Leaves*, "A Labor Problem", August 1919, p. 399)

The permanent laborer proved to be proficient at beet work and general farm work. At the end of the 1918 season, the Great Western Sugar Company and the farmers began to realize the benefits to having permanent experienced workers.

The Great Western Sugar Company in *Through The Leaves*, August 1919, p.379, "Beet Laborer at $20.50," wrote, "Steps will be taken to prevent misrepresentation on the part of solicitors and sub-agents regarding the principle requirements of the labor contract, both as to work and as to pay and concessions to be allowed."

Improved living conditions became a major concern of Great Western and the

farmers when migrant workers became year-round residents. In November of 1919, in a *Through The Leaves,* editorial page, N. R. McCreery wrote,

> During the past year or two a great deal has been done in the way of building better houses, but there are still a large number of shacks that are not fit habitation for human beings... The facts are, that if we are to continue to grow beets, labor for the hand work must be secured aside from the American help. And if these people are to come back year after year they must receive fair treatment at the hands of the people they work for... We want to make a plea for tolerance and fairness on the part of the growers.

By the end of 1919, the treatment of the laborers had not changed significantly. Many farmers still refused the Great Western Sugar Company's advice, and their uncaring mentality toward their laborers resulted in lower crop yields and serious economic repercussions. Great Western continued to admonish the farmers in article after monthly article and repeatedly emphasized the Biblical golden rule.

In the December 1919, p.603, *Through The Leaves* article, "If You Treat 'Em Rough," illustrated two farmers' treatment of their laborers. One farmer was hard-headed, believing he owed no man anything except the wages he had agreed to pay. The matter of treatment never occurred to him. He furnished a place to sleep and food, both of which were low-cost and lacking in variety. The houses were tumbledown, often without glass in the windows, dirty, and un-kempt.

The second farmer, a neighbor of the first farmer, was exactly opposite in character. He was a careful businessman, but he was noted as an exceptional farmer in his methods of cropping and caring for his land. He employed a number of men throughout the year, and at harvest time, the number increased considerably. His laborer housing was a model of neatness. He provided good housing, healthy food, and fair compensation.

As long as there were more men than jobs, the first farmer got along well, but when labor was scarce, the laborers could choose where to work. In this case, the second farmer had all the labor he needed and got his crop in, while the first farmer lost his entire crop.

This example illustrated that farmers with a prejudicial mentality paid a price; on the other hand, the laborers stayed with caring farmers year after year. The Mexican laborers proved they could competently perform the farm work, and with proper training, the farmers could utilize them to their full potential.

> The day has gone by even on the farms when hired men can be treated like beasts of burden. The practice never did pay even in the worst of times, for the best men invariably drifted to the best places and no one ever made much profit out of low-grade labor. (*Through The Leaves,* "If you Treat 'Em Rough", December 1919, p.606)

The June 1924, p. 339 article, "The Mexican as a Farm Hand", *Through The Leaves*, commented,

> Generally speaking, we have had the notion that the Mexican was no good with a team… Those who want to work usually learn quickly and, with a little time and patience on the part of the farmer, they develop into good farm hands.One farmer said... 'I never had a better farm hand than this Mexican. He takes interest in all farm work and that is more than you can say for some of our farm hands.'… The Mexican has played an important part in getting the crop in this spring and he will be worth a great deal during hay and wheat harvests. It is true that they are "green" and awkward at work with which they are unfamiliar, but those who are willing and anxious to learn will soon reward an employer for a few days of his time and patience spent instructing them.

Taken from *Through The Leaves* April 1928, p. 174. Photos of Hispanics performing a variety of jobs in the fields. Courtesy of City of Greeley Museums.

In 1920, Ynez Lopez Sr., with his five children including his oldest child, Francisco, and daughter-in-law, Martina, and their children, Juanita Lopez and Augustine "Gus" Lopez, were contracted as laborers for Mr. David Kelly who owned several farms in the Greeley area. Ynez began working on Kelly's farm near Galeton and worked for Mr. Kelly nine years.

Mrs. Katherine Casey Stewart of LaSalle, Colorado, told Gabriel Lopez, "My grandfather, David Kelly, had a lot of respect for your grandfather, Francisco Lopez, and cared about the whole family. When I arrived with my mother in 1929, I got to meet the Lopez's. Your great grandfather, Ynez Lopez, gave me my first pet, a lamb, which I named George. I really liked that man. Your people worked very hard. I remember my grandfather and grandmother cared for the Lopez family, and the farmers around us cared for their help, because they needed good workers, or their farms would not prosper as well. My grandfather and your great grandfather cared for each other a lot, and that is why I remember the Lopez family. I remember my grandfather and grandmother brought Mr. Lopez and

8

family into our house to eat. That is how much my grandparents liked the Lopezes."

From 1920 through 1931, the Great Western Sugar Company's articles in *Through The Leaves* encouraged farmers to care for their help, patiently teach them farming skills, respect them and their families, and provide good housing. A good worker-farmer relationship would result in mutual respect and prosperity.

Those who came before 1920 were migrant workers. They lived in primitive, sub-standard summer-only shacks lacking in most amenities. As most migrant workers would go home after the beet harvest, there was no need for farmers to improve seasonal labor housing.

It was in these seasonal houses the new permanent stoop labor force was housed. Workers complained bitterly of the terrible housing conditions. They stuffed the cracks in the walls with paper and rags to keep warm and dry in the winter. The workers constructed furniture, shelving, and other household items from wooden crates.

As the sugar beet industry boomed, good housing was an incentive that enabled beet growers and the Great Western Sugar Company to recruit, train, and keep their skilled, productive workers happy on a permanent basis, no longer needing to rely on migrant workers with little or no experience with sugar beets.

These are examples of the kind of beet houses provided by some farmers. Last year beet labor was asked to and did live in all three of these shacks. It was impossible to get good labor for these contracts.

Through The Leaves, March 1920, p.186. Courtesy of City of Greeley Museums.

References

1. Maddux, Hazel C. (1932, June). *Some Conditions Which Influence the Mexican Children in Greeley, Colorado, and its Vicinity.* (Masters Degree thesis, Colorado State College). pp.18, 19.

2. Rolph. George M. (1917). *Something About Sugar*

3. Steinel, Alvin Theodore. (1926). *History of Agriculture In Colorado 1858-1926.* pp. 284, 285.

4. Shwayder, Carol Rein. (1987). *Sugar Beet Story 1901-1907. Weld County Old and New.* Vol. 11. p. 1, 2, 3.

5. Rolph, George M. (1917). *Something About Sugar:* p. 159.

6. Shwayder, Carol Rein. (1987). *Sugar Beet Story 1901-1907. Weld County Old and New.* Vol. 11. p. 6

7. Shwayder, Carol Rein. (1987). *Weld County Old and New People and Places 1870 through 1881.* Vol. 3. p .403.

8. Hugner, Henry. (1927). A *History of the Beet Sugar Industry of Northern Colorado.* p. 173, 185,190, 192.

Chapter 2

The Founding of the Colony

From *Through the Leaves*, November 1924, p. 571. Picture shows adobe homes being built or already built. Photo courtesy of City of Greeley Museums.

In order to secure a better class of beet worker and market Northern Colorado as the ideal place to work in the sugar beet fields, the Great Western Sugar Company responded to the need to provide desirable living conditions for laborers and their families. The resulting colonies supported the reconstruction of the farming system. The Company decided to build colonies in, Colorado, Wyoming, Nebraska, and Montana for highly skilled workers who would become year-round residents.

In 1922, Lester Maddux, the manager of the Great Western Sugar Company of Fort Morgan, Morgan County, Colorado, established the first "adobe Mexican beet workers' Colony in the U.S."[1] Providing Mexican beet workers with inexpensive but satisfactory colony housing proved successful in Morgan County. This led to the construction of other colonies in Weld County at Ault, Eaton, Fort Lupton, Gilcrest, Gill, Greeley, Hudson, Johnstown, Kersey, Milliken, and Wattenberg.

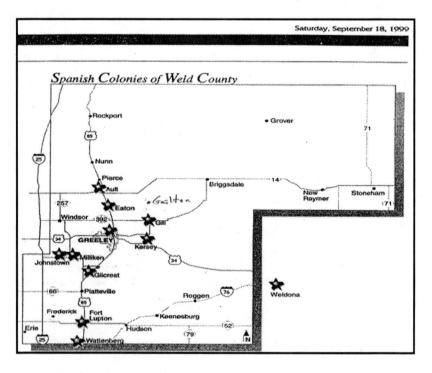

Map of Spanish Colonies in Weld County. Courtesy *The Greeley Tribune* September 18, 1999, p.5.

The Great Western Sugar Company, in 1924, purchased land northwest of Greeley, Colorado, for a *colonia* or colony. It became known as the Spanish Colony and is representative of the communities established by the Great Western Sugar Company. It is located northwest of Greeley at the intersection of O St. and 25th Avenue which isolated or segregated Mexican residents in the Colony from the town of Greeley. The townspeople did not wish to have the Mexican residents near the town.[2]

Only families highly recommended by the sugar beet foremen were invited to live in the colony. No one was allowed to lease or purchase a building site until a field supervisor vouched for his character. *Through the Leaves,* in a November 1924 article, "Practicing a Labor Preachment", p. 562, reported,

The better class of labor will undertake to build a home of their own and persist until they have completed it and paid for it, a preferred class of workers is secured for these colonies. In the communities where colonies have been located appreciation of the movement has been general. 1. It gives added assurance that the community will have a number of experienced beet workers from year to year. 2. That class of beet help cannot only raise a better crop than inexperienced labor but it can do more and better general farm work, such as harvesting hay and grain, irrigating and cultivating. 3. It keeps in the district the money earned there. Colonists do not take their wages away after the beet harvest.

Those not selected to live in the Colony found housing in nearby towns; for example, Hispanics settled in north and east Greeley. Those who worked on farms miles away from any town lived in tenant houses on the farms.

The Spanish Colony was planned to have one 16' wide and three 30' wide streets. There were three one-way streets which connected to form a large square. The first road, North 25th Avenue Ct., was 30' wide and used for northbound traffic. The 16' wide street at the north end of the Colony had no name, and it was a one-way street going west to 26th Avenue. The next street, North 26th Avenue, 30' wide, was used for southbound traffic. The fourth street, 30' wide, named M street, was a partial one-way street going east until it intersected North 25th Avenue Ct. and became a two-way street to North 25th Avenue. (See illustration below)

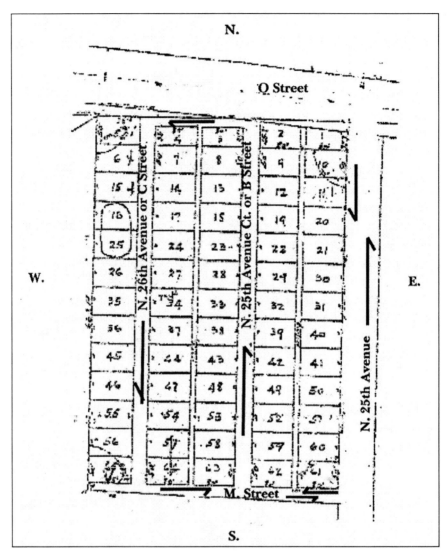

Espanola Sub-Division (Spanish Colony of Greeley, Colorado). The photo shows the number and sizes of the Lots. Map courtesy of Palmer Lopez.

The colony land was platted into 65 Lots 100' deep x 50' wide with 10' on each end for easements. Of the 65 Lots in the Colony, four Lots were allocated for two parks, Lots 40 and 41 on the west side of the colony and Lots 37 and 44 on the east side. Wells were drilled and hand pumps installed in each park for drinking and household water. A third pump for irrigation was on Lot 5. The water pump was a Model-T engine and pumped the water into the irrigation ditches in the Colony. The Colony exists today with the original platting, although some street names have been changed.

Permission from the railroad was needed to construct the irrigation ditches. The ditches crossed railroad property located at the north end of the Colony. The Colony's residents used the Model-T engine irrigation pump on Lot 5 to divert water from the main ditch into smaller ditches in the alleys and streets in front of the homes to water gardens, trees, and flowers. Residents shared the expenses for the gas and oil that the pump needed to run.

The Great Western Sugar Company contracted with the beet laborers to build their own houses of two rooms or more. The contract required the laborers to lease their homes for five years and establish permanent residence. At the termination of the leases, the Great Western Sugar Company required the homes be purchased. Some residents bought multiple homes and rented them to those who could not afford to buy their own homes.

In 1924, plans for two-room adobe dwellings, along with the supplies to build the homes, were given to the laborers. (See illustration below.)

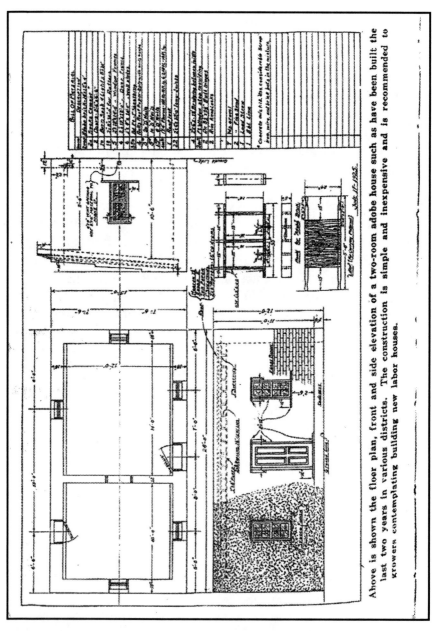

Plan of an adobe home used by the colonists to build their homes. From *Through the Leaves, October 1923, p. 395 and July 1925,* p. 319. Photo courtesy of City of Greeley Museums.

To achieve a uniform appearance, the houses were built 10' from the front property line in north-south rows. The front doors faced east or west, and all exterior walls were painted white. (See illustration below.)

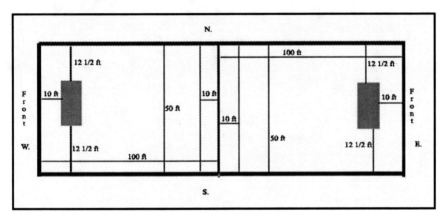

Graphic created by Gabriel Lopez.

Beginning in April 1924, adobe bricks were made and baked for forty homes using sand, dirt, short straw, and water. Wooden brick molds were approximately 18" long by 12" wide by 4" or 5" thick.

Adobe bricks being stacked and sun dried. *Through The Leaves,* October 1923, p. 395. Courtesy City of Greeley Museums

A September 22, 1924, *The Greeley Tribune* article, "Adobe Houses Being Built," reported on forty adobe structures under construction in the "Mexican village" just across the Dixon Bridge, north of the Cache La Poudre River and northwest of Greeley on the Windsor road. Rain and snow did not diminish the colonists' dreams to build their homes; the residents of the Spanish Colony worked to build houses even in very cold weather.

The *Through the Leaves* article "Ingenuity and Perseverance Shown by Mexicans in Constructing Adobe Homes", November, 1924, p. 569, related that, although believed otherwise, adobe farm soil did not make good adobe bricks because of cracking; however, other kinds of farm soil could be used. "Soil with a large admixture of sand makes the best brick."

The article in *Through the Leaves*, November 1924, p. 571 continued with photos and texts illustrating construction steps as shown below.

"Fig. 1 shows the first operation in brick making. The wet mud must be puddled thoroughly with a mortar hoe or by tramping it with bare feet. At the same time straw is mixed with it. Some prefer to mix a large batch and let it stand over night others haul it as soon as it is mixed to where the bricks are moulded."

"Fig. 2 The moulder presses the mud into the eight corners of the twin mould with his fists and then smooths off the top of the wet bricks."

"Fig. 3. The next operation is to pull off the mould form letting the two green bricks lie in that flat position to dry out for two to three days. At the expiration of this time they are tilted into the position of the bricks immediately behind the moulder."

Fig. 4

"Fig. 4, in order to expose more surface to the drying effect of the air...Note that they are piled on edge and air spaces left between the bricks to permit their drying out thoroughly. These piles are covered with straw and boards to prevent damage by rain. Piles should be made from north to south, so that the sun can shine on two sides and one end of the pile. Usually the bricks were left in the pile for two weeks or more, before they were laid into the wall, as shown in Fig. 5."

Fig. 5. "A cement foundation one foot high is set on top of the ground and the bricks are laid onto it. The door frames and window frames are made of 2 x12 planks with outside edge flush with the outside wall line. The walls are made from 1in. to 18 in. thick, (according to the size of brick) and are usually run to the same height on all four sides of the house."

"Fig. 6 and 7, all four walls extend above the roof. Most of the houses have been built in that manner. Those pictures also show method of placing rafters, sheathing, and dirt roof covered with 1 ½ in. of cement plaster. The galvanized iron spouts that project conduct the water from the roof through the rear wall and drop it far enough beyond that wall to prevent any washing."

Fig. 8

"An ingenious device pictured in Fig. 8 is used to elevate bricks, mud and mortar to top of building."

Fig 9

"Fig. 9 shows houses complete with roof in place, ready for outside plaster or stucco. Usually 6-penny nails were driven into the - brick with heads protruding ¼" to serve as a binder like lath to retain the stucco." (Rocks were used as well as nail spikes in the Greeley Spanish Colony)

The first 40 homes of the Greeley Spanish Colony were built from September to December 1924. The first trustees were either appointed by the Great Western Sugar Company, or elected by the residents of the colony. The trustees of the Colony had assembled four groups of men to build each row of homes.

The roofs were 13½" thick and consisted of 1" sheathing on the bottom of 2" x 8" x 15" joists, with additional 1" thick sheathing on top of the joist. Next, tarpaper was laid and a 1½" thick layer of mortar was spread over the tarpaper. Stucco 2" thick was spread over the entire structure inside and outside to complete the house.

The women and older children helped if they were able. The competition to finish each row was intense. The simple two-room plan made it possible for the families to move out of their inadequate farm housing and into better constructed permanent homes.

In the beginning, most homes had only hard-packed dirt floors. Women sprinkled water evenly over the floor to control the dust and refresh and preserve the hard-packed surface so it could be swept. Later, when it became financially possible, wooden floors were constructed with 2" x 6" x 12" joists, overlaid with wood planking or sheathing when available.

The majority of the colonists built two rooms the first year and later added other rooms and decorative features. The colonists also took exceptional interest in cultivating flowers and bushes in their yards.

Finished stuccoed adobe, by its nature, deteriorates over time when exposed to the elements and requires constant repair. At times, economic difficulties prevented a resident from painting or making the needed repairs, especially during the Depression Era of the 1930s.

The Carbajal family in front of their adobe home in the Colony. Back row L to R: Sara and Manuel. Front row L to R: Maggie, Connie, and Gil. Notice the stucco is gone, exposing the bricks' mortar. Photo courtesy of Gilbert "Gil" Carbajal.

Shortly after the homes in the Spanish Colony were built, the trustees called a meeting of the residents to discuss writing a constitution. The trustees wrote the Constitution for the Spanish

28

Colony, and it seemed as legal to the Colony residents as the Constitution of the United States. They were very proud of their Constitution. It is interesting to note the title of their Constitution: *Constitution and Rules of the Spanish Colony Neighbors of Greeley, Colorado.* (See Appendix B.) It was not called the Mexican Colony, as most Greeley residents referred to it, but was officially named the Spanish Colony.

Children were sent door-to-door to notify the residents of the Colony of any public meetings. Each family had a right to bring up matters related to the Colony at these meetings. The Constitution called for at least three annual meetings, scheduled when important matters needed to be brought before the people. The Colony had commissioners or trustees and school commissioners. The Colony Commissioners' duties were: 1. Keep law and order, 2. Report violations of the law to the County Sheriff, and 3. Keep the Colony clean.

Five of the trustees elected in 1929 have been identified. (See Appendix B.)

(See following illustrations.)

Ynez (Inez) Lopez Sr., President, lived on Lot 42 and was born in Mexico circa 1870. He died in Greeley on July 3, 1938.

Ynez Lopez   Photo courtesy of Arnulfo "Nudy" Lopez.

Dimas Salazar, Secretary, lived in the colony on Lot 20 and then moved to Denver, where he later died.

Dimas Salazar. Photo courtesy of Beatrice Salazar.

(Photo Unavailable)

Daniel Martinez, Treasurer, lived on Lot 34. He moved to Erie, Colorado, and was believed to have died there.

Esperidion Gonzales, Trustee, lived on Lot 61. He moved to California and then to New Mexico where he was believed to have died.

Esperidion Gonzales. Photo courtesy of Josie Garcia.

Rufino Ortiz, Trustee, lived on Lot 54. He died on December 12, 1947, in Greeley, Colorado.

Rufino Ortiz. Photo courtesy of Sam & Viola Lopez.

From its beginning, many responsible men of the Spanish Colony filled the roll of trustee or commissioner. Eventually, Alvin Garcia took over all responsibilities for the management of the Colony, and, under his direction, the Colony received natural gas, electricity, sewer and water services.

In 1929, the five-year contract between the Great Western Sugar Company and the colony residents expired. The processes to move the ownership of the colony residents began with a letter sent by the Great Western Sugar Company. The letter sent to Ynez Lopez on April 25, 1930 by the Great Western Sugar Company stated:

I am handing you herewith Warranty Deed covering Lot 32 in Espanola Subdivision. You should have this deed filed with the County Clerk and Recorder.

A copy of the letter follows.

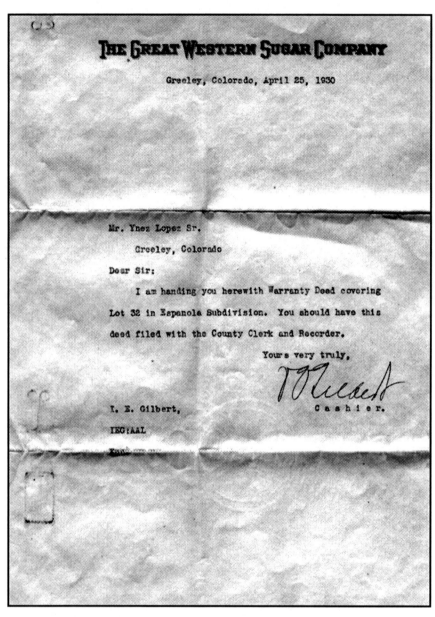

THE GREAT WESTERN SUGAR COMPANY

Greeley, Colorado, April 25, 1930

Mr. Ynez Lopez Sr.

Greeley, Colorado

Dear Sir:

I am handing you herewith Warranty Deed covering Lot 32 in Espanola Subdivision. You should have this deed filed with the County Clerk and Recorder.

Yours very truly,

Cashier.

I. E. Gilbert,

IEG:AAL

A letter from the Great Western Sugar Company to Ynez Lopez Sr. telling him to take the deed to the County Clerk and Recorder. Photo courtesy of Palmer Lopez. (See Appendix C)

The Spanish Colony, or Espanola Subdivision, was incorporated, and the plat of the Colony filed with the Weld County Clerk and Recorder on June 20, 1929. The colonists then began to purchase their homes and record the deeds at the Weld County Clerk and Recorder's office. A copy of Ynez Lopez's deed follows.

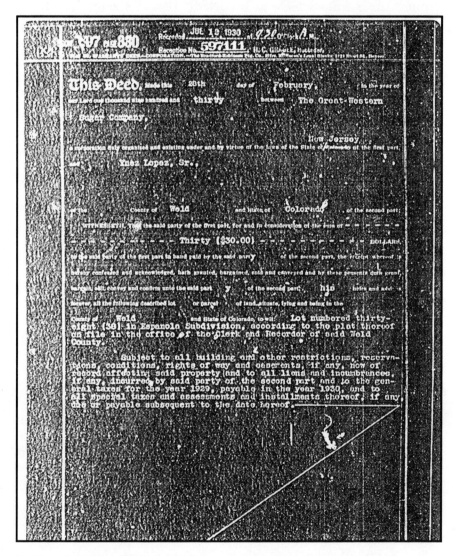

Ynez Lopez's deed from 1928 for Lot 38. Copy acquired from the Weld County Clerk and Records Office. Photo courtesy of Gabriel Lopez.

For the first fifteen years the colony's needs were meet by its residents. As time passed, improvements were needed which were beyond the capabilities of the colonists.

In the spring of 1940, the residents of the Spanish Colony approached the County Commissioners asking them to make improvements at the Colony, especially regarding sanitation. In 1941, the County Commissioners sent Dr. John Fountain, a county physician, and Roy Davidson, a county health engineer, to assess what improvements were needed. Based on their findings, they suggested the Spanish Colony petition the Farm Security Administration (FSA) for funding to make improvements.

The Greeley Tribune printed an article on Sept 9, 1941, p.1, "FSA Spanish Housing Plan Is Explained", which reported:

FSA officials and engineers who investigated the possibility of making the improvements said reconstruction to provide water and modern sewage disposal in the houses would be inadvisable and not accepted by the FSA office in Washington. They gave crowded conditions in the Colony and improper heating in the houses as two reasons why plumbing could not be installed in the present Colony, and proposed that the entire village be eliminated and a new one constructed to provide the better living conditions which the colonists desired ... "Everyone in the Colony would be benefited from the health standpoint by this movement which grew out of attempts to improve sanitation and has grown bigger." Dr. Fountain said, 'I am all for it from the standpoint of health and improving living conditions.'

The 1924 Colony would have been demolished and a new one constructed. Alvin Garcia said, "I remember that day. They were going to build us a new Colony just north of where it is now across O Street and up the hill a ways." In a meeting, colonists were given the choice of remaining where they were or relocating to a new colony. Alvin continued, "We voted to have the new Colony. Everyone was so excited to have new homes, and I wanted a new store. They showed us plans for the new Colony. It would have been beautiful."

After the vote, the construction began on the new colony. Property lines were staked out, and roads were built. Just as construction began, the tragic events of December 7, 1941, the bombing of Pearl Harbor, halted all development.

The construction of the new Colony would have cost approximately $160,000. There would have been a maximum of 80 homes, with Lot sizes of 100' by 200'. These homes were to vary in size from one to three rooms with rent approximately $8.00 a month, including all utilities, a refrigerator, and a stove. The children would still have attended the Gipson School. The plan for the new Colony included a community hall, a clinic with a part-time nurse and a craft shop so residents could build their own furniture.[3]

Although the new colony was not built, gas service was installed in 1942 in the original Colony, followed by water and sewer service in 1956. Cisterns were used from 1940 to 1956 for water, because the wells and pumping equipment deteriorated, allowing the river water to contaminate the drinking water. Thereafter, water was delivered to the Colony's cisterns in barrels by wagon.

Alvin Garcia said, "I don't know for sure, but because of the bombing of Pearl Harbor and the war starting, I think they forgot about the new Colony. I am sure the money and material went to the war effort, but we endured, and the Colony eventually got sanitation and plumbing, and it is still there."

2004 print of Map of Greeley Spanish Colony.

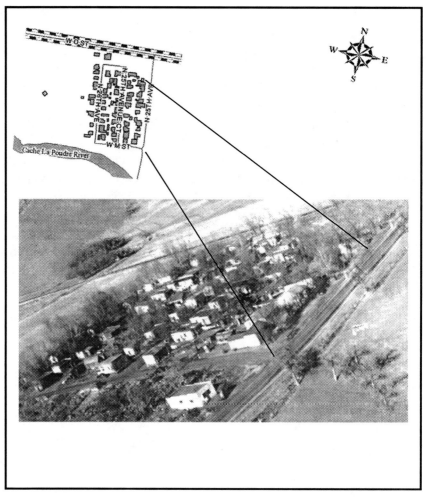

1949 Aerial photo of the Greeley Spanish Colony. Photo courtesy of Alvin Garcia.

References

1. Maddux, C. V. (1924, June). Beet Workers Colonize. *Through the Leaves,* p. 323.

2. Ford, Peggy A. Employment Brought Most Migration. (1999, September 18*). Weld County Past Times, The Greeley Tribune.* p. T16.

3. FSA Spanish Colony Rebuilding Costing $160,000 Gets General Okeh, Decision Up to Colonists. (1941, September 9). *The Greeley Tribune.* pp. 1, 2.

Chapter 3

Field Work and Relations with the Unions

"Stoop laborers" thinning the sugar beets, using short handled hoes. This is a good visual illustration of the meaning of the word "Stoop Laborers." Photo courtesy of Colorado State Archives.

Field Work

The seasonal work of the sugar beet field worker, or stoop laborer, began in late March or early April after the farmer properly cultivated his grounds by plowing and disking. After the sugar beet seeds were planted, the stoop laborer was contracted to care for the fields.

Most laborers took their families to the farm for the work season. The first job was to clean and air out the tenant house and to stock it with food, bedding, and household items for the season. The wife often stayed and cared for the younger children while the laborer and his older children cleaned the fields of tall weeds, pulling them by hand. She also brought water and meals to her family working in the field.

Ed & Jess Esparza eating burritos in the back of a truck in the late 1930s. Photo courtesy of Gilbert "Gil" Carbajal.

For some contract laborers, the fields were close to their homes, which allowed them to get water and meals from the house and to use the outhouse.

As the fields of sugar beets grew, the laborers began their backbreaking work in the hot sun, which involved several time-consuming and important steps. These included the *first hoeing* when beets were blocked and thinned, the *second hoeing* which cleaned out any *doubles* left from the first hoeing and new weeds which had sprouted, and the *third hoeing* which consisted of cleaning between the beets.

Harvesting was the final step in the beet cultivation process. Before the work began, it was necessary for the farmer and laborer to have a complete understanding of not only the distance between plants, but also how the farmer wanted the field worked.

Each step completed properly contributed to the strength of the sugar beet stand and created less work for the laborer. These important steps are outlined in the contract located at the end of the chapter.

The first hoeing consisted of hoeing all weeds from around the beet plants. The thinning and blocking began after the beet had four well-developed leaves. The farmer told the laborers when to start hoeing and thinning, and the laborers started to work within 24 hours.

Using either a long handle-hoe or, if preferred, a short-handle hoe, the laborer began the backbreaking job of blocking and thinning.

The laborer either stood or squatted to hoe around the plants, first to get rid of weeds, and, at the same time, thin out beets from the cluster

From *Through the Leaves*, July 1941. Photo courtesy of City of Greeley Museums.

From *Through the* Leaves, July 1941. Photo courtesy of City of Greeley Museums.

of the beet plants, making sure each plant had plenty of dirt around each stand so as not to expose any roots. The laborer was to leave one plant stand, separated by 12-inches from each other, for the most satisfactory results.[1]

The work was time-consuming and back-breaking because of stooping over to complete the job, thus the term *stoop laborer*. From Monday through Saturday, the length of the workday varied depending on what needed to be done in the fields. It usually began at 5 a.m. and could end at dusk or when workers could no longer see.

Moses Espinosa of the Spanish Colony said, "We started about late March or early April cleaning the ditches, putting the weeds in a pile, and then setting them on fire to burn the seeds, so they would not spread into the fields where the crops were being planted. By then, the farmer had the fields tilled and disked and the beets planted, and my dad and the older children would start hoeing and cleaning the fields. Thinning the beets was hard work, especially on the knees. We had to pull the smaller beet plants so the big plant would grow and produce a big or average size sugar beet, depending on the separation."

To insure a better crop, the farmer visited the laborers daily during the blocking and thinning season to make sure the work was done properly. During each hoeing, the laborer needed to take care not to drag too much dirt away from the beets to the center of the row, so as not to cover other small beet plants. Thinning beets early when they had four to six leaves produced up to approximately 19 tons per acre; however, if thinning was done when the plants had more leaves, the yield was less tonnage per acre.[2]

By 1918, the sugar beet industry was booming. They experimented with ways to perfect the size and quality of beets. The first seeds used were 3/16" in diameter. When watered, each seed sprouted and dispersed into several beet plants. This produced a heavy row of seedlings.

The farmers started to segment the 3/16" seed into several individual seeds to be planted, and, as a result, less seed was needed. Thinning was a major concern. If the rows weren't thinned enough, crowded beets would be too small. Seeds planted too far apart resulted in overly large beets.

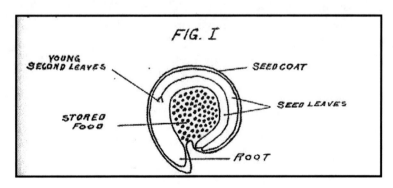

From *Through the Leaves*, April 1923, p. 121. Photo courtesy of City of Greeley Museums.

The second hoeing began as soon as the first hoeing was completed, usually in June.

Moses Espinosa explained, "Along with the thinning, we also pulled the weeds that were a little big, so when it came time to hoe the weeds again, there wasn't much hoeing to do."

The second hoeing removed any doubles left from the first hoeing. During this hoeing, care was taken to cut deeply enough between the beets to kill the weeds, deeper than the first hoeing. This was a crucial step in the growth cycle of a good beet crop.

By the third hoeing, the sugar beet plant was about 1½" tall with enough foliage to block the sun and prevent weed growth. The laborers then only needed to pull an occasional weed.

Moses Espinosa remembered an incident when he was about 5 years old. "I was the water boy and carried water out to the fields so my dad and the rest of the children could have a drink." Laughingly he said, "I remember several times I fell asleep waiting to take the water which was already in the bucket. The water was warm or hot when I arrived. Dad took a drink, got mad and disciplined me. I still did that off and on. You would think I would have learned from the spankings my dad gave me."

Beets were planted in rows ¼ to ½ mile long. Laborers walked several miles a day tending to the fields under the intense heat of the sun, day after day. Several family members worked as a team.

Ricardo "Rico" Lopez recalled, "Dad had us working together doing about ten feet of beets per person. Then when we reached where the person in front started, we would go to the front of the line and start another ten feet."

The harvest usually began in late September. The farmer hitched a team of horses to a beet puller, and the puller was adjusted to lift the beets out of the ground without breaking the root.

Harvesting beets. Photo courtesy of City of Greeley Museums.

The harvest was a challenge, because the farmer had to get the crop loaded and into the factory before it froze. The Great Western Sugar Company would not accept frozen beets or beets with a lot of dirt on them. The farmer or his foreman talked to the laborer to ascertain how much the laborer could handle daily and how many beets to roll or pull to prevent frozen beets. The stoop laborer topped the beets and loaded them into wagons or trucks.

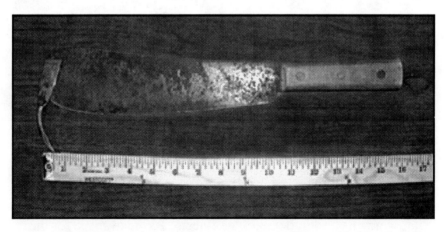

Beet topping knife used to top the beets during harvesting time. Knife is owned by Peggy Ford. Photo courtesy of Gabriel Lopez.

Topping beets was hard work. Rico Lopez, a young boy, said that the topping knives were scary. Workers used a 10" to 14" blade with a hook on the end. The worker hooked the beet and brought it up to the free hand and sliced the leaves off the sugar beet.

The foreman assigned four laborers to a row, and they rotated about every ten feet. The adults held the beet in one hand, and with the other hand cut the leaves off with a single swipe. The younger ones held the beet between their legs in order to top it. Alvin Garcia began working the beet fields at age 12. When asked if he was ever scared of cutting his leg or hand, he said with a chuckle, "We were more worried about the weather and getting the job done, so Dad could get paid, than hurting ourselves."

Manuel Carbajal, on left, and his two unidentified friends, topping beets in 1939. Notice the beets, on the left side of them, and the leaves that were cut off, on the right side. Beets that were topped are in the middle of the row and ready to be picked up by the man following them. Photo courtesy of Gil Carbajal.

Moses Espinosa said, "Now the time was getting close to start worrying about the topping of beets. To make space for the topped beets, we used a harrow or a *rastra* as it was called in Spanish. It is three boards chained together and pulled behind a horse or a tractor to level the ground; some called it *dragging*. This was done between rows of sugar beets. When we topped them, we laid them on this leveled ground, and later the farmer hired other laborers who used pitchforks to load the beets into the back of a wagon or truck."

Alvin Garcia also remembered, "We knocked the dirt off of the beet by hitting it on the ground, then we topped it and laid it in the middle of the rows. You see, we took six rows and put the topped beets in the middle or third row. This allowed the wagon or truck to come alongside to load the beets."

Manuel Carbajal and son, Lupe, standing next to a load of beets ready to go to the beet dump in 1949. Dog is unknownbut was excited to have his photo taken. Photo courtesy of Gil Carbajal.

Ricardo Lopez added, "The topping of the beets was done from September to the end of October. The weather could be cold and snowy. My father wrapped the boys' shoes with burlap sacks to keep our feet warm. Beet work was hard work, but it was work."

It was in the best interests of both the farmer and the laborer to contract with each other year after year. The longer the laborer remained with one farmer, the more he understood the farmer's methods of beet production. This harmonious relationship would ensure many years of prosperity for both.

Beet laborers from the Spanish Colony, posing in a beet field, ranging in age from 16 to the mid-twenties. Photo taken in 1937 or 1938. Standing, L to R: Edward Lopez, David Lopez, and Tim Garcia. Sitting, L to R: Moses Espinosa, Domingo Duran, Elfigo Duran, Augustine "Gus" Lopez. Photo courtesy of Robert Duran.

Many laborers contracted with farmers for other seasonal crops such as onions, potatoes, green beans, hay, and wheat. These laborers didn't return to their homes in the Spanish Colony until all crops were harvested. Moses Espinosa, one of five children said, "My family would work beet crops as well as all the other crops. My dad [Otavio Espinosa] was always working the farms. He worked for a farmer in Pierce, Colorado. The farm life was all he knew. When the first hoeing was done on the sugar beets, my dad and the family went to the other fields and worked on hoeing the other crops, if time permitted. You see, sugar beets were not the only crop grown at that time, and money was hard to come by. We were constantly hoeing or working the fields. Dad always kept us busy."

The Esparza family working an onion field in Weld County the late 1930s. Photo courtesy of Gil Carbajal.

Moses Espinosa continued, "By the time we noticed that the summer was almost over, it was fall. We had already stacked the hay in a big mound. You see, they didn't bail the hay. Later, they had the machinery to do that type of work. Everything we did was manual and hard work. Sometimes we stacked hay two or three times a year. When harvesting came, it was for all crops. Dad picked potatoes and put them in a basket [for the farmer] and later in [his own] bags [since the farmer allowed workers to take left-over, smaller potatoes]. The same thing was done with the onions. We also picked the green beans, we did this on our knees or bent over. By the time dad was done, he was so tired his back hurt. But that didn't stop him; he continued working. We harvested some of the crops simultaneously, since most of the crops were ready for harvest at the same time. We would not get home to the Spanish Colony 'til November or December."

At the end of the season, when all crops were harvested, the laborers were ready to go home. At this time, the farmer was required to make his final seasonal payment; however, there were a few farmers who took advantage of their tenants and didn't pay them. Many farmers felt that giving the laborers staples such as potatoes, beans, and onions constituted their wages. The farmer failed to realize that his laborers still needed cash, as per contract, to purchase additional food, clothing, and other non-edible items.

In Hazel C. Maddux's thesis, *Social Conditions of Immigrant Mexicans of Weld County*, she noted that the average annual income per family was $600 to $1000.[3] Moses Espinosa said, "Dad got paid and went into town for three or four big sacks of flour. We ate nothing but beans and potatoes and tortillas. There were a lot of children to feed, but Dad made sure we had enough flour to make all the tortillas we wanted. Also, Dad would get several big cans of lard and other things we couldn't get on the farms. The farmers allowed us to get the small potatoes that were left on the ground. We gathered them, put them in sacks, and took them home. We did the same with the onions and beans. Dad always had food for us to eat. The work we did was hard, and this was done every year." Moses laughed," When I told my children what we did and how we worked, they wouldn't believe me. But we did work hard and suffered a lot because of the Depression and prejudice. We had to do it or starve."

The Colonists also took care of their own. They gave food and other essentials to help needy families in the Colony make it through the winter or hard times.

As technology improved, there were many changes in the care and harvest of crops. The August 18, 1939, p. 187, article in *The Greeley Tribune,* "Stoop Labor In Thinning May Be Cut" reported, "Beet growers in Colorado and other states will be able to practically eliminate stoop labor in thinning sugar beets next spring, by replacing the regular plates on a standard beet planter with new single seed-ball plates that will be available."

The farmers continued to need workers for fieldwork, and, by 2004, the migrant and permanent workers were still a much needed labor force for the agricultural community. The stoop laborers continue to work today in Greeley and the surrounding areas in the sugar beet fields and with other crops such as onion, potatoes, peas, beans, and carrots.

Loading topped beets into a truck to take to the beet dump in the early 1940s. Photo courtesy of Gil Carbajal.

In 1942, Warren Monfort Feedlots, a large cattle-feeding company, recruited many of its workers from the beet fields; Tito Garcia Sr. was the first to be hired. Seventeen year-old David Lopez, the second person hired, remained with Monfort of Colorado, now Swift and Company, for over sixty-one years. David Lopez received the Colorado Outstanding Older Worker Award on September 26, 2003, for the longest employed person in one company. Both Garcia and Lopez had been beet laborers.

When the U. S. entered World War II in 1941, many of the young men joined the military, which created a shortage of agricultural laborers. On August 4, 1942, the United States and Mexico signed the Bracero (meaning *strong arm*) Treaty for the recruitment and employment of Mexican Nationals to alleviate the shortage of manual labor in the fields and to help maintain railways. The Bracero Treaty remained in effect until May 30, 1963.[4] By the end of WWII, sugar beet farming was a leading industry, with Colorado producing a quarter of the nation's sugar.[5]

Labor Issues

In *The Greeley Tribune* in an April 30, 1928, article, "Many Mexicans Must Get Work Out Of District," it was reported that,

> A large part of the Spanish-American and Mexican population of northern Colorado must seek work outside of the district or be idle, so trustees of the Colony northwest of Greeley told the county commissioners and newspaper men here Monday. They said that practically none of the residents of the Colony have work but that most of them have been promised work at Wheatland, Wyo. Farmers in some sections who are raising beets are taking advantage of the surplus of beet labor to contract acreage at $20 or $3 less than the price, which the workers had expected. The Spanish Americans say that they were assured there would be plenty of work here until very recently when some of them were told they must go to Wheatland if they are to be employed for the summer.

The older men and women and mothers cared for the Colony during that time. Some of the older children helped when they were not in school.

Stoop laborers were not always contented with their wages and working conditions. The first known strike occurred in May 1932. A May 17, 1932, article in *The Greeley Tribune*, "7 Agitators Jailed Here Today" noted,

> First official move in the Northern Colorado beet labor strike came Tuesday noon with the arrest by the force of Sheriff W. W. Wyatt of seven alleged agitators who, Wyatt said, will probably be charged with intimidating workers... The following who claim the Spanish-American colony northwest of Greeley as their home: Ramon Deleo, 24; Pete M. Duran, 26; E. Padilla, 28; Henry Padilla, 18; Pablo Maes, 18. [They were] arrested in one group on the Pearson place located five miles northwest of Greeley. The reputed agitators had been riding around, talking to groups of laborers here and there, making threats in some places, Wyatt declared. "Quite a few"

51

laborers have left the fields on account of the strike propaganda, Wyatt learned... Some workmen being promised that if they would strike for three days that the leaders would secure from the sugar company better pay for the labor. This was patently a false promise in that the sugar company has no control over the price paid for the labor.

An article in *The Greeley Tribune,* "Beet Strike Situation In County Quiet," on May 21, 1932, commented,

The strike was called May 16 by the United Front committee representing workers of all nationalities and from all sections against intolerable conditions in the beet fields. Wages have been repeatedly cut during the last three years and the present scale of between $8 and $15 an acre or less, means absolute starvation. The United Front committee is demanding a return to the 1930 scale of $23 an acre and also a guarantee of wages from the sugar company, since frequently after a summer's work a contractor receives nothing or a small percentage of his wages because the money from the beets has been used to pay the farmers mortgage to the bank. Often too, he finds himself in debt to the merchant and farmer for his summer's living expenses and is held on the farm under literal conditions of serfdom to 'work it out.'

The strikers were very aggressive and some picketers were arrested. The laborers, who did not have a contract, continued to work and were harassed by the strikers.

In 1932, many Spanish Colony residents left and moved to New Mexico, California, and Arizona due to a labor strike against the Great Western Sugar Company and area farmers. Also, at the end of the May strike, many of the Mexican Nationals were taken back to Mexico. Some were forced, and others volunteered to go back. They left by train and later by buses, cars, and trucks. The Great Western Sugar Company provided food for the trip home.

A headline in *The Greeley Tribune* of May 28, 1932, "500 Mexicans Leaving Here by Rail Today", noted that two parties, of 500 people each, left Weld County, thus removing a burden from the Pauper Fund.

Another strike reported during the summer of 1938 was for higher wages for picking peas. *The Greeley Tribune* July 2, 1938 p.1 article, "WPA Employee Is Leader of the Agitators" reported,

Attempt of Mexican farm labor agitators to enforce a pea-pickers strike for higher wages failed in the Greeley district Saturday morning when deputy sheriffs acting under instructions of Sheriff Gus G. Anderson ordered the rural picket lines dissolved and warned that if any further attempt is made to prevent willing workers from going into the fields the agitators will land in jail. There was no show of violence. Strike attempt, the first of the season reported here, was on the Ray Riggs place, one and one half miles east of Lucerne, where 10 acres of peas are being picked for Glen Hubbell to be shipped in refrigerator cars to eastern markets. Shortly after Deputy Sheriffs Guy McGinness and Guy Ballinger arrived and informed the agitators that interference with the right to work would not be countenanced, from 10 to 15 pea pickers went back into the field. They are employed at a rate of 83 and one third cents per basket, on which basis Hubbell told officers, they can make from $3 to $4 per day… The spokesman for the group attempting to enforce a strike for higher wages was Vincente Vigil, bespectacled resident of the Greeley Spanish Colony… Hubble came to the sheriff's office and asked for help shortly after the attempted strike was called. He told officers that he asked Vigil the reason for the attempt to call a strike. 'Because $3 a day isn't enough to live and feed our babies on,' Vigil answered according to Hubbell.

Parked in Shade in Midmorning at Lucerne, green pea shipping capital of Weld county, this string of cars of pickers is the tipoff that another strike is on. Women and children and some men loll around the cars, but most men gather in groups where they are harangued by leaders or those with special grieves such as the two row bosses discharged Friday. This Friday morning snapshot was taken when all was peaceful, later a group led by John Lopez marched on the nearby office of Glen Hubbell, demanding the 5-cent holdback pay, retained until crop is harvested. Lopez was arrested by Sheriff Gus Anderson, whose orders soon dispersed the string of cars shown here. Observers expected most of the workers back in the fields by afternoon, picking by reduced crews continuing all day. The Tribune has prepared a six-column pictorial layout of the green pea deal, from vine to iced car, to be printed soon.—Tribune photo and engraving.

From *The Greeley Tribune*, July 8, 1938, page 1.

In the photo above, the caption mentions, in part, that

...the string of cars of pickers is the tipoff that another strike is on. Women and children and some men loll around the cars, but most men gather in groups where they are harangued by leaders or those with special grieves such as the two row bosses discharged Friday. This Friday morning snapshot was taken when all was peaceful, later a group led by John Lopez marched on the nearby office of Glen Hubbell, demanding the 5-cent holdback pay, retained until crop is harvested. Lopez was arrested by Sheriff Gus Anderson, whose orders soon dispersed the string of cars shown.

'Don't Serve as a Squirrel,' is the literal translation of the picketeer's sign. "No Sirva de Esquirol." held by Sheriff Gus Anderson, but it means in Spanish slang, "don't work as a scab," exactly what the sign at the right in English reads: "Fellow Workers, Don't Scab." The sheriff, credited with holding the pea strike to a minimum, is pictured here with two leaders of the strikers—Ed Madrid, left, and Arthur Lopez, right, arrested Sunday. Arthur is not to be confused with John Lopez, the first arrested in the pea strike. John being accused of leading a march on the office of Glen Hubbell at Lucerne. Ed Madrid and Arthur Lopez are the two "row bosses" whose discharge as "incompetent" caused the trouble among the pea pickers. Photo and engraving by the Tribune.

From *The Greeley Tribune,* July 11, 1938, page 1.

The two picketers in the photo above are Ed Madrid, left, and Arthur Lopez, right, with Sheriff Gus Anderson holding two picket signs. In *The Greeley Tribune* on July 11, 1938, the article, "Pea Strike Is Broken" noted,

> 'Don't Serve as a Squirrel' is the literal translation of the picketeer's sign, "No Sirva de Esquirol" held by the sheriff Gus Anderson, but it means in Spanish slang, "don't work as a scab," exactly what the sign at the right in English reads: "Fellow Workers, Don't Scab."…. Arthur is not to be confused with John Lopez, the first arrested in the pea strike. Ed Madrid and Arthur Lopez are the two row bosses" whose

discharge as "incompetent" caused the trouble among the pea pickers. Sheriff Gus Anderson arrested 16 CIO pea strike pickets, all of them Mexicans or Spanish Americans, in the Lucerne area north of Greeley early Sunday morning. At the county jail here, two of those arrested – boys, 15 years old, were turned loose while the 14 adults held in the jail were booked for obstructing the highway, threats and intimidation, and disturbance. Those held in the jail were booked as: Pete P. Barela, 46; Eugene Ganzolas, 18; Estanistada Dominguez, 22; Momula Marquez, 24; Tadro Jaques, 23; Frank Garcia,19; Pablo Maese, 35; Manuel Japolli, 17; E.B. Martinez, 45; Arthur Lopez, 28; Ed Madrid, 38; Joseph Cruz, 30; Ernest Marquez, 20. Most of them are residents of Greeley Spanish Colony.

On July 15, 1938, p. 1, an article in *The Greeley Tribune,* "Union Accepts Contract for Picking Peas," commented,

The final agreement made Thursday night is for a wage of 90 cents per cwt. The union had originally asked for $1.25 per cwt. Hubbell had been paying 831/3 cents. The new scale went into effect Friday morning. Strikers are to be reinstated in jobs. A number of them appeared at the fields Friday morning and as many of them were given jobs as could be used, but there were so many picketers available that not all of those who were out on strike could be used Friday.

The Colonists, men, women, and children, were hard workers who took pride in their accomplishments. They knew that their sweat and toil earned their wages.

Union Accepts Contract for Picking Peas

Final agreement on the terms of the settlement of the pea pickers strike in the Lucerne fields was reached Thursday night when the agricultural union of the CIO accepted modified terms offered by Glen Hubbell, contractor and shipper of the peas.

The principal item at issue in the arbitration, conducted by John W. Kelly, national labor relations board examiner, was the wage for picking.

The final agreement made Thursday night is for a wage of 90 cents per cwt. The union had originally asked for $1.25 per cwt. Hubbell had been paying 83½ cents. The new scale went into effect Friday morning. Strikers are to be reinstated in jobs. A number of them appeared at the fields Friday morning and as many of them were given jobs as could be used, but there were so many pickers available that not all of those who were out on strike could be used Friday.

Mr. Hubbell said that about 400 pickers were on hand Friday morning. Picking was in progress in the fields of Charles Adams and H. T. Hull. Thursday two cars were shipped, bringing the total to 24 cars.

By Tuesday when the harvesting will be finished, Hubbell expects to have shipped 30 cars, he said Friday.

Union officials accepted final terms Thursday night and Hubbell confirmed his own acceptance, thus closing the negotiations. Among other terms is included recognition of the union by Hubbell, but the agreement applies only for the pea harvest in the Lucerne area this year.

CIO union officials here this week said that they expected to be active in Weld county in other agricultural harvests this fall including potato digging and beet harvesting.

How far the National Labor Relations Act will apply to these harvests is a question being discussed here. The National Labor Relations Board claimed jurisdiction here in the pea strike on the basis that Hubbell classified as a packer and processor employing workers. The labor relations act, however, specifically exempts "agricultural workers" from the jurisdiction of the act. As potato and beet harvesting is done by workers employed by the farmers themselves, the situation is not the same as in the pea strike where the workers were employed by a "processor."

The Greeley Tribune, July 15, 1938, page 1.

57

ORIGINAL

LABOR CONTRACT

CONTRACT FOR HAND LABOR FOR SEASON 1917

74-48

MEMORANDUM OF AGREEMENT, Made and entered into this_____day of_____
A. D. 1917, by and between_____ of _____
hereinafter designated the GROWER, and_____ _____
of_____, hereinafter designated the CONTRACTOR.

WITNESSETH; Whereas, the GROWER has entered into a contract with the Windsor Factory of THE GREAT WESTERN SUGAR COMPANY for the growing of sugar beets, and is desirous of contracting with the CONTRACTOR for doing the hand work on said crop; now, therefore,

IN CONSIDERATION of the sum of One Dollar in hand paid by the GROWER to the CONTRACTOR, the receipt of which is hereby acknowledged, the CONTRACTOR hereby covenants and agrees with the GROWER to do the hand work on_____acres, more or less, of sugar beets, planted or to be planted on_____¼ of Section_____, Township_____North, Range_____ West of the Sixth P. M., for the season of 1917, in accordance with the rules and regulations printed on the back hereof and made a part of this contract.

The CONTRACTOR further agrees to receive as full compensation for said work the prices hereinafter specified, and the said GROWER hereby agrees to pay the said CONTRACTOR for said work as fast as the respective classes of work have been completed and approved by the agricultural superintendent or field man of THE GREAT WESTERN SUGAR COMPANY, Windsor Factory, at the prices specified below; except that it is mutually agreed between the parties hereto that $_____per acre shall be withheld from the first payment falling due under this contract until after the crop has been harvested, as a guaranty of the faithful fulfillment of this contract.

	Per Acre.	Per Ton.
For bunching and thinning	$ 7.00 or $	
For second hoeing	$ 2.00 or $	
For third hoeing	$ 1.00 or $	
For pulling and topping	$10.00 or $	

The GROWER further agrees to provide reasonable living accommodations for the CONTRACTOR without expense to him, and to furnish said CONTRACTOR with water near at hand for drinking and domestic purposes without expense.

This contract shall bind and benefit both parties thereto, and its fulfillment shall be a charge and a lien on the crop on which the labor is performed.

IN WITNESS WHEREOF, The parties hereto have subscribed their names the day and year first written above.

_____ Grower

_____ Contractor

Copy of a 1917 beet labor contract (the back of the document). Courtesy of City of Greeley Museums.

1920 SUGAR BEET CONTRACT

The Mountain States Beet Growers Association, at its Annual meeting held in Denver, December 8-9, 1919, unanimously adopted the following clause to cover price for sugar beets for season of 1920:

"To pay for beets delivered the flat price of Ten Dollars per ton, and an additional consideration at the rate of $1.50 per ton of beets for each $1.00 advance in price of sugar above $7.00 per hundred pounds at U. S. seaboard markets, fractions to be reckoned in proportion, and said seaboard price to be determined by the average of said markets for the twelve months between October 1st, 1920, and September 30, 1921. Payment of said additional consideration, if any shall result hereunder, shall be made to the grower on October 15th, 1921."

Example:

Sugar at	$ 7.00,	seaboard,	$10.00	per ton for beets
"	8.00,	"	11.50	" "
"	9.00,	"	13.00	" "
"	10.00,	"	14.50	" "
"	11.00,	"	16.00	" "
"	12.00,	"	17.50	" "
"	13.00,	"	19.00	" "
"	14.00.	"	20.50	" "

Or, for an example involving a fractional seaboard price, $8.50 sugar would make a price of $12.25 for beets, and, for a more probable figure let us suppose the year's average to result at $11.85 for a hundred pounds of sugar at seaboard; then the grower would receive $17.27½ per ton for his beets.

Copy of a 1920 beet labor contract. Courtesy of City of Greeley Museums.

This is an example of a 1937 labor union certificate given to its members.

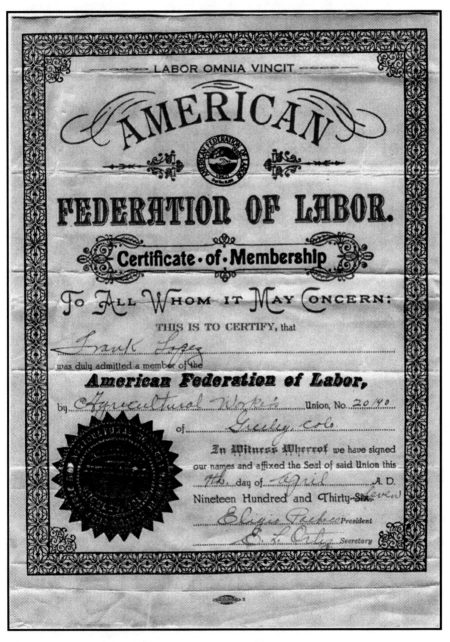

Labor Union Certificate issued to Francisco "Frank" Lopez Sr. on April 7, 1937. Courtesy of Palmer Lopez.

References

1. On Thinning Sugarbeets. (1923, May). *Through the Leaves.* p.185.

2. The Second Hoeing of Beets. (1923, June). *Through the Leaves.* pp. 226, 228

3. Maddux, Hazel C. (1932, June). *Some Conditions Which Influence the Mexican Children in Greeley, Colorado, and its Vicinity.* (Master Degree thesis, Colorado State College). p. ii

4. *The Bracero Program.* (www.farmworkers.org/benglish.html).

5. *Denver Mile High Magazine.* (2003, June/July). p. 161.

Chapter 4

Memories of Home, Music, and Moonshine

Ynez Lopez Sr. home in 1929. From: Hazel C. Maddux , Masters Degree Thesis, 1929.[1] Courtesy of University of Northern Colorado

By 1925, within a year of the houses being built, changes were already underway in the Colony. Families added rooms on to their original two-room dwellings, and later installed floor covering such as, e.g. wood, linoleum, carpet, etc. The flat-style roofs were replaced with gabled roofs, and, in some of the yards, separate cellars were dug to store vegetables and other food, while others had tiny cellars under their homes. The Colony houses were painted white. Alvin Garcia, a Colony resident since 1924, related, "The adobe houses were so white that when it snowed or was snowing, you could not find or see the Spanish Colony."

Mary Martinez recalled a story about her dad, Vicente Jojola. "Warren Monfort, who owned Monfort Feed Lots, gave my dad a good size shed to use at home. My dad and older brothers rolled the shed three and a half miles. They used poles and laid them under the shed as rollers. As the shed rolled over the poles, the boys picked them up and returned them to the front of the shed, so it could continue to roll forward. They rolled it down the Windsor road [O Street] to 25th Avenue and then to our house in the Colony. This shed was attached to the back of the house and is still used as a bedroom."

Alvin Garcia mentioned that 100 trees were donated to the Spanish Colony. An article in *The Weld County News,* April 13, 1928, reported that 1,000 trees were donated to the Greeley area, and, most likely, 100 of these were given to the Colony by the City. Each resident received two trees which were planted in the front yards in alignment with the corners of each home. The east park had two rows of trees; there were bushes and flowers planted in the west park, but no trees. As the trees grew, they created a pleasant canopy for people to walk beneath. One can imagine the children running in and out under these trees chasing each other. The colonists sat in the shade of the trees, visiting and watching the traffic go by.

Carmen Lozano Weekley, who was raised by her grandparents, Frank M. and Isabel R. Lozano, lived in the Colony from 1935 until 1955. She remembered, "My uncle, Frank Lozano, would take us kids out in the yard and tell spooky stories at nighttime. We had a pile of leaves in the yard, and all us kids sat around the pile while Uncle Frank told his stories. One day, Uncle Frank was going to tell us a spooky story in front of the pile of leaves. Earlier, before we went outside to hear the story, Louie Ortiz crawled under the leaves and covered himself with them. It was getting dark, and all us kids were seated around the pile of leaves waiting to hear Uncle Frank's stories. Uncle lit the leaves on fire, and, as they started to burn, out jumps Louie, screaming and yelling. He didn't get burned, but we thought it was a ghost. We screamed and jumped all over the place. The next day Louie came over and said, 'I'm going to hell; from now on I will never hide in the leaves again.' We laughed so hard. He really scared us."

Some residents had small gardens in their back yards. They grew pumpkin, zucchini, corn, peas, and other vegetables. The Colonists also planted several kinds of flowers. Morning glories were popular in front of the homes. A small bush, *la Rosa de Castillo*, was planted in the parks, churches, and back yards. Josie Garcia remembered when she was a young child that tall plants with red and white flowers and other colors called St. Joseph's Flowers [hollyhocks] were planted in front of all the houses. She also remembered everyone had lots of potted plants, shrubs, and a few flowers.

Arnulfo "Nudy" Lopez said, "My grandpa, Ynez Lopez Sr., had cherry and apple trees planted in his yard [located on lot 42]. There were only a few fruit trees planted in the colony."

Esther Schillinger's 1929 Colorado State College Masters Degree thesis, *Social Conditions of the Immigrant Mexicans of Weld County*, documented some of the homes in the Spanish Colony. Schillinger, who visited the Colony, said the homes were furnished as well as an average American home and were as neat. They had tables and chairs, and attractive spotless linoleum covered the floor. She also mentioned that the Spanish-speaking people had a lot to contribute to this country with their drawing, painting, and musical talents. Nearly every home in the Colony had some kind of musical instrument. Family portraits or religious pictures were displayed in many homes. Like any other average American home, the drawings and artwork of the children were proudly displayed.[2]

Left to right: Isabel Lozano, Bob Medina, and Carmen Lozano Weekley playing in the Colony in front of the Lozano home, 1946. Courtesy of Carmen Lozano Weekley.

Josie Garcia commented, "There were many good artists in the Colony, but not me, I couldn't draw a thing. There were also good singers; we always had nice school programs."

Robert Duran, 5 years old, in the summer of 1942, in front of his grandfather's, Efren Duran's, home on lot 17 on N. 26th Ave. Photo courtesy of Robert Duran.

Many colony residents, old and young, were talented. They excelled at playing the guitar, piano, harmonica, and violin. When asked how they learned to play instruments, the consistent answer was, "We were all self-taught."

Ricardo "Rico" Lopez, 15 years old, playing piano at home in the Spanish Colony, lot 42, circa 1949. Courtesy of Rico Lopez.

Nudy Lopez said, "Mom [Martina Lopez] played the guitar really well, and Rico and Sam [brothers] played the piano. Mario [brother] played the guitar and piano." When asked what instrument he played, he chuckled and said, "I played the radio."

Frank Lopez, Jr. related, "I played the harmonica and can still carry a good tune with it today, and I will be 76 this year [2003]."

Moses Espinosa remembered, "My dad used to play the piano well, and we banged on it also. Dad got an organ at an auction held at Island Grove Park. That is how he learned to play."

"My dad played the violin," Mary Martinez remembered. (See the wedding march photo in Chapter 9; Mr. Vicente Jojola, Mary's father, is the violinist.)

Criselda "Kate" Espinosa Cassel said, "During the Depression, my dad didn't have much for us to eat. Dad went fishing in the Cache la Poudre River, and my stepmother would boil the fish he caught and then fry them for us to eat. Also, during the war [World War II], my sister, Eloysa, and I worked at the Spud Chips factory making potato chips for the soldiers. We also shared in watching our children. I had one, and Eloysa had three. I worked the day shift, and Eloysa watched the kids. When she went to work in the evening, I watched the children. We had to survive, so we did what we could at the time."

Referring to the role of women in the Colony, Kate said, "Traditionally, the women were more sheltered than the men. The women stayed home, while the men went to work or to find work. The women kept the Colony going. They fed the animals, tended to the flowers, bushes, and trees, and did much of the yard work around the house. We cared for the Colony the best we could."

L to R: Kate Espionsa Cassel holding son, Gus Lopez, Eloysa Espinosa Tellez holding son, Sam Tellez circa 1943. Photo courtesy of Jerry Lopez.

The first Colony residents who arrived from New Mexico and Southern Colorado spoke Spanish; although most knew English, they preferred to speak Spanish. When asked what the primary language was in the Colony, Kate said, "Spanish was the language most used and is my first language. In the Gipson School from about 1931 to 1937, we had to read and speak English. When school was out, we spoke Spanish in the Colony. My stepmother's Spanish was different from Dad's Spanish and ours. She [Bibliana Rios Espinosa] was from Mexico and spoke Old Mexico Spanish, whereas my dad was from southern Colorado. It was just different than ours."

During Prohibition, many colonists made moonshine [beer] at home. Esther Schillinger wrote, "The offense most frequently committed by Mexicans are violations of prohibition"[3] Patronage from the Anglo community for bootleg liquor was so prevalent [in some colonies] that the Hispanic was willing to take his chances and produce it.

Delilah Gomez Fiechter, who grew up in the Colony, remembered a story about her grandpa. "My grandma went to church one Sunday and left my grandfather home alone [in Gill, Colorado]. There was a sheriff who was always trying to catch Grandpa with the moonshine. The sheriff searched the house inside and out and couldn't find any liquor there. The sheriff told grandpa he could smell the liquor, but he couldn't find any evidence to arrest him, so he left. When grandma arrived home and took down a *ristra* [a string of dried red chilies] to make chili, she found a bottle of moonshine in it. Grandma asked Grandpa why the bottle was there, and he said, 'I had to hide it from the sheriff, and I knew he wouldn't look there.' You see, the ristras were covered with a net that would hold the chilis together. He put the bottle in the ristra, knowing it would not fall out."

Kate Espinosa Cassel said, "Daddy [Otavio Espinosa] made his beer in barrels in the basement under the new addition to the house. He made it with raisins, yeast, and barley, and then let it ferment in the barrels for a while. Daddy put the raisins in a pan when he was done with them and told Jenny [Rios] and me to throw them away. Jenny and I loved to eat raisins, so we ate a few while walking to the trashcan. After eating a few, we got dizzy and were walking all over the place. Later, when we got older, we realized we were drunk. We were around ten or twelve years old. Daddy went to Dewald's Cash Grocery store [owned by C. F. Dewald, 807 8th Street Greeley, Colorado] to buy little bottles to put the beer in. When it was ready to drink, Daddy and the older men of the colony gathered in the basement or kitchen and drank the beer and had a good time."

About 1939, dressed up to go to town. L to R: Kate Espinosa
Cassel, age 15, Ernest "Lico" Espinosa, age 20, Jenny Rios,
age 16. Photo courtesy of Jerry Lopez.

Alvin Garcia mentioned that most of the colony residents
made their own beer. He laughed and said, "We kids would make
beer too. We would take turns making it in barrels in our garage. I
would do it one time, and then the next turn would be Martinez's or
Duran's. We would make about 10 gallons for the weekend. We used
raisins, malt, yeast, and five pounds of sugar per 5 gallons of beer.
Then it fermented for five days. On Saturday night we would party!
You knew it was good when you popped the cap off the bottle and
steam or smoke came out. If there was alot of smoke, then it was
good beer! We made our own beer until 1941 when I got married
and had to stop making it. I don't remember anyone in the colony
ever getting caught making their beer."

The children of the original colonists, like Alvin Garcia, grew up,
married, and had their own families. Families began to change as

modern times brought new stresses and responsibilities; for example, Jess Gomez, who raised his family during the 1940s and 1950s, commented, "I worked all day, six days a week. On Sunday, my only day off, I found it more important to spend time with my family. My children were a joy to me, and we would do things on that day. I didn't drink or smoke, and that is why I had no time to socialize and drink and smoke with the Colony men. My kids were more important than that. Yes, I did say 'Hi' every now and then and have short visits with them, but mostly I spent the time with my kids. I still do now that I'm retired. I spend one day with each of them; Delilah, my daughter, and I spend every Thursday together."

Tito "Butter" Garcia, Jr. said, "Do you know who brought the Zoot Suit to the Spanish Colony? It was Inez "Neddie" Lopez. He spent a year in Arizona with his family picking lettuce [in 1942]. His older brother, Gus, was stationed at Luke Military Base in Phoenix, Arizona, training for the Army, where he married Kate Espinosa. Neddie wore his Zoot Suit to their wedding. When Neddie returned to Greeley, he wore his Zoot Suit at the dances in the Salon. Every guy there wanted a Zoot Suit like Neddie's, so we just folded each pant leg over tight and then cuffed them a couple of times. It looked like we were wearing a Zoot Suit, and we were cool, man! We also used Vato language." (See Appendix D.)

The Zoot Suit had been known to represent a gang. In Los Angeles, there was a riot about the Zoot Suit. Zoot Suits were eventually banned. (See Appendix E.) Because of that, another style, the semi-Zoot Suit evolved. The pant leg was not as tight around the ankles as the original Zoot Suit."

L to R: Henry Quezada and Mario Lopez modeling his Zoot Suit
pants. Photo courtesy of Gabriel Lopez.

Rico Lopez remembered, "The boys, Edward "Lalo", Mario, Frank Jr., Neddie and Lucio Duran, and others always took their pants to my mom [Martina Lopez] for alterations. She tightened the cuff around the ankle and made them look like the Zoot Suit."

By the late 1950s, as the early residents began to leave and new residents moved in, the demographics of the Colony changed. It was no longer the same community. The new residents came from Texas and from different states in Mexico.With the growth of Greeley to the west, the Colony was no longer an isolated, insular community. It became a typical American neighborhood, with many of the neighbors unknown to one another. When interviewing the remaining original family members, they all said they didn't know their neighbors anymore, as they now tended to keep to themselves.

References

1. Maddux, Hazel C. (1932, June). *Some Conditions Which Influence the Mexican Children in Greeley, Colorado, and its Vicinity.* (Masters Degree thesis, Colorado State College). p.32.

2. Schillinger, Esther K. (1929, August). *Social Contacts of the Immigrant Mexicans of Weld County.* (Masters Degree thesis, Colorado State College). pp. 10, 39.

3. Ibid. pp. 25, 26.

Chapter 5

Religion, Traditions, and Folklore

The Pentecostal Church is still at the Colony on N. 25th Avenue Ct. Courtesy of Gabriel Lopez. Photo taken in the summer of 2003 at the Spanish Colony in Greeley, Colorado.

Religion

Religion played an important role in Colony family life. *The Bible* and its teachings were widely applied by the colonists in training their children. Common biblical proverbs, along with short sayings or aphorisms, were frequently spoken (See Appendix F). When asked what kind of reading material people had in their homes, the answer was inevitably "*The Bible*".

The Spanish Colony had two churches, the Catholic Church and, later, the Pentecostal Church.

Catholic Church

A reference to the Catholic Church in a store in the Colony was found in the 1948 dedication program for Our Lady of Peace Catholic Church located at 1311 3rd St., Greeley, Colorado. "At the Greeley Colony, a hall built by the [Ynez Sr.] Lopez family, later purchased by the [Hiailliro] Tellez family, was donated to the diocese for church purposes, in 1930."[1] Several colonists interviewed said some services started in the store about 1928.

The first catholic priest in the Colony, Reverend Trudel, came from Fort Collins, Colorado, and conducted the Mass one Sunday a month. Reverend Casamiro Roca, who replaced Reverend Trudel, and Reverend Dominic Morera were the last known to serve the Colony Catholic Church, which closed when the Our Lady of Peace opened in Greeley in 1948.

Josie Garcia said, "Doña Serapia Tellez, a little lady who lived in a house behind the [Colony Catholic] church, always made sure the children went to catechism classes which she taught. Sometimes Frances and Monica Garcia and missionaries came to help. She always had us girls go around the Colony ringing the bell to remind the children to go to catechism. In May, she would take us across the field every evening to dedicate flowers to the blessed Virgin. Serapia always wanted to know why I brought ugly flowers. I explained that Mom [Santitos Lopez Garcia] always said, 'God loves the pretty and the ugly,' so I always made sure I brought some wilted and ugly flowers. I remember once that missionaries from Ireland worked in the Colony. They were very interesting, and we learned a lot about different cultures from them."

75

Having their own Catholic Church benefited the Colonists. They saved gasoline by not having to travel to Saint Peter's in Greeley. After six days of hard labor in the fields, going to Mass in the Colony was more convenient.

Although catechism classes were conducted in the Colony, baptisms and confirmations were first performed at St. Peter's Catholic Church in Greeley and then at Our Lady of Peace Catholic Church in Greeley after it was built in 1948.

The Most Rev. H. M. Newell laying the cornerstone, assisted by Father O'Sullivan and Father Doran.

Laying the corner stone, 1947. Photo in the pamphlet of the dedication of Our Lady of Peace Church. Courtesy of City of Greeley Museums.[2]

Communions were sometimes performed in the Colony Church. Josie Garcia remembered, "There were three of us who did our communion at the same time in the Colony - Mary Jojola Martinez, Dewey Ortiz and I. Reverend Casamiro Roca performed the communion services."

Arnulfo "Nudy" Lopez, who was born and raised in the Spanish Colony, recalled, "Doña Serapia was a strict disciplinarian in her catechism. We had to keep our heads looking forward, we could not eat candy, gum, or even talk to anyone during catechism. We respected her, so we did not give her any trouble."

Catechism class in front of the Colony Church with Sister Martina and Sister Mary. Photo courtesy of Alvin Garcia.

When asked about hymns sung during church services, most agreed there were some hymns which colonists brought from New Mexico, such as: *Himo A Cristo Rey, Mandamientos De La Ley De Dios, Bendito, Bendito, Del Cielo Bajo, Oh María! Madre Mía.*[3]

Of the church, Josie Garcia said, "I remember it being a small but beautiful church. It had a few benches and some chairs. A movie star donated the church altar, but I don't remember who. I do remember Bing Crosby and Bob Hope sent donations to our church."

Alvin Garcia recalled, "I received a letter in my [mail] box from Bing Crosby addressed to Doña Garza for the Colony church, and I gave it to Padre Dominic."

Nudy Lopez talked about the altar. "[It] was about the width of the church, with a cloth over the top. From behind the altar, the preacher gave his sermons. There was a small cross on the wall behind the altar."

Discrimination occurred frequently at church, which hurt the Hispanic people the most. Alvin Garcia remembered, "They [Hispanics] were met at the door and then ushered to one side at Saint Peter's Catholic Church in Greeley." They were the only parishioners segregated in church. Josie Garcia verified this treatment, "I heard about a lot of prejudice at St. Peter's. My parents and uncles would tell me that they were seated on one side of the church in different chairs and benches." The Hispanics wanted to be with other people. They disliked isolation and believed they should be treated the same as others in church; however, this was not the case.

Esther Schillinger, in her 1929 Masters thesis, commented on religion among the Hispanics. She observed social, economic, and discriminatory treatment of the Hispanics by the church. A woman interviewed by Esther Schillinger echoed Josie Garcia's memories, "If they insist on separating the Mexicans why don't they separate the Germans and Russians? Many of the Mexican people go to church only occasionally because of the way they are treated... I started going to the Baptist Church ... When I am clean and neatly dressed and act like others, I want to be treated like the others ... We all go to the same place when we die. Why should we be separated here?"[4]

The highest values and ideals embraced by Hispanic Americans and Mexicans were from the Catholic religion. Many enjoyed the beautiful rituals and traditions of the Catholic Church, but they refused to attend if they were made to feel inferior and unwanted. Many converted from Catholicism to Protestantism, because they were welcomed and treated better in the Protestant churches.

In 1947, a new Catholic Church was built in Greeley on the southeast corner of 2nd Street and 14th Avenue. It was officially named Our Lady of Peace.

About 1974, Alvin Garcia, a very devout Catholic, wanted a place of repose and reflection for himself and others. Mr. Ramon Marquez was commissioned to build an 8' x 8' x 10' shrine which contained religious statues and a small bench to kneel on. The shrine was built behind Alvin's store on Lot 10, which he sold in 1999 to Jose Marquez.

78

Alvin Garcia standing at the door of the shrine in his back yard at the Spanish Colony. Photo courtesy of City of Greeley Museums.

Jose Marquez said, "My dad built the shrine for Alvin in the mid 1970s. On December 12th, they have an annual commemoration for it. Throughout the day, anyone is welcome to come in and visit with Alvin and the Marquez family. In the evening, we have a nice picnic or meal for all who want to come."

A popular celebration today is the *Quinceañera*, a religious presentation of a Mexican girl on her 15th birthday to the Hispanic Catholic community. It signifies the young girl taking responsibility for her religious life. There is an hour-long bilingual Mass in honor of her *Quinceañera*. After the Mass, the guests and attendants join the girl for her birthday party. A gala reception and dance is usually held. An elaborate dinner, along with a traditional dish, chicken *molé*[chicken with chili], is served. When asked about this celebration, Josie Garcia and others said the *Quinceañera* wasn't performed in the Colony until about the 1950s. Over the years, American influences have changed some of the meaning and formality of this celebration.

Criselda "Kate" Espinosa Cassel fondly remembered a play in the Salon (The Community House in the Colony). "My half sister Jenny Rios and I sat under the benches in the Salon and watched a play called *La Pastores*. This play was about Christmas, and I remember in the play they used tall poles with a ball made out of paper and painted really pretty. They walked or danced around in a circle. Then they would stop and bang the poles against the floor. It was a nice play."

La Pastores was a popular Nativity play presented in two acts. In the first act, shepherds are watching their flocks at night when an angel appears and announces the birth of Christ. The shepherds decide to go to Bethlehem, and, on the way, a hermit joins them. Satan, in disguise, also joins them and manipulates the hermit into running away with the wife of a lazy shepherd named Bartolo. Bartolo alerts the rest of the shepherds who find the couple and proceed to Bethlehem. Meanwhile, Satan is vanquished by the angel Miguel and rushed off the stage. In the second act, the shepherds arrive at the manger and present their gifts to the newborn child.

Los Pastores[5] (Traditional *Pastorelas* or Song)

LETRA (7)	Song (7)
Hermanos pastores,	Brother shepherds,
Hermanos queridos	Brothers beloved
Vamos caminando	Let us journey on
Por nuestros caminos.	Following the road.
Vamos poco a poco	Let us go slowly
Arrodeando el Ganado;	Herding the flock.
No se desanimen	Do not lose heart
Ya vamos llegando.	For we are there almost.
Que por esos montes,	I see a light
Que por esos riscos,	In yonder mountains,
Que por esas sierras	In yonder boulders,
Una luz diviso.	In yonder peaks.
Camina Gilita	Come on, Gilita,
Que vendrás cansada	You must be tired;
Al pie de esa selva	At the edge of the forest
Haremos majada.	We shall set up camp.
Anda un lobo fiero	A ferocious wolf
Muy encarnizado.	Is roaming about
No haga algún destrozo	And could well cause destruction
	Among the fold.
En nuestros ganados.	
	And the little lambs
Y los corderitos	Which have lingered behind
Que atrás se han quedado	Can be carried in arms
Echenlos al hombro	Until we arrive.
Mientras que llegamos	And as for the kids
Y los más chiquitos	That can scarce make time
Que atras se han quedado	Let's carry them, too,
Vayanlos alzando	As we drive the flock.
Y arreando el ganado.	
	At the foot of the sierra
Al pie hay esa sierra	We shall set up camp
Haremos majada	While Gilita
Mientras que Gilita	Sits down and rest
Descansa sentada.	
	Now we have arrived
Y pues ya llegamos	Joyously and happily
Con gusto y placer	Having come to see Jesus
A ver a Jesus	Mary and Joseph.
María y José.	

Throughout the play, there is a good deal of humorous dialogue between the shepherds and the lazy Bartolo who is always asleep on his pallet. Every scene opens with a song called a *letra* which introduces each character. At the end of the presentation of gifts, all the shepherds join hands and sing a lullaby to the Child and then depart with a farewell song. The songs or *Pastorelas* are principal features of the *La Pastores* folk drama.

Nudy Lopez remembered Arthur Lopez playing the role of Bartolo. "He had us all laughing so hard. He played the role so well."

Also at Christmas, the children at Gipson School would participate in Special activities. One such activity was making a dollhouse to be sold. Other activities were programs in which many parents and friends participated. An article in *The Greeley Tribune*, dated December 23, 1937, mentioned one such program.

Gipson Children Will Hold Christmas Sale

A Christmas sale of toys and small articles made by the children at the Gipson school near the colony, will be held Saturday at the Gates Wardrobe shop on Eighth street opposite the postoffice. The money will be used to buy many needed things for the school.

The children have worked for several weeks making and painting toys, calendars, holders for small articles to be offered for sale.

The doll house that was built at the school last year and exhibited last winter will be offered for sale. It was made by the upper grade children. It is 3 feet by 2 feet in floor diameter.

The sale will start at 10 o'clock.

From *The* Greeley *Tribune*, December 23, 1937.

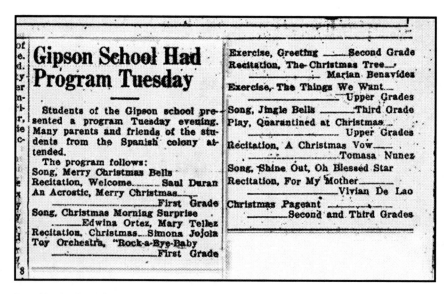

Gipson School Had Program Tuesday

Students of the Gipson school presented a program Tuesday evening. Many parents and friends of the students from the Spanish colony attended.

The program follows:
Song, Merry Christmas Bells
Recitation, Welcome_____ Saul Duran
An Acrostic, Merry Christmas____
_____First Grade
Song, Christmas Morning Surprise .
_____Edwina Ortez, Mary Tellez
Recitation. Christmas__Simona Jojola
Toy Orchestra, "Rock-a-Bye-Baby
_____First Grade

Exercise, Greeting _____Second Grade
Recitation, The Christmas Tree__.
_____Marian Benavides
Exercise, The Things We Want____
_____Upper Grades
Song, Jingle Bells _____Third Grade
Play, Quarantined at Christmas __
_____Upper Grades
Recitation, A Christmas Vow____
_____Tomasa Nunez
Song, Shine Out, Oh Blessed Star
Recitation, For My Mother_____
_____Vivian De Lao
Christmas Pageant _____
_____Second and Third Grades

From *The Greeley Tribune,* December 23, 1937, p. 4.

83

Pentecostal Assembly of God

1943 photo shows the Temple Bethel congregation celebrating the church's 10th anniversary

1943 Temple Bethel congregation standing in front of the Pentecostal Church in the Spanish Colony. Photo courtesy of Rico Lopez.

The second church established in the Spanish Colony was the Pentecostal Assembly of God. It was completed and dedication services were held in 1930. An article in *The Greeley Tribune,* January 12, 1930, "Church Dedicated at Spanish Colony" noted,

Dedicator service was held for the new Pentecostal Assembly of God Church, recently completed at the Spanish–American Colony, two and one half miles northwest of Greeley, on Wednesday evening. The church, financed and built entirely by folk in the colony, measures 26 feet by 40 feet and has cost $620. New circulating heater has been installed, as have four gasoline lamps. The Church fund was started by Women's Mission Society, which made and sold a quilt and other articles. The pastor, A.T. Lopez, continued the interest and as soon as the beet harvest was completed, young men in the community built the church. Two hundred dollars is yet to be paid, but residents of the colony have pledged to pay off the debt the next year.

Josie Garcia remembered, "Pentecostals sang beautiful hymns. My girl friends and I would stand across the street at the Salon [Community House] and listen to them. A few hymns were sung by the people in the Catholic Church, but not as many as in the Pentecostal Church."

Standing L - R, Unknown, Johnny Gordiani, Mrs. Gordiani, Adelia Duran, Tilly Duran, Hilda Duran, Leyba, Unknown, Unknown, Sarah Torrones, Torrones, Flora Mares, and Carmen Lozano Weekley. Sitting L-R, Augustine Gurrola, Frank Torrez, wife Lilly Torrez, and Helen. Circa 1948 at KFKA Radio Station. Photo Courtesy of Carmen Lozano Weekley

Carmen Lozano Weekley recalled, "I played the piano and sang at KFKA radio station at 6:00 in the morning with the Pentecostal Church group. Our official song was, *En Golgota a Villa una Cruz*. Johnny Gordiani directed at the radio station."

Carmen Lozano Weeley and Bob Lozano standing in front of Frank and Isabel Lozano's house in the Colony. Photo courtesy of Carmen Lozano Weekley.

Carmen also recalled the Pentecostal Christmas play about King Herod. "My uncle, Bob Lozano, played King Herod, and I was an angel. The story is about King Herod looking for Christ after he was born. King Herod was looking for Christ to kill him. Of course, I played the good angel."

Today, the church still stands on Lot 3 in the Colony. Attached on the west side of the church is a section of a classroom from the Gipson School, which was salvaged and added onto the church when the school was demolished on April 4, 1963.

Traditions

Frank Lopez, Jr. remembered, "*Mañanitas* were sung early in the morning for birthdays. If they [friends and relatives] knew what window you were sleeping by, they would sing at that window. When the person whose birthday it was heard them singing, he [or she] would stick his [or her] head out of the window."

Josie Garcia also recalled the *Mañanitas*, "I was born on St. Joseph's day, March 19, and early in the morning. I would be serenaded by friends and family. My mom would make a cake, but it had no candles. She would prepare a favorite dish for us. Mine was red chili with pork."

"The *Mañanitas* were never sung for me," Nudy Lopez recalled. "I think it was sung for the older ones [adults] and any whose birthday fell on the day of a saint. The singers were usually

Paul Maese, Anastacio "Tacho" Tellez, Pantaleon Delao, Ramon Delao and Vicente Jojola, and anyone who wanted to join them. Food and drinks were served after the song to all who were there."

During his interview, Nudy and his brother, Rico Lopez, sang the song of the *Mananitas* that was sung to them in the Colony. Following are the lyrics they remembered for *Las Mananitas*.

Las Mañanitas
(Traditional song from Mexico)

Estas son las mañanitas, que cantaba el Rey David. Hoy por ser día de tu santo, te las cantamos a ti.	These are the mornings that King David sang. Since today is your Saint's Day we sing them to you.
Despierta mi bien despierta. Mira que ya amaneció. Ya los pajaritos cantan. La luna ya se metió	Awaken, my loved one awaken and see what the morning brings. The birds are singing and the moon has set.
Que linda está la mañana en que vengo a saludarte. Venimos todos con gusto y placer a felicitarte.	How beautiful is this morning that brings me to greet you. We come with energy and joy to congratulate you.
El día en que tu naciste, nacieron todas las flores y en la pila del bautismo cantaron los ruiseñores. Ya viene amaneciendo.	On the day of your birth the flowers were born. On the baptismal font the smiling ones sang.
Ya la luz del día nos dió. Levántate de mañana. Mira que ya amaneció.	The morning is breaking and the light of the day touches us. Get up this early morning and see what the morning brings.
Quisiera ser un San Juan, quisiera ser un San Pedro. Para venirte a cantar con la música del cielo.	I wish I was a St. John, I wish I was a St. Peter, to sing for you the music of heaven.
De las estrellas del cielo quisiera bajarte dos. Una para saludarte y otra para decirte adiós.	Of the stars in the sky I would like to bring you two - one to greet you and one to say goodbye.
Ya viene amaneciendo, ya la luz del día nos dió.	Either it comes day break, or the light of the day is given to us.
Levántate de mañana. Mira que ya amaneció	Arise in the (Levántate) morning. Look at what already has risen

Interestingly enough, the two most common celebrations among Hispanics and Mexicans in 2004 are May 5 or *Cinco de Mayo*, a commemoration of victory for the Mexican army over the French in 1862, and September 16, a holiday commemorating independence from the Spaniards in 1810. These celebrations were revived in many places in the U. S. during the Chicano movement of the 1970s.

Mexican Independence Day Being Observed

Mexican Independence day was being celebrated in various parts of Colorado Tuesday and Wednesday by citizens of Old Mexico.

The only Weld county celebration of which local authorities had been advised is at Gilcrest. There the celebration was scheduled to start Tuesday night and last thru Wednesday. Sheriff Gus Anderson prepared to send deputies to Gilcrest where celebrations were arranged.

There is no celebration at Greeley. The Greeley Spanish colony has only three Old Mexico families out of a total of 60 families. The rest are American born, or Spanish American.

From *The Greeley Tribune,* September 15, 1936, page 2.

Folklore

There is the wailing woman called the "*La lloróna. (ya-rón-a). The Dictionary of New Mexico and Southern Colorado Spanish* (1984) by Ruben Cobos gives several definitions of La Lloróna:

1. The ghost of a woman seeking her children who died at birth. The ghost wails in the night as a sign of danger or impending death; 2. a soul from Purgatoryatoning for its sins; 3. the spirit of an Aztec goddess to whom babies were sacrificed, and who is heard during the night looking for children to carry off; 4. the ghost of *La malinche,* the "tongue" or interpreter and mistress of Cortes, conqueror

89

of Mexico, who betrayed her people for her lover; 5. the ghost of an unmarried young woman who, to spite her paramour and father of her two children, drown them when she discovers that he is making plans to leave her in order to marry a wealthy society lady whom his mother has chosen for him.

Some people say *La Lloróna* was a young woman who drowned her baby. When the woman died, St. Peter told her she couldn't enter heaven until she brought the soul of her baby with her, so her spirit came back to earth. She cries as she searches the river, looking for the child she can never find. In a poem of *La Lloróna*, she can be heard weeping and sobbing aloud, especially when it is stormy, and the wind is high. No small child is safe alone on the banks of the river.

LA LLORÓNA[6]

Don't go down to the river, child
Don't go there alone;
For the sobbing woman, wet and wild,
Might claim you for her own.

She weeps when the sun is murky red;
She wails when the moon is old;
She cries for her babies, still and dead,
Who drowned in the water cold.

Abandoned by a faithless love,
Filled with fear and hate.
She flung them from a cliff above
And left them to their fate.

Day and night, she heard their screams,
Borne on the current's crest;
Their tortured faces filled her dreams,
And gave her heart no rest.

Crazed by guilt and dazed by pain
Weary from loss of sleep,
She leaped in the river, lashed by rain,
And drowned in the waters deep.

She seeks her children day and night,
Wandering, lost, and cold;
She weeps and moans in dark and light,
A tortured, restless soul.

Don't go down to the river, child,
Don't go there alone;
For the sobbing women, wet and wild,
Might claim you for her own.

The story scared the Spanish Colony children and kept many of them away from the Cache la Poudre River at night. If the children heard a noise coming from the river, they ran home screaming "*La Lloróna!*" Whenever there is a gathering of old friends, the story of the *La Lloróna* is always told.

This story was remembered even when the children became young adults. Sally Lopez recalled an occasion when her husband, David, was in his twenties. She said, "On the farm [south of C Street NW, between N. 23rd Avenue and N. 21st Avenue], David walked down the long driveway to the C Street for his ride to work. Early one morning around 5:00 a. m. it was still dark, yet light enough to see a figure on the road. He left home and forgot to take his lunch box. I saw the lunch box on the floor next to the door. I picked it up and ran out after him. I was still in my white night gown when I turned and ran up the driveway, screaming in a soft yell, 'David, David.' David turned around and saw this figure running after him calling out his name and my nightgown and long black hair billowing in the wind. The first thing he thought was, *La Lloróna*! He screamed '*La LLORÓNA*!!' and started running, never looking back again. He didn't have much to eat at lunchtime that day."

There were maxims or sayings used to teach the children to respect their elders and others. Most were scary stories to keep the children from doing wrong.

Gabriel Lopez related a lesson taught by his mother, Kate Espinosa Cassel. She told him, if he talked back to her, the ground would open up and swallow him. "The older kids told the story of a boy who constantly talked back to his mother. One day he was walking down the dirt road and the ground opened up and swallowed him half way. When they attempted to dig him out, they only found half his body. I never talked back to my mother from then on. I also walked on the sidewalk. I figured the cement would not open up like the ground would."

Frank Lopez, Jr. reminisced, "To keep the children from staying out late at night, the parents told them a story about how the devil would form himself into a ball of light or fire. There were many fireflies in the Colony. At night these fireflies flew around, and when they came together, it was just like a ball of fire. The children would scream and run home and tell their parents they saw the devil."

Carmen Lozano Weekley also remembered, "One night in October, on the last street of the Colony where we lived, it was getting dark, and we were sitting outside. My uncle was getting ready to tell us a spooky story when we saw what looked like a ball of fire going from one tree to the next. The scary stories told to the children served their purpose well. The children stayed home. If children ventured outside at night, they were always aware of the stories, and they walked or ran quickly to get where they were going. They looked behind themselves and around every corner and into open garages hoping not to see anything scary."

"Salt was a commodity and scarce," David Lopez recalled. "If one spilled it, the parents said they would have bad luck. The child had to throw salt over his right shoulder to reverse the bad luck. It taught us to hold the salt shaker carefully and not spill any on the floor when we salted our food."

Delilah (Gomez) Fiechter shared her recollections of an architectural feature in the Colony. "There were these big diamond shapes mounted on the outside of all four walls of my dad's house. They were a light green and about 2 feet wide and 2 feet long. Three were put on the front and back and one on each side for a total of eight diamonds. I couldn't believe someone would mount these diamonds on a house, because they were ugly. When I was visiting in Taos, New Mexico, I saw similar diamonds on a house. A lady was standing outside of the house, and I asked her what they meant. She said, 'They represent protection against wicked spirits.' She also said, 'The frames around the windows were painted forest green or turquoise for protection against something which I don't recall.' The frames around our windows were painted forest green. I now have a different attitude towards those big diamonds on our house. They are not too bad looking. We were the only house in the Spanish Colony that had the diamonds on the outside walls."

Viola Gomez Merrill standing by her house. Notice the green diamond on the wall behind her. Photo courtesy of Delilah (Gomez) Fiechter.

Religion, traditions, and folklore passed down from generation to generation have been the foundation of the lives of the Spanish Colony residents. Descendents of the early colonists can look back at the evolution of their heritage with pride, and, in turn, pass on their knowledge and experiences to future generations.

References

1. (1949). *Our Lady of Peace Dedication Pamphlet.*

2. Ibid.

3. Morera, Dominic, Reverend SF. (1955, February 21). *Alabemos Los Dulces Nombres.*

4. Schillinger, Esther K. (1929, August). *Social Contacts of the Immigrant Mexicans of Weld County.* (Masters Thesis, Colorado State College). p.34.

5. Echevarria, Evelio, and Otero, Jose. *Hispanic Colorado Four Centuries: History and Heritage.* p. 191.

6. Anaya, Rudolfo. (1999). *My Land Sings Stories from the Rio Grand*, p.19.

Chapter 6

The Store of the Colony

Alvin Garcia at his store with children buying candy, *The Greeley Tribune* September 7, 1980. p.C3.

Ynez Lopez Sr. owned the store on Lot 1 that was remembered as the first structure built in the Colony in 1924. Alvin Garcia, remembering the first post office which was located in the store, said with a little chuckle, "The mail was delivered, and around one o'clock in the afternoon, one member from each family came and got the mail. It was like a swarm of ants running to the store. Sometimes distributing the mail ran smoothly, and other times it was a mess."

About 1926, Ynez made Salvino Lopez a partner in the business. Ynez later sold his share to Salvino [no relation to Ynez], who operated the store until about 1927. Mr. Salvino then sold the store to Mr. Hillario Tellez and left the Colony. As mentioned in Chapter 5, this building was donated to the Denver Arch Diocese for the Spanish Colony church.

Shortly after he built his store, Ynez Lopez installed a gas pump for the residents who owned cars. Alvin Garcia said, "Hillario ran the gas pump for a couple of years. He charged about 10 to 15 cents for a gallon of gas. It had a hand pump on it; you had to pump the gas to the top and then pull the trigger, and the gas would flow down into the gas tank." The company that installed the pump removed it when the store was donated to the Catholic Diocese.

Ynez Lopez opened another store in 1930 in his four-room adobe residence on Lot 42. He used the front living room as his store. Gene Maese said, "My dad [Paul Maese] told me Grandpa [Ynez Lopez] had a drug store in his store on Lot 42. He didn't sell prescription drugs. He did sell *conicos* (marbles), and books from Mexico. "Grandpa was the first to read all the stories in the books. When the customers wanted to buy a book, he would tell them all about it. The customers would tell him, 'Why should I buy this now? You have told me all about it!' That is why Grandpa couldn't sell a book from his store."

Gene also remembered when the gypsies came to the Colony. "The gypsies would go into Grandpa's store and buy cases of sodas from him. Grandpa charged them the deposit knowing they might take off with the bottles. The next morning, he would send Neddy [Ynez Lopez, another grandson] and me to collect the empty bottles and cases. The gypsies were asleep in their tents and wagons by the Cache la Poudre River, and they didn't hear us collecting the bottles.

We took them back to Grandpa, and he gave us candy for doing the work."

Nora Antonelly, Ynez's granddaughter and a Colony resident, has memories of her grandpa's store. "Grandpa let me help him for the first time after I nagged him for weeks. I worked behind the counter. Ice cream cones were 4 cents for a small scoop of ice cream. A little boy came in and asked for an ice cream cone, but he only had 3 cents. So I said 'No' at first, and the young boy started crying. I then whispered to the child and said 'O. K., I will give you an ice cream cone for 3 cents'. Grandpa Ynez was napping on the sofa, woke up, and told me he had heard everything I told the young boy. He looked at the little boy and told him to go home and get the other penny from his mom or dad. The little boy went home and did return with another penny and bought the ice cream cone from Grandpa. That was the only time Grandpa let me work for him in the store. Grandpa told me he knew what this child was up to, and he didn't fall for his pleas anymore. The young boy needed to learn he couldn't weasel his way through life."

"Aunt Jenny helped my Grandpa, Ynez Lopez, when he had the store," Dorothy Garcia Rodman said. "Grandpa wanted Gus and Jenny [Ynez' grandchildren] to know enough English to read and write, so they could help him with his books and write letters. Both my grandpas [Ynez Lopez and Abram Garcia] were able to write in Spanish and English. He encouraged Gus and Jenny to someday take the store and run it."

Just prior to his death in July 1938, Ynez gave the store to his oldest son, Francisco Lopez Sr.. Francisco operated the store for about six months and then offered the business to his son, Augustine "Gus". Gus, however, preferred farm work to running the store. Francisco's daughter, Juanita [Jenny] Lopez Garcia, on the other hand, had recently married Alvin Garcia in August 1938. She and Alvin accepted the business and changed the name to "Garcia's Store." In the beginning, the store was a part-time venture for Alvin and Juanita [Jenny]. They continued to work on farms for their primary income. Alvin commented, "I worked on the farm, and Jenny worked in the store. One year Jenny helped me pick potatoes along with my brother and sister-in-law, Tito and Santitos. We worked the Everett Johnson farm just west of Lucerne, Colorado. Jenny helped me all the time. We had the store, but Jenny helped me on the farm too. We traveled back and forth from the Colony to the farm every day. In the 1940s, we also worked on Harvey Mathias' farm picking pickles. I took Jenny and Josie Garcia along to help and also the kids, Robert Duran, Steve Garcia, and my sons, Abe and Claudie. They were small, but they picked really well. During the winter of 1941, I had nothing to do, so I worked for the railroad on a section gang putting in track from Eaton to Ault."

During the years 1938 to 1999, the Garcia's operated the store in six successive locations. They moved the store from Lot 42 to Lot 31 in 1938, and operated it out of their home. In 1943, Alvin's uncle, Tito Garcia Sr., who lived on Lot 50, moved into Greeley. Alvin and Jenny purchased Tito's larger house and moved their home and store there.

In 1949, the Garcias built a new structure located south of W Street just outside of the Spanish Colony and near the Cache la Poudre River. Alvin and Jenny got supplies to stock the shelves from stores in Greeley when they had extra cash on hand.

In the back of the store was a pool hall. It became a popular place for both young and old. People gathered to play pool, cards, and checkers, and some gambled on the games being played.

New store built across from the Spanish Colony. Back row L to R: Alvin Garcia, Domingo Duran, Ricardo "Rico" Lopez, Louis Hernandez. Front row L to R: Martina Lopez, Josie Garcia, Jenny Lopez Garcia, Sally and Monica Garcia. Photo courtesy of Alvin Garcia.

In 1951, Alvin Garcia had a stroke. This left him with some paralysis on his right side. Prior to Alvin's stroke, he worked for the Union Pacific Railroad in Cheyenne, Wyoming, as a laborer in the stores department. So that Jenny could care for their family, Alvin, and run the store, they moved Garcia's Store back into their home on Lot 50. At this time, they had Rufino Ortiz build a basement under their home for the store. Alvin said, "I stayed in the house that year [1951]. I couldn't do anything while recovering from the stroke" Alvin was unable to return to full-time work. In order to meet the financial needs of the family, Jenny looked outside the store and the Colony to supplement the family's income. Jenny went to work for Weld County General Hospital in 1954 as a cleaning lady. Later, she was promoted to work in the operating rooms. Weld County General Hospital trained her to become a surgical assistant. Alvin said, "I managed the store from 1953 to 1999. I threw away my crutches and managed the store, and Jenny worked at the hospital."

From 1952 to 1954, Jenny and Josie Garcia [niece] worked for Harvey Mathias. Harvey said, "I would rather have them [Jenny and Josie] than the boys work for me. Jenny and Josie shucked barley; the machine would cut the barley down, and Jenny and Josie would pile it up. They worked hard harvesting barley." Josie said, "We had to clean sugar beets and do other things on his farm."

The store was moved in 1982 for the sixth and last time to Lot 11. Alvin had his son, Claudie, build a new frame home with a basement. Alvin mentioned, "I had the store in the basement on Lot 11, but when I moved it upstairs in the same house, the City of Greeley charged me $150.00. I didn't think that was right, but I paid it anyway."

When Jenny retired from the hospital in 1985, she helped Alvin manage the store until her death in February 1992.

Jenny Lopez Garcia at her retirement party in 1985 in her work clothes. Photo courtesy of Alvin Garcia.

After Jenny's death, Alvin managed the store with the help of his children - Abraham ["Abe"], Claudie, Annabelle Canzona - and his grandchildren. Alvin retired in 1999 at the age of 87. He leased and then sold the store in 2001. The new owners converted it into a store and a restaurant with takeout dinners.

Gabriel Lopez has vivid memories of the store when he was a kid in the late 1950s through 1960s. "On top of the shelves were all the trophies won by the Greeley Grays baseball teams. There was only one aisle, and it was extremely narrow. On the north side of the aisle were coolers that held sodas, milk, butter, eggs, and other cold items, plus a freezer for ice cream bars and frozen steaks, hamburger, and ham. I, my cousins, and other children in the Colony crowded up to the counter on the south side of the aisle to buy candy. With a big smile, Uncle Alvin would ask what we were doing. Of course, we were there to buy candy such as Sixlets, red cinnamon-flavored Hotdog Gum, Candy Cigarettes, Taffy, Dixie Sticks, small Waxed Pop Bottles filled with flavored water, and other varieties of penny candies at three for a penny. When it came time to pay, occasionally someone was a little short, but Uncle Alvin would pretend that it was the correct amount, as he liked to see children happy. As children, we used to say, 'Let's go to Uncle

102

Alvin's and get some candy.' We would run down the alley and through yards to get to Uncle Alvin's store. We thought we had run for miles, when in reality we ran past only a few houses to get to the store."

Delilah Gomez Fiechter remembered, "The bus stop was next to Alvin's store, and Alvin had a pinball machine. He never minded the kids waiting in his store, and we would play with the pinball machine and buy gum, candy, and sodas. It was fun and nice to have the store nearby. There was a bus for grade school, junior high school, and high school."

When talking to Alvin Garcia, he said with a pleased and satisfied smile, "Because of the store, I saw all the children who were born in the Colony from 1938 to 1999. I watched them grow up and move away. But all of them still call me 'Uncle Alvin.'"

Jenny's brother, Rico Lopez said, "I remember seeing Jenny at the Safeway store [in Greeley, on 11th Avenue] buying soda pop on sale for their store. Jenny and Alvin worked hard to keep the store operating. I am proud of what they did for the Colony."

Jenny Lopez Garcia and Alvin Garcia in the store at the Spanish Colony. Photo courtesy of Alvin Garcia.

Tito 'Butter' Garcia, Jr. [nephew] told a story about when he tried to steal money from Garcia's Store. "Some other boys and I were playing craps, and I was losing money big time! I lost all of my money but wanted to play some more. I said to my buddies that I would get the money from my Uncle Alvin's store. I told my buddies to look out for Uncle Alvin. Alvin had installed a window, so he could look into the store to see if someone was there. I didn't know this at the time. So there I was sneaking into the store, and Uncle Alvin was watching all of this. I thought that Uncle Alvin couldn't hear me. All of a sudden I heard the door open and out came Uncle Alvin. He yelled at me, and asked me what I was doing. I was so scared that I dove through the window. As we ran away, I yelled at my buddies, 'Why didn't you warn me about Uncle Alvin?' Alvin was so mad at me at the time. Uncle said later he knew what I was doing, and he just wanted to scare me."

During this interview with Alvin and Butter, Alvin was laughing so hard that Butter had difficulty telling his story. This story held many fond memories for the two of them. Butter lived briefly in the Colony until his family moved into Greeley, but he spent all of his spare time with his relatives in the Spanish Colony.

Carmen Lozano Weekley remembered, "I used to play store. When we moved from Eaton, Colorado, to the Colony, we had a trailer. My grandpa put it in the back yard. In half of the trailer my grandpa made me a *tiendita* (store), and in the other half was my playhouse. I had 50 dolls in the trailer. I used to buy the penny candies at Alvin's store. I took them to my little store and the kids came to buy them from me. Nora Marquez was the one who took care of the store. I was the owner. I didn't do anything, because I was the boss, and she was my worker. I don't know who came, but Nora said, 'Carmen, this girl doesn't want to buy the candy. She said she can go to Alvin's store and get 10 candies for a penny.' I said, 'Tell her to go to Alvin's store and get them, but forget about coming to my store and playing with us.' I was a naughty little girl. The girl bought the candy from my store, so she could play with us."

Jose's dad is Ramon Marquez, who has lived in the Colony since 1969. He moved from New Mexico to Colorado to work in the sugar beet fields. When asked why he chose to live in the Colony. Jose said, "The homes here made it feel like our old home, and Spanish is still spoken."

Today, the site of Alvin's and Jenny's last home and store is still a lively place. Alvin Garcia sold the store to Jose Marquez in 1999 [no relation to the Marquez of the Colony]. Jose first came in 1970 and didn't care for the Colony. He returned to Albuquerque and married Beneranda. Jose and Beneranda moved to the Colony in 1978 from Albuquerque, New Mexico. He said, "I think the Colony looks nice now, and I have learned to love it." Two of their three children were born in the Spanish Colony. Alvin sold the house on Lot 20, located next to the store, to Jose in 1986. Jose's family worked the beet fields in the 1970s and 1980s. Jose worked for a construction company in Denver and then started to work for Markley's Furniture Company in Greeley and occasionally for Weld County. Jose has lived in the Colony for 17 years and intends to stay. They continue to operate the store, although it is not as big. They installed a kitchen and sell burritos, tacos, and other Spanish foods to go. Jose and Beneranda renamed the store *La Tienda* (Spanish for The Store*)*.

The Garcia's store on Lot 11, renamed *La Tienda* in 2001. Photo taken by Gabriel Lopez.

Chapter 7

Maintaining the Colony

Looking north on Second Street in the Spanish Colony, circa 1940. Photo Courtesy of Gus and Mary Jojola Martinez.

The Colonists maintained attractive, clean homes and yards, took pride in their belongings and respected their neighbors' property and belongings. The rules and regulations they adopted protected the health and safety of the Colony residents.

Criselda "Kate" Espinosa Cassel said, "My stepmother and us girls untied the mattresses and took out the stuffing or wool. We washed the coverings and dried them on the clotheslines. Then we put the stuffing back in and tied up the mattresses and used them that night. My stepmother told us, 'If your oven is clean, that means you are a clean person.' This taught the children to keep the oven and house clean. Now, whenever I see dust or a spot, I stop right away and clean it. This was what we were taught to do."

In spring and fall, the Colony scheduled clean-up days, and everyone participated as directed in the Constitution.[1]

Section I:

That all the habitants of this town that are owners or renters: shall have the best cleaners possible so as to save the honor of the town.

Section II:

That each owner of property or residents of the colony is prohibited to dump rubbish in private property or in others property unless he may have the permission.

Section III:

That each property owner shall have a regular sized box to deposit said rubbish, which shall be made in line with the others so the same owner may be able to clean it when necessary and throw it to a place where the Commission may say.

Section IV:

That each property owner may be obliged to maintain the costs in benefit of the town for which they should pay a due of $1.00 a year each one being $.50 the 15th day of July and $.50 the 15th day of November of each year.

Residents were required to clean up the Colony and repair the irrigation system, churches, outhouses, Salon, etc. The community shared both work and laughter in conducting these civic projects.

Every family in the Colony, or a representative of that family, participated in the clean-up days. Families who did not participate were charged $5.00. This money was used for maintenance costs. After the families completed their yard work, they voluntarily helped others. Moses Espinosa compared the Colony to an "Indian village". It was a community where everyone cared for it and each other.

The carpenter of the Colony was Rufino Ortiz. He helped others as much as he could, and his rates were reasonable. Rufino also made coffins, which he stored in his yard.

To maintain discipline and order among the Colony youths, the Trustees met with the children in the Salon to review and remind them of the rules. Well-behaved and mannerly children helped ensure order and harmony. Most parents disciplined their children and taught them good manners; children were polite and respectful. Adults were addressed as Mr., Mrs., Miss., or, in Spanish, Don and Doña.

Mary Martinez remembered an occasion involving the colony children. "The trustees gathered all the children together in the Salon and explained what we could and could not do, and what the curfew times were. Curfew was strictly enforced. One trustee explained that if someone pointed a finger at a person and said, 'There goes a bad person,' that was being impolite. If one pointed his or her finger, they were to say, 'there goes a good person.' They were very strict about this gesture, because they wanted the children to grow up respecting others."

An example of obedience, duty, and respect taught to the children of the Colony involved serving adults a drink of water. Many who were interviewed commented on this custom. Whenever an adult in the house - a father, mother, grandparents, or guests - wanted a drink of water, a child was asked to get it. After the glass of water was delivered, the child stood with arms crossed, and waited patiently until the person finished drinking. Then the child took the glass and asked if he or she wanted any more. If so, the child refilled the glass. If not, the child took the glass back to the sink and, in most cases, washed it and put it back in the cabinet. Only then was he allowed to go play.

Mary Martinez said, "If the child wanted to stay, he or she was to sit and keep quiet and listen intently to the conversation. The child was also taught to wait to participate in the conversation. Interrupting someone who was speaking was forbidden. This taught the child to always listen to others' conversations and not ignore them or interrupt them as they spoke."

Alvin Garcia demonstrated this childhood lesson during his interviews. He always patiently waited for the interviewer to write down his words.

The good manners and the respect for others taught these children were evident in their adult years. For example, Gabriel Lopez remembers his father, Gus Lopez, never left a dirty glass or dish. "If you did not drink from a glass or a can of pop within a few minutes, he would take the glass away, even if it wasn't empty. He washed it and put it away, thinking you were finished."

To enforce and maintain safety and protection for the Colony, the Commission or Trustees selected one man, respected by all as if he were a real policeman. His duties were listed in Section III of the Constitution.[2]

Section III:

> Said person elected by the Commission will have the right to prosecute the boys if they should play ball games, and at the streets of this town, and in all things that may bring trouble to them and to the parents, and at the same time not let them crowd in or by cars or trucks going through the streets of this town, and in all things that may bring trouble to them and the parents of said boys. All persons driving inside the Colony must not exceed the Speed Limit of 15 miles an hour (3 Chapter, Section II, Paragraph II).

Alvin Garcia said, "This arrangement lasted until 1949 or 1950 when the City of Greeley appointed Arthur Lopez and Jose Sedillos as policemen."

The constitutionally-elected policeman was in charge of the Curfew, which applied to the children and teenagers in the Colony.

The bell was rung in the morning for school and again for lunchtime. As a policeman, this person maintained security in the Colony, at dances, weddings and parties. He broke up fights and kept the gypsies out as well as he could. In most cases, the residents helped the policeman patrol the Colony.

A bell house was placed on top of a tower built to tap the artesian spring which supplied the water pump in the east park. Usually a trustee or someone assigned by a trustee rang the bell for curfew and other events. Curfew in the summer was 9:00 p.m., and in the winter 8:00 p.m., and it was strictly adhered to. For the children who were not at home at the time the bell rang, the Colony police officer or a trustee would take them home and scold both the child and the parents. Dave Lopez recalled an incident when some of the kids climbed the ladder to the bell and put a sock over the clapper so the ring was not heard.

The tower was razed in the latter part of 1939 or the spring of 1940. The bell was dismantled and sold for scrap by one of the residents in the Colony.

(Augustine "Gus" Lopez) The tower in 1939 as it was being taken down. Photo Courtesy of Palmer Lopez.

Nora Antonelly recalled, "When I was a small child, I thought the bell tower and water pump belonged only to Grandpa Ynez Lopez Sr., because it was directly behind his house. I thought he was the Mayor of the Spanish Colony. I sat by the tower and felt like royalty. Many of the colony residents stopped by and visited with me. I thought Grandpa had given them permission to get water from the pump. The girls and I went for walks around the Colony and ended up sitting at the water pump. I felt like a special person, because I thought the tower and well belonged to Grandpa. Now it makes me feel silly, because the tower and pump belonged to the Colony and not just to Grandpa Ynez. The tower and water pump will always be special to me."

The tower had benches inside where the colonists sat, visited, and shared fond memories. "The Place" in the Colony to meet the boy or girl of their dreams was at the water pump under the tower. Many volunteered to fetch the necessary water, as it gave them a chance to visit. Romances and even marriages resulted, as there was no shortage of volunteers to carry out this household chore. The second water pump, located a block west of the east park, didn't

112

have a tower or benches. This well served the homes on North 26th Avenue.

Due to the seasonal nature of their work, the colonists didn't plant grass. The yards of the homes consisted of hard-packed soil with trees, bushes, and flowers planted as accents. Josie Garcia said, "We sprinkled water on the dirt and swept it nice and clean before we played in the yard."

Residents who remained in the Colony, during the sugar beet season, due to age or other circumstances, took care of the gardens and animals, such as dogs, cats, chickens, goats, etc. while the majority of the residents worked the farms.

Many interviewed recalled how the gypsies camped along the Cache la Poudre River south of the Colony. Kate Espinosa Cassel recalled, "They came one day and usually left the next day. They stole things from the homes closest to their camp. They also stole Dad's chickens from his pen." The chicken pen was located across the street from his home on Lot 63.

In a field south of M Street, some residents constructed small corrals for cows or pigs. When it came time to butcher one, the whole Colony was invited to help.

Mary Jojola Martinez mentioned, "Don Otavio Espinosa invited all the residents to come and enjoy the day at his house to carve up a pig. He gave a portion of the pig to each family who came. They played music and enjoyed each other's company all day long. Others in the Colony did the same thing. We were a people who liked to give and who helped others as much as we could." With a sad smile Mary said, "You don't see that happening as much today, if at all."

According to the 1930 Federal Census,[3] the majority of the Colony residents spoke English. Sixteen of these residents came from Mexico, and four of these Mexican Nationals became naturalized citizens. In M. Darling's 1932 thesis, she noted there were 355 residents in the Colony.[4] The majority of the residents came from Southern Colorado and New Mexico.

Many of the workers who settled in the Spanish Colony had their own vehicles, such as Model T's or trucks. Those with cars generously provided transportation for those who had no vehicles. Sometimes car owners lent their vehicles to others.

Copy of Frank Lopez's Sr. Colorado automobile registration. Courtesy of Palmer Lopez.

Alvin Garcia laughed as he recalled, "My father-in-law, Francisco Lopez Sr., loaned his car and driver's license to a family on the other side of the Colony, which is now N. 26th Avenue. On the way to get some food, the car was pulled over by a policeman. The officer looked at the driver's license and asked if he was Mr. Lopez. He was so scared he told the officer, "No!" The officer put him and my father-in-law in jail that night and released them the next morning. My father-in-law was given a strong warning not to do that again. He said, 'Okay, I won't.'" Laughing harder, Alvin continued, "My father-in-law loaned the car again to the same person, but not his driver's license!"

Arnulfo "Nudy" Lopez mentioned, "The older boys, my brothers, took my dad's car to the river [Cache la Poudre River]. They drove it, bouncing all the way down the riverbank, until they reached the water. Then they washed the car and cleaned it really good. When they were done, they carefully drove up the riverbank to keep the dirt and dust off of the car. The boys then cleaned themselves up and drove into town. Those Model T's were really good at climbing, especially the riverbank. Today, one would need a four-wheel drive to do it."

Shown in the model below, a yellow model T car is being driven into the river for a wash.

The Spanish Colony Model board located in Centennial Village Museum, Greeley, Colorado. Photo Courtesy of City of Greeley Museums.

By adhering to the guiding principals of their Constitution and supporting each other, the Greeley Spanish Colony held to a high ideal of cleanliness and law and order. In this environment, colonists prospered, and their children grew up in a safe and sanitary community despite their relative poverty.

References

1. Schillinger, Esther K. (1929, August). *Social Contacts of the Immigrant Mexicans of Weld County.* (Masters Degree thesis, Colorado State College). pp. 57-60.

2. Ibid. p. 60.

3. Federal Census: Department of Commerce-Bureau of the Census Fifteenth Census of The United States: 1930 Population Schedule; State Colorado; County Weld; Gibson Precinct 16 Enumeration District No. 62-30; Supervisor's District No. Sheet 6A, 6B, 7A, 7B, 8A; Pierce Precinct 50; sheet 2A; Crow Creek Precinct 18; sheet 4B. (See Appendix G).

4. Colony Reports Show Great Interest Here. (1932, February 18). *The Greeley Tribune.* p.8.

Chapter 8

Recreation in the Colony

Children in back row L to R: Abraham "Abe" Garcia, Sam Lopez, Martin Hernandez. Front center: Claudie Garcia. circa 1948-1949 Photo Courtesy of Alvin Garcia.

As in any community, the children of the Spanish Colony amused themselves with a variety of activities and games. Sam Lopez recalled, "There were a lot of children in the Colony, so it was easy for us kids to find someone to play with and something to do. We sometimes just ran and chased each other up and down the alleys."

Gene Maese said, "The children in the Colony had to be creative, because they couldn't buy any toys. They made their own. I made my own sled with wood I salvaged from the Colony."

Josie Garcia recalled, "We used to create our own carnivals. We used an old tub for a swing and a loop-o-plane, at least that is what I called it. We threw a rope over a tree branch and my cousin, Marion Maese, tied the knots. I was the creator of our carnival!"

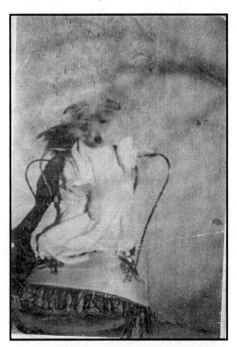
Duran Family dog, Queeny, dressed up like a doll.
Courtesy of Robert Duran

The children played many different games. The boys played baseball, marbles, and kick-the-can. They walked on stilts, and played a game called "war."

"War" required several participants. Each team consisted of two boys with the smaller of the two perched on the shoulders of the bigger boy. Each twosome would pull and tug until only one pair remained standing.

The girls played hopscotch, dolls (if they had them), and tag. They often watched the boys play baseball or other sports or played baseball themselves.

Criselda "Kate" Espinosa Cassel remembered, "My half sister Jenny Rios and I played jacks, dressed paper dolls with cut outs from magazines and made dolls out of socks by tying some cotton in the end of a sock and painting a face on it. We played on a

118

little teeter-totter my dad made from a piece of wood. We were always so jolly in the Colony."

Mary Martinez recalled, "We had a small wheel and all the girls took turns pushing it up and down the road with a rod. Both the girls and the boys rolled car tires up and down the street, sometimes with someone in the middle of the wheel hanging on for dear life."

Gene Maese said, "We used clothesline wire and bent it into a "u" shape and put it through the hole of a small wheel. While the wheel was on the ground, we bent the other end into a handle of the right height. We gave the wheel a shove and ran behind it as fast as we could up and down the street."

Edna Espinosa Aragon said, "We played *bolitas negro y blanca*; this was Chinese checkers played with black and white marbles. We also made our own playing cards out of paper."

Both girls and boys played "hide-'n'-seek." Without fences, they had the whole Colony to hide in.

South of the Colony across M Street was a sand pit where the children climbed trees and made tunnels and roads in the dirt mounds to play with their cars. It was also used for sledding in the winter.

On Lot 26 located on the west end of the Colony, the residents built a 12' high by 8'-10' wide brick "L" shaped wall to play *rivalote* or handball (similar to racket ball). The walls were made of adobe brick and stucco, and the floor was cement. The ball was hit on one wall, and spectators often stood or sat along the other wall.

Ricardo "Rico" Lopez, who played *rivalote* as a teenager, said, "For the young or old, *rivalote* was very competitive. You had to play to win! There was no mercy for the other players, including yourself! The girls were equally as competitive, as they wanted to impress the boys."

The Spanish Colony maintained a baseball diamond for its semi-pro team. The children also used these baseball diamonds for their own games of baseball. In 1942, the Colony had a little league team.

Otavio Espinosa's pool hall on Lot 23. Picture taken in February 1943. Starting from the left: unknown man, Louis Espinosa, Joe Rios with cigar, Sam Rios in uniform, Leroy Gurula, Mario Lopez with a hat on, Efugo Duran sitting looking at camera, Moses Espinosa, and Nanie Espinosa. Photo Courtesy of Jerry Lopez.

The pool hall in the Colony provided recreation for the older boys and men and, for some, this was their first opportunity to learn to play pool. They also played cards and gambled at the pool hall. It was purely penny-ante gambling with the pot ranging from twenty cents to one dollar. The men also played craps against the wall outside the pool hall.

Alvin Garcia said, "We would play for pennies or matchsticks just to pass time. We were not making that much money by farming to have high stakes. I remember a man came from California who played cards professionally and wanted to play for big money. He left for another town when he found out how little the ante was."

The pool hall was a convenient place for the men of the Colony to discuss old times, current events, politics, baseball, boxing, and other sports. Most Colony residents were Democrats.

Gabriel Lopez remembered, as a young boy growing up in the 1960s, how his father, Augustine "Gus", taught him to play marbles in the back yard of the family's home in Cheyenne, Wyoming. Gus was an infant when his parents arrived in Greeley in 1920 and growing up in the Spanish Colony he learned to play marbles.

Gene Maese said, "Frank Lopez, Jr. and I walked over to Tolito's, a nickname for Carlitas Martinez (*tolito* means impatient in English). His house was on the northwest corner of the Colony. In back of the house, his dad had a small adobe house, similar to a chicken coop. Inside was a potbelly stove and a kerosene lantern minus its glass chimney. We would start a fire in the heater and light the lantern and play cards. We gambled for marbles. It was something to do, because the winters were very cold, and we couldn't play outside."

"The older ones played marbles along with the children in the colony," Moses Espinosa recalled. "They enjoyed it just as much, and they also bet against each other. Their betting was often with matchsticks. At night they used the matchsticks to light the area to play cards. They played until their fingers were black from the burning matches, and they could no longer strike or hold onto them."

The Cache la Poudre River, which bordered the Colony on the south, provided many opportunities for entertainment, including swimming and fishing. Frank Lopez, Jr. remembered as a young boy how he and his friends fished in the river. When they caught a fish, they made a fire on the bank, cooked the fish, and ate it.

A tree branch hung over the river, and a rope was attached to it. With a running jump, the children grabbed the rope and swung out over the river and let go of the rope, falling into the water.

A photo of the Spanish Colony model at the Centennial Village Museum. Children are walking across the Cache la Poudre River on stilts while playing follow-the-leader. Photo Courtesy of City Greeley Museums.

In a game of follow-the-leader on stilts, the leader led the group to the river and walked across it on stilts. Gene Maese said, "Lalo [Edward Lopez] was the champion of the stilts. No one could outdo him. He was the only one who could walk on stilts as tall as a house. He would climb up to the top of the roof, and somebody would give him his stilts which he had made. He walked on them all over the Colony. He was the best."

During the winter when the river froze, the children ice skated into Greeley. Moses commented, "Sometimes we fell through the ice up to our knees or waist. Sometimes we were so wet, we couldn't walk, because our pants were frozen. We also cut the ice into blocks and stood on them as they floated down the river until they broke or dissolved. We would cut more blocks and continue playing. We were like animals. We would always be so wet, and yet we never got sick."

East of the Spanish Colony, in a pasture, was an artesian spring with water which constantly flowed into a pond. During the winter the children ice skated and played games such as crack-the-whip, which was a line of children holding hands and skating all over the pond making sharp turns in order to break the line and send them flying. Another game was jumping barrels. Several who were interviewed expressed admiration for Edward Lopez who could jump over 13 barrels and was the best skater.

The Cache la Poudre River and the artesian spring provided food for the Colony.

Moses mentioned, "I went down to the river and hunted for mourning doves, pheasants, ducks, wild rabbits, and jackrabbits with my dad's .10 gauge shot gun. My friends and I sat on a branch that hung over the river and shot carp with my .22 caliber gun. Sometimes we ate the fish and meat at the river. We built a fire and cooked them. We had fun doing that and telling stories. I took some home, so we had something different to eat other than beans, but, of course, beans and potatoes were served with the meat or fish. I also trapped muskrats along the river. I skinned them, stretched the pelts, and sold them for seventy five cents each. I would catch three to four a day. When Dad was only bringing home ten cents an hour, I made more than he did. I sold wood for five cents a bag to the Colony residents. I gave dad all my money to help him. I collected old rags, copper, aluminum, and bones, and took them to the junkyards and was paid a penny per pound. The bones were used for fertilizer, and the rags ... I don't know what they were used for."

Asparagus and spinach and another form of spinach called *kelites* grew wild along the river, irrigation ditches, and barrow pits. *Kelites* was commonly used to flavor the beans.

Kate Espinosa Cassel remembered frequently having *kelites* mixed in with their beans. She said, "My sisters went to the river's edge to pick them until I was 12 years old, then it was my turn to collect the *kelites*. They grew on the river's edge and we had to be old enough so we wouldn't fall in. My stepmother [Bibliana Rios Espinosa] boiled them and then fried them with onions, little pieces of tomatoes if we had some, and salt and pepper. We added just a little bit of *kelites* to the cooked beans, which made them very good!"

Josie Garcia remembered, "My mother was a very good cook. One of the dishes she made was beans and spinach. She would fry the spinach with onion, tomato, salt, and pepper."

Most of the fuel came from the trees along the river. It was usually one of the children's chores to gather the wood. Frank Lopez, Jr. recalled, "We got the wood along the river for the wood-burning stoves. There were a lot of trees with fallen branches, which made gathering wood easy. There were a lot of beaver dams along the river, and we took wood from them. That was a lot easier to do. Then the beavers would redo their dams, and we always had a fresh supply of wood!"

Occasionally, colonists went into Greeley to Lincoln Park or to see a movie. Many of the young children walked to the theater. They patronized the Rex, one of Greeley's first theaters, renamed the Chief on September 1, 1934. They also went to the Kiva and Park movie theaters.

Gene Maese said, "At Christmas, the Park and maybe the Kiva had big boxes out front, and donated toys were placed in these boxes for the needy. If you brought a toy and dropped it in the box, you could see the movie for free." He laughed and continued, "We had no good toys. Ours were homemade and worn out, but we took them anyway and dropped them into the box. They would say, 'Okay, you can go in.' We ran into the show and had a good time."

The adults also went to the Kiva. On Tuesday nights, the Kiva showed movies in Spanish for the Hispanics and Mexicans.

Gabriel and Jody Lopez recalled Gus Lopez saying, "My dad [Francisco Lopez Sr.] said to me '*mi hijo, vamos a cine*'. In English this means, 'My son, let's go to the show.' My grandpa [Ynez Lopez Sr.] and Dad loved to go to the shows. If my grandpa and dad had had a VCR, they would have never left the house." Gus, like his father and grandfather, also liked to go to the movies and especially enjoyed John Wayne films.

Kate Espinosa Cassel mentioned, "We went into Greeley once in a while on Saturday or Sunday, because we worked all week. We would have a piece of watermelon and eat it at Island Grove Park. We went to the Gilbert-Bishop Drug Store at 820 8th Street, to get a banana split and then walked to Lincoln Park to eat it. Dad always gave us 50 cents to use for candy or soda pop."

Carmen Lozano Weekley remembered, "We played hopscotch, hide-and-seek, and kick-the-can. I want to tell you something, but it is kind of embarrassing. My brother and sister and I got on top of my aunt Nellie's house. My dad was doing construction, and he had a pile of sand in the yard. My grandma had washed clothes, and she hung the sheets in the front and other clothes in the back of the clotheslines. The "unmentionables" were always in the middle, because it was bad for people to see the undies, you know. She used to make her own bloomers, BIG BLOOMERS! My brother and I tied strings and attached a rock to her bloomers. We climbed onto Aunt Nellie's roof to toss our parachute bloomers in the air to float down. Grandma came out, and I thought she was going to have a heart attack. She screamed, '*Aye dios mio, Aye ya yah*!!!! We laughed and hid for a bit."

While the residents of the Colony worked hard to care for the community and their families, they also knew how to entertain themselves. The children were creative and imaginative with their toys and whatever other materials were available to them, and they always had someone to play with in the Colony. The adults balanced their responsibilities with recreation and enjoyed dances in the Salon, games of pool and cards, and going to the movies.

Chapter 9

The Salón

Greeley Spanish Colony Salon or Community House in 2002. Photo courtesy of Gabriel Lopez.

Jose Marquez owned the Colony's community house or *Salon*. Dances, box socials, beauty pageants, boxing matches, wedding receptions, and plays such as the *Pastores* were held there. The Colony Trustees and the House of Neighborly Service also conducted their meetings and activities in the Salon.

Greeley Spanish Colony wedding march. Courtesy of Alvin Garcia.

Several former residents had fond memories of wedding festivities within the Colony; for example, after a wedding at the church, the colonists traditionally joined in a processional march with the newlyweds. The procession with the bride and groom began at the south side of the Cache la Poudre River. A violinist and guitarist led the procession north over the bridge and back into the Colony marching through all the streets. When they arrived at the Salon, the festivities began. Everyone in the Colony participated.

During the afternoon and early evening, a reception meal made by the bride's parents was provided. Commonly served dishes included beans, tortillas, potatoes, rice, *molé,* and *meñudo*.

Mary Martinez remembered, "My mom worked all day before my wedding and even the morning of the wedding day making all kinds of dishes – beans, rice, chicken, *molé*, tortillas, *tamales*, sweets like cakes, and bread pudding. She worked so hard. She made my wedding day so wonderful."

At twilight, the dancing began. The adults were ready to party. Traditionally, the bride and groom began the dance either by themselves or leading a march with all the members of both families joining in.

Mary Martinez continued, "I remember when the dancing was going on, and, as it got late, the children were lying under the counters on mattresses the parents brought into the Salon and placed in the corners of the room. They didn't take the children home, because there was no one old enough to watch them, so they came to the dance. It was a lot of fun."

To raise money for the baseball team, a beauty pageant was held in the Salon. Half of the proceeds went to the Greeley Grays and the other half to the winner of the pageant. The beauty pageant contestants represented teams in the Northern Colorado Baseball League. Young women came from Fort Collins, Gilcrest, La Salle, Jownstown, Cheyenne, Wyoming, and other teams. A dance was held at the conclusion of the pageant.

Greeley Spanish Colony Beauty Pageant held at the Salon or Community house. Photo courtesy of Alvin Garcia.

128

The City of Greeley required a license for any group or organization holding an event. During the Depression, money was scarce, and Louis Espinosa asked the City to waive its event fees. The March 30, 1932 edition of *The Greeley Tribune*, "License Waived for Two Spanish Dances," noted, "Louis Espinosa pointed out that due to present conditions, the task of furnishing clean entertainment for local Spanish-American people is difficult." The City waived the $25.00 fee since the proceeds went to buy uniforms, equipment, trophies, and to pay for other team expenses.

In the late 1930s, boxing events were held in the Salon. Dave Lopez reminisced about boxing. "The fathers had us box against one another, and each bet on his own son. We still played with each other after the boxing match. In some cases, it made better friends out of some children. We tended to respect one another more after an event, especially if we won a lot and were pretty tough." Wrestling matches were sometimes held in addition to the boxing.

Boxing match in the Salon, circa 1954-55   L to R: Claudie Garcia and "Pungy" Garza. Photo courtesy of Alvin Garcia.

Claudie Garcia remembered, "In the photo [above], I was about 12 or 13 years old. I won by decision. We trained for months and boxed against the other boys for this tournament sponsored by Our Lady of Peace church. I guess we drew to fight against each other, "Pungy" Garza and I. We fought the one time that day. There were others who fought too - Tommy Lopez, Billy Lopez, and others I just can't remember now. You can see [in the picture] there wasn't much room for spectators in the Salon. This was the only year I boxed, because I was more interested in baseball."

Box socials were held to raise money for Colony repairs and expenses. For this event, girls and young women each made a lunch and placed it in a decorated box to be auctioned. Boys and young men bid on the lunches. They raised the bid until it got pretty high, but usually the bidding stopped, so the boyfriend could win the lunch. The successful bidder then took his lunch and the young woman who made it to the Colony Park or stayed at the Salon.

Edna Espinosa Aragon remembered a funny story about a boy who cared for her. She said, "I made donuts for the box lunch. I took them out of the oven too early, and they were a little raw. Ernesto Marquez bought the box of raw donuts. I had to sit and eat them with him at a desk in the Community House. That was the thing to do. We had to eat what we made with the person who bought it. The *masa* (dough) came out of the donut as you bit into it. I pretended to bite into them, but then I threw them behind the desk when Ernesto was not looking. Ernesto Marquez didn't throw them away. He said, 'They are not too bad,' and he ate them. He must have liked me, and I felt so sorry for him."

"Box socials were held to raise money for the Greeley Grays," Dorothy Garcia Rodman fondly remembered. "Aunt Jenny [Juanita Jenny Garcia] loved to decorate boxes. Out of a little box, she made a little diamond-shaped piano and other wonderful boxes of unusual and interesting designs. We fixed lunches in these boxes with special sandwiches, cakes, and other favorites. You had to sit with whoever bought your box. It might be an old man; you never knew who was going to buy your box. A dance was usually held afterward."

Dancing in the Salon in the Colony. Lucia Hernandez, Otavio Espinosa, Levina and Felipe Lucero. Photo courtesy of Jerry Lopez.

The colonists held many dances in the Salon. There were so many people at the dances, it was necessary to make cards or tags in different colors to control the number of people in the small Salon. Several colors of tags were used for the dances. When one group's turn was up, they left the Salon, and the next color group began. If folks with the wrong colored tags tried to sneak in when it was not their turn and were caught, they would be thrown out for the rest of the evening. Usually two men guarded the door to turn away any uninvited guests.

Laughing very hard, Alvin Garcia recalled, "They [uninvited guests] would not come and cause trouble because of the Colony's reputation of having good fighters. If they picked a fight, all the colony folks jumped in to fight against them."

An article in *The Greeley Tribune*, "D.C. Royer Is President of Spanish Work," dated November 8, 1933, page 1, noted,

An economically planned budget was adopted and the board hopes to begin work at the colony Nov. 15. During the

131

summer, the board, with the help of the county commissioners, was able to repaper and recalcimine the community house at the Spanish American colony, and the House of Neighborly Service in Greeley. The board is working for social life among members of the Spanish American colony. A library to be established in the colony is one outgrowth of this plan... Another activity will be introduced of a primitive course in home economics, in rhyme, and song.

Alvin Garcia remembered, "There was a library that was started in the Salon, and it had some books, but it didn't last long. The health clinic was put there also, and that stayed until the early 1940s. They did paint the Salon and made it look really nice, but the library only stayed for a year or two, that is all." In asking others who lived in the Colony about the library, they did not remember, but remembered most of what the House of Neighborly Service did for them.

The article of November 8, 1933 also described other activities the House of Neighborly Service provided for the Spanish Colony (See the following article).

New President

—Photo by Gardner

D. C. Royer, who is new president of the House of Neighborly Service, working among the Spanish speaking people of the community.

D. C. Royer Is President of Spanish Work

D. C. Royer was Tuesday night elected president of the House of Neighborly Service, at a meeting of the board at the Chamber of Commerce rooms. Serving with him will be Sue Beattie, vice president; Mary Hutchison Seem, secretary; William R. Baab, treasurer.

The following new board members were elected to serve: Mrs. D. M. Faris, Marion Van Dyne, Elizabeth Doten, Iva Newman, Rev. R. C. Speer, Dr. Tracy D. Peppers.

The board is greatly encouraged by the fine spirit, the cooperation, and the financial aid already received and that which has been promised by citizens of Greeley, which together will cover the $300 asked for.

An economically planned budget was adopted and the board hopes to begin work at the colony Nov. 15. During the summer, the board, with the help of the county commissioners, was able to repaper and recalcimine the community house at the Spanish American colony, and the House of Neighborly Service in Greeley.

The board is working for social life among members of the Spanish American colony. A library to be established in the colony is one outgrowth of this plan. People are asked to give their old or disused books, especially books for people under the age of 16, to this library. Even tho the books may be old and worn, they will be mended and can be put to excellent use. Anyone who wishes to donate either books or money or their preparation may communicate with Mary Hutchison Seem at 1220 Ninth avenue or telephone her at Greeley 439W.

Another activity will be introduced of a primitive course in home economics, in rhyme and song.

Activities of the colony, under the direction of the worker, Jane Wilson, are: kindergarten, Mondays, Tuesdays and Fridays at 9 a. m.; home economics, Mondays at 2 p. m.; quilting, Tuesdays at 2 p. m.; music appreciation, Fridays at 2 p. m.; baby clinic directed by Sue Beattie, community nurse, Wednesdays at 9 a. m.; camp fire under the direction of E. Gertrude Lee, Wednesdays at 2 p. m.; library Thursdays at 2 p. m.; story hour Saturdays at 9 a. m.; boys' work, Sundays at 2 p. m. church and Sunday school in Spanish, Sundays.

The Greeley Tribune, November 8, 1933, page 1.

The first shelter for the homeless in Greeley was established in the building which had been the Spanish Colony Salon or community house. It was built in 1924, and until 1981, housed

Chapter 10

Schools and Education

Art by Mary Martinez, Gipson School, 6th grade. Photo courtesy of Gus and Mary Martinez.

colony events. "Poor Housing, Poverty Plague Migrants," in *The Greeley Tribune*, July 19, 1979, described the need for such a shelter.

A migrant farm worker is by definition a poor person, according to the U.S. Civil Rights Commission. Indeed, Labor Department statistics show that children of migrant workers are born into some of the worst poverty in this country; born into families whose income is often several thousand dollars below the poverty line for a much smaller family.

Another *The Greeley Tribune* article, March 21, 1999, "I Know," noted, "When the Guadalupe Shelter opened in 1987, it was intended to house migrant workers." The shelter's location on the outskirts of Greeley was ideal for migrants who worked in the fields outside town all day. The March 21, 1999 article also stated,

The building doesn't look like much. On the corner of 25th Avenue and 0 Street in north Greeley is a 50-year-old house in need of a paint job. On summer nights, migrant workers sleep in its yard. In the dead of winter, people line up at its door.

During recent growing seasons, migrants have faced a housing shortage. Farmers, fearful of fines imposed by the Department of Labor's housing inspectors, have continued a trend to terminate traditional living arrangements, where once they provided housing for their laborers.

Alvin Garcia, who lived next to the shelter and was active in issues concerning Spanish Colony residents said, "People don't say too much about it [the homeless shelter], but they support it. It's a pretty nice thing that will do some good."

The Salon served many purposes; from 1924-1980, it had been a meeting place for decisions made to benefit the Colony, a recreational hall for the residents, and a place for celebration. Circa 1987, it became Greeley's first homeless shelter, and it remains so today.

If a person can speak, read, and write the official language of the country in which he lives, it becomes easier, even routine, rather than frightening, to deal with medical personnel, civil authorities, or bank employees. In the early years of the Colony, however, educating the children was not a main concern of the farmers or laborers.

The farmer needed his fields cultivated and his crops harvested. On the other hand, the laborer needed to get his contracted fields finished in order to get paid; with the help of his children this was possible. The children, in addition to the adults, played an important role in the agricultural and economic growth of Greeley and Weld County.

Some parents, however, were advocates for education. In 1923, Colorado passed a compulsory school law that mandated children had to attend school from ages 7 to 14, or until they finished the eighth grade. An article in *Through the Leaves,* August, 1924, p. 412, noted,

> It was quite evident, owing to the large number of children in most of the families, that compulsory school attendance must be overlooked or some plan adopted which would enable the children to assist in making a living and also meet the requirements of the school law. From the agricultural superintendent of the Great Western Sugar Company, Mr. E.C. Walter, it was learned that about seven weeks are required to harvest a crop of beets. Consequently, school has been opened seven weeks earlier, about the middle of July, for those pupils who must or who desire to work during beet harvest. It is a matter of choice with pupils whether they start to school in July or September, but it is absolutely necessary that a choice be made as the compulsory school attendance is enforced.
>
> This school opening in July continues until beet harvest opens which is usually the latter part of September. A seven weeks' vacation is then given for both teachers and pupils. At the close of the vacation period schoolwork is resumed with the same organization as before the vacation... The results of this plan may be summarized as follows: The average attendance in days per pupil has increased from forty-five in

1917 to 162 in 1923. The enrollment 210 in 1917-18 has increased to 501 in 1923. In 1917-18 there were no pupils doing work above the fourth grade. Graduation was a matter of reaching the age of sixteen. Neither parents nor pupils considered school as being worth while.

Arnulfo "Nudy" and Augustine "Gus" Lopez are two examples of Spanish Colony children who worked beets to supplement their parents' income. Nudy remembered an occasion when his father clashed with a farmer about his 8-year-old son working in the field rather than being in the classroom. "Dad [Francisco Lopez Sr.] was getting really mad at Mr. Sigurd Carlson, the farmer he was working for. Mr. Carlson told Dad that I could not work the fields, because I was too young and by law required to go to school. Dad told Mr. Carlson that nobody told him what to do. Dad started chasing Mr. Carlson around the field; he wanted to beat him up. They ran around, while my brothers Gus and Dave chased after Dad to stop him. They finally caught Dad and held him down. Gus told him the farmer was right. Nudy had to go to school, or Dad would be in trouble with the law. Gus said, 'Nudy can work after school and on weekends, but he has to go to school.' Dad got up and said 'o.k.' and they went back to work."

Sheriff W. C. Tegtman made the arrests. Oct 8, 1925 Thursday

RELEASE OF CHILDREN FOR BEET HARVEST IS PROBLEM OF F. A. OGLE

Numerous requests have been made of the county superintendent of schools for the release of children from the schools of the county for work in the beet harvest which begins on Thursday, but as yet F. A. Ogle has granted none of the requests.

A steady stream of Mexicans for the most part has been besieging the office in the court house in an effort to get their children out of school for a term. These people claim that they are entitled to the release under the law and Mr. Ogle is checking up on the cases in the various districts. He is determined to issue permits only in the most stringent cases. Children under 14 are not dismissed for work in any case under the state law. Between 14 and 16 the case is up to the county superintendent of schools.

The Greeley Tribune, October 8, 1925.

This illustrates how parents relied on even very young children to meet the financial needs of the family. Many hands were required to complete the fieldwork, and the absence of even one child meant economic loss and potential hardships for the family.

La Grange school circa 1940. Courtesy of City of Greeley Museums.

There was a continuous demand by the parents that the kids be allowed to stay out of school to work.

Gus Lopez attended the La Grange School at Weld County Road 66 and 59th Avenue for a short time. Whenever he passed the school, he recalled "This is where I went to school for a half year while we [the family] worked on the farm north of the school house."

Nudy Lopez remembered, "La Grange school was used to house us when school was dismissed during the harvest." At the age of 15, Gus Lopez quit school to help earn money for his family. After returning home in 1945 following WWII, he worked the farms until 1948 when he moved his family to Cheyenne, Wyoming, to work for the Union Pacific Railroad. He operated a crane for many years. When the railroad installed an overhead crane, he operated it, self-taught. He retired from the Union Pacific Railroad in 1978.

Gus Lopez's school card, courtesy of Greeley, Colorado School District 6.

Moses Espinosa said, "I finished the fifth grade at the age of 16. I didn't even go to sixth grade. I worked the fields and helped make money for Dad and the family." Mr. Espinosa was a carpenter for the Wyoming National Guard in Cheyenne, and worked at F. E. Warren Air Force Base. He retired from there and now restores old automobiles as a hobby.

Both Gus Lopez and Moses Espinosa worked for the CCC camps and WPA and served their country in World War II.

> According to Hazel Maddux's (1932) thesis ...
> Educational difficulties arise from the strong opposition of
> farmers and citizens. They think efforts to educate the
> Mexican children is a waste of time and money.[1]

Socially, the Mexican laborer was considered an outcast by many. The children associated with the Anglo children only in school. Even this opportunity was often denied them when they were segregated in separate rooms or buildings.

The children who lived in the Spanish Colony went to Gipson School located at 21st Avenue and 2nd Street from 1924 to 1928. All the grades were taught in one room. The primary grades had by far the largest percentage enrolled. Here there were no language

140

handicaps. All of the children were taught to speak English, and the lessons were taught in English.

Gipson School, circa 1900, prior to being moved to the Spanish Colony Courtesy of City of Greeley Museums.

The children of the Spanish Colony walked and rode bikes to school. Some became very sick from walking to school in inclement weather. Instead of busing the children into Greeley, the school district decided to move Gipson School closer to the Colony. Greeley did not want the Hispanic children in the Spanish Colony interacting with the Anglo children.

In 1928, the Gipson School was moved south of the Cache la Poudre River, near the 25th Avenue Bridge and within view of the Colony. Another room was added onto the front and on to the back for a classroom and for shop classes. The school received electricity in 1947; however, by the time of the school closure in 1949, it still had no running water.

Remodeled Gipson School for the Spanish Colony on North 25th Avenue. The room to the right was for 1st and 2nd grades; the room to the left was for 3rd and 4th grades. The building on the back is not shown; it was for 5th and 6th grades and a woodshop.   Courtesy of City of Greeley Museums.

Gipson became Greeley's only segregated school. English was taught even though most of the children knew how to speak some English; however, they preferred to converse in Spanish. Spanish was mostly spoken in the Colony, yet many older residents knew how to speak, read, and write in English.

Criselda "Kate" Espinosa Cassel remembered, "In Gipson School, from about 1931 to 1937, we would have to read and speak English. When not in school, we spoke Spanish. My stepmother's Spanish was different from Dad's Spanish and ours. She [Bibliana Rios Espinosa] was from Mexico and spoke Old Mexico Spanish, whereas my dad was from southern Colorado. It was just different than ours." An example of the differences is the word bathtub. The word bathtub used by Gilbert "Gil" Carbajal, whose parents came from Mexico, was *tina*; however, Ricardo "Rico" Lopez, whose parents came from New Mexico, used the word *baño*.

Reading class in session at Gipson School. Art Jojola standing and reading. Photo courtesy of Palmer Lopez.

When the students were asked if they learned a lot at Gipson School, their comments were that, it was difficult for the teachers to teach them with their limited Spanish and the variety of Spanish dialect spoken in the colony plus the students, limited English. But the teachers tried and did the best they could.

Even though Gipson School was moved for segregation purposes, it proved to be beneficial for the Colony residents. It was closer to home, which allowed for a safer walk and helped keep down winter illnesses. As the Colony was a close-knit community, having the school only for them strengthened the tradition of closeness and caring.

Spanish Colony children at Gipson (Gibson) School, circa 1930. Photo courtesy of Barbara Grantland.

In the 1930s, the average school attendance was approximately 60 students, with an average of 3 to 5 teachers. An article in *The Greeley Tribune*, September 3, 1938, reported that Gipson School had 3 teachers.

The February 17, 1931, p.8. *The Greeley Tribune* article, "Woman's Club Milk Service in Public Schools Putting Bone and Muscle on Many Underweight Boys and Girls" noted,

> '...I made four extra points on my last report card!'... Gibson school began to be served milk in 1926, and, at first had 10 bottles daily...As their enrollment has increased rapidly until they now number nearly 80 children, the Girl's Association of Greeley High School is helping this year with 20 more bottles.

A mandatory grooming and hygiene inspection required every child's head to be checked for lice. Nudy Lopez refused to let the teacher check his head. He said, "I will let you check me only if I can check your head first." The teacher let Nudy check her head, and then he said, "Okay, you can check mine now."

Carmen Lozano Weekley remembered, "One day at school a nurse came, and Nudy Lopez sat at the front of the class. The nurse had a fine-tooth comb and combed his hair for *piojos* (lice), because he had a tolerance for them. After she combed Nudy's hair, Nudy would say, 'Ma'am, ma'am, I think one is biting me here,' and point to his head."

"I would run home, because having my hair checked for lice was very traumatic for me," Josie Garcia recalled. "Mrs. Wood, my teacher, and Mom [Santitos] got to be pretty good friends; she would check my hair at home. I was so afraid she would find something and wash my hair with hot vinegar. I remember Nudy would not let the teacher check his head until the teacher let Nudy check hers first. He did this with a magnifying glass! You see, lice were a problem for us, as we went from farm to farm to live and work during the season. We were so busy working hard in the fields. With the living conditions on the farm, it was difficult for mothers to get kids ready for school."

Of course, there was always a prankster. Nudy Lopez remembered, "One day in school, I was so tired and wanted to go home. I turned the clock ahead one hour so school would end early. When the teacher saw the time, she sent everyone home. The teacher later found out, so the next day the students had to stay an hour later to make it up."

Carmen Lozano Weekley stated, "The teacher asked, 'Okay class, who discovered America?' Nudy said loudly, 'Aye, *carambus* (*caramba*), *no mi querdo,* (I don't know), teacher." The teacher said, 'You are right Nudy, and you are smart.' Nudy said, 'What did I do? What did I do?' The teacher said, 'You told me who discovered America.' Nudy said, '*Aye, carambus, no mi querdo.*' The teacher said, 'See, you repeated it; Columbus discovered America,' Nudy said, 'I did that!' We all laughed at him."

"Someone was always running away from school," Frank Lopez, Jr. remembered. "The teacher would chase after them yelling, 'Come back to school' as they were crossing the river. They were found and brought back to school." The children walked over the bridge, or, when the river was low, they waded across to get to school.

Many of the students were excellent artists. Their paintings were displayed in school halls and other buildings in Greeley. The children were also taught crafts such as woodwork, art, and other hobbies.

Carmen Lozano Weekley remembered, "At Gipson School, I learned to oil paint from Miss Schultz. I am now an oil and acrylic painter, and my work is in private collections in the U.S. and Europe."

A Work Shop
Simple instructions in wood-carving and carpentry are given to these boys. They are taught the correct use of tools and materials through the construction and finishing of toys and small articles of furniture.

Manuel "Piniones" Benavidez and Edward "Lalo" Lopez. *The Greeley Tribune,* March 26, 1938.

The Greeley Tribune article, May 23, 1937, "Gipson Children Will Hold Christmas Sale," noted,

The children have worked for several weeks making and painting toys, calendars, holders for small articles to be offered for sale. The doll house that was built at the school last year and exhibited last winter will be offered for sale. It was made by the upper grade children. It is 3 feet by 2 feet in the floor dimensions.

146

Mary Darling visited Gipson School. In her 1932 thesis she wrote, "Miss Fink, the principal of Gipson school which is maintained for the Spanish-Americans, says that the children have learned to appreciate the library which is being built up there, and that they often read for pleasure."[2]

At the time Gipson School was organized, the parents were more interested than the children; however, when the children completed the sixth grade, they preferred to remain there for junior high.

The Greeley Tribune in an August 10, 1949 article, "Gipson School Children Will Be Taken by Bus to Lincoln," reported,

> Gipson School will not be reopen. Students will be transported by bus to Lincoln school, the only building in which there is space for them at present. A report by teachers who made a survey showed that Gipson would have opened with actually only 35 students and six grades with three teachers. Superintendent Moore said that is not an economic method of running a school… Teachers believe that the transfer of students to Lincoln will greatly speed up their education. One important point is that the Gipson students talk Spanish on the playground. This is natural. That delays by that much their learning English, Superintendent Moore pointed out… Besides the salaries of teachers at Gipson with the very low teaching load due to the small number of pupils, the cost of janitor, fuel, lights… Incidentals in operating Gipson would bring annual cost to $10,00.

From 1954 onward, the Colony children were given a better opportunity to complete school and graduate. Many pursued college educations and became lawyers, doctors, and college professors. Others pursued careers in real estate, military, health and human services, construction, and with local industries, such as Monfort Feed Lot.

Busing enabled Spanish Colony students to complete 12 years of schooling. Rico Lopez, who graduated from Greeley High in 1954, said, "I felt that in the 1950s, busing helped me and the other children finish our education. Sure, some dropped out of school, because they liked to do the farm work and wanted the money right away. But for those who wanted an education or whose parents insisted on their getting an education, the busing program played a major role."

Gilbert "Gil" Carbajal said, "When I attended school in 1942, my parents [Manuel and Sara] never took us out of school to work the beet fields. My dad always made us go to school. One day I was really sick and had just vomited on the floor. I told my dad I was really sick (*No me siento bien*) and couldn't go to school. My dad said," Get going, get going to school, and if you die, I will come get you (*Vamos, vamos a la escula y si te mueres, yo voy por ti*). (See Appendix F.) He wanted all of us to get all the education we could. I went to school and made it through the day. We worked hard in the evenings after school and on the weekends, but when it was Monday, we went to school. I helped out by delivering *The Greeley Tribune* newspaper in the mornings before school and on weekends. I worked for the Greeley Bowl-A-Rama setting up pins. I finished my school years and went on to college. I received a Bachelor's degree in Educational Guidance from Colorado State College (University of Northern Colorado) in Greeley, Colorado, a Master's degree in Language and School Administration, and my PHD in Educational Guidance and School Administration, from C.S.U. in Fort Collins, Colorado."

Gil Carbajal taught physical education in Douglas, Wyoming, and coached football and basketball for the same school. In the summer, he returned to Greeley and played for the Greeley Grays Semi-Pro baseball team. He then moved to Fort Collins and taught school and coached the same sports for Lincoln Junior High [Poudre School District].

This is an example of how important education was to the parents of the Spanish Colony, who themselves had limited education but wanted better for their children.

Delilah Gomez Fiechter, who graduated from Greeley West in 1969, commented, "I think busing helped the children get a better education, even though all the buses used for the Spanish Colony were the worst buses the district had. One time, the bus broke down on the railroad tracks. The bus driver needed to push the bus out of the way, so he made the children help him push it off the tracks. When my mother found out, she was so mad she wrote the school district and complained. Also, the buses used had no heaters, or they didn't work during the winter. It was cold going to school."

When Delilah was asked where the bus picked up the children for school, she said, "The bus stop was next to Alvin's store. Alvin had a pinball machine. He never minded the kids waiting in his store, and we would play with the pinball machine and buy gum, candy, and sodas. It was fun and nice to have the store nearby. There was a bus for grade school, junior high school, and high school. When I started kindergarten, it was at Washington School. Mrs. Wolf was my teacher and met us at the door. When I started going to Aims Community College, located at Lincoln School, the first person I saw on my first day was Mrs. Wolf. She chuckled and commented on this strange coincidence. Mrs. Wolf asked me what I was going to pursue in college. I wanted to become a watercolor artist. She said 'I knew that, because when I asked you children in kindergarten what you wanted to grow up to be, some said a ballerina, fireman, policeman, but you stood up and said, "You wanted to be an artist'. Mrs. Wolf made me so happy when she told me that." Today, Delilah is a freelance watercolor artist whose award-winning art appears on greeting cards produced by Leanin' Tree and other national greeting card companies.

In 1963, Gipson School was demolished with one portion of it being moved and attached to the west side of the Pentecostal Church in the Spanish Colony.

The Greeley Tribune in an April 4, 1963 article, "Demolition Work Started at Gipson School," reported on the fate of the school. After the school was closed, the school district rented the building for several years to the U.S. Public Health Services, C.D.C Laboratory.

Another type of school was The Americanization School.[3] A woman's club in the 1920s established an Americanization school in Greeley which was in session three nights a week for eight to twelve weeks during the winter. The school provided citizenship classes for aliens and reading and writing classes for adults.[4] The differing educational backgrounds and the ability to learn determined how long individuals would attend these classes. This school was free to all, and many men took advantage of the opportunity, as they appreciated the value of an education. Women, since they were needed to stay at home and care for the children, generally didn't attend these night classes. English fluency and a better

149

understanding of financial, business, government, and medical matters afforded the Hispanic Americans better opportunities to succeed in the dominant Anglo-American culture.

The February 18, 1932 *The Greeley Tribune* article, "Colony Reports Show Great Interest Here," explained,

> Total of 355 people now live in 47 houses at the colony. They include 180 adults, 80 school children, 50 of kindergarten age and 45 babies. Average attendance at the classes has been: kindergarten 31, cooking 18, sewing 13, school work 15, singing and social hour 17, children's story hour 23. Money given by the Woman's club and the Rotary club pays for milk served to the children at each kindergarten session, three times a week. One graham cracker is also served; the children are all seated for the lunch, wait until all are served, and eat in orderly and mannerly style. More is being done at present for the girls than the boys, for they have sewing classes and their Red Cross work. Organization of Camp Fire Girls group is also being considered. The boys have a basketball, but they need a leader who understands recreational work... Cooking classes, held once a week, run on about $1 a week, held at different homes. Sewing classes are held Tuesdays in the Community Center.

Fieldwork, with its long hours, gave the field worker relatively little opportunity or time to pursue educational advancement. The Americanization School had to be conducted at the convenience of the workers.

Martina Lopez exemplifies the desire to learn. She raised 14 children, the last seven on her own as a widow. While she could read and write, she still valued schooling and held on to her dream of receiving a formal education. She received her GED from Aims Community College in 1975 at the age of 76 with a 4.0 grade point average.

Martina Padilla Lopez. Photo courtesy of Palmer Lopez.

References

1. Maddux, Hazel C. (1932, June). *Some Conditions Which Influence the Mexican Children in Greeley, Colorado, and its Vicinity.* (Masters Degree thesis, Colorado State College). p. 29.

2. Darling, M. (1932). *Americanization of Foreign-Born in Greeley, Colorado.* (Masters Degree thesis, Colorado State College). p. 92.

3. Ibid. p. 87.

4. *The Greeley Woman's Club Scrapbook.* (1924-1948). Volume 1. City of Greeley Museums and Archives.

Chapter 11

Greeley Helps the Spanish Colony

Community Center Run by La Casa de Amistad at Mexican Colony

This photo by Gardner shows some of those who are greatly assisted thru efforts of the House of Neighborly Service, gathered about the Community center at the Spanish-American colony.

The Greeley Tribune, February 18, 1931.

When charities and relief societies need to extend services to those impoverished by inadequate wages, America pays for its cheap labor. No nation can prosper when it holds one group a slave to its industrial development.

Hispanic people from the southwestern United States were enticed to move to Weld County to work the beet fields with the hope of bettering their lives and the lives of their families. When they arrived, they had few physical comforts and struggled to be recognized and accepted by the local community; despite poor conditions, they stayed and played an important role in American agriculture and industry.

Often, newly arrived field workers found only a life of poverty and a lack of education. Private and government relief organizations helped meet both the immediate and the long-term economic, social, and educational needs of the Hispanic people. In Greeley, social workers studied the needs of the Spanish-speaking people, solicited help from the community, and developed social and educational programs.

Mary Darling, in her 1932 Colorado State Teachers College Masters Thesis, *Americanization of Foreign-Born in Greeley, Colorado,* wrote,

> Americanization in our city is recognized as taking place in many ways. It is found in the service to humanity which is rendered by our churches; it is a part of the program of some of our organizations; it is shown in the training provided in our young people's organizations where worthwhile activities are being carried on, … it has its part to play in welfare and relief work, for always there is need; but most directly is it seen to function in the Americanization school whose object is to train the alien so he may become a citizen, …Our Spanish Colony is a place where the real spirit of America should be shown, and is being shown, in the earnest effort of those who seek to relieve present physical distress, and to improve cultural and educational conditions.[1]

Mary Darling and Esther Schillinger in their 1929 Master Theses, noted that it would take generous and on-going cooperation of not just one, but all churches to sufficiently improve the standard of living for Hispanics in the Greeley area. They observed that some protestant churches provided social service programs and training such as weekly sewing and cooking classes. The goal of Greeley's Americanization classes was to enlighten Spanish-speaking people [American-born and Mexican Nationals] about the political, economic, and social customs of the area in which they lived.[2]

This was an interesting concept during the 1920s and 1930s, and it illustrated the pervasive lack of knowledge concerning Hispanic people; for example, all Hispanics were referred to or thought of as "Mexican" when in reality only four of the original 40 families who settled in the Greeley Spanish Colony were from Mexico. All others were American-born citizens, and most were bilingual.

Under the auspices of the National Board of Mission of the Presbyterian Church, the First United Presbyterian Church of Greeley established centers for social and welfare work among the Spanish-speaking people in its church district in Weld County. Each center was known as a House of Neighborly Service.[3]

The House of Neighborly Service Association of Greeley (HNSA) was one of three relief agencies that provided service to the residents of the Colony. It was founded on May 28, 1926 to help Spanish Colony residents adjust to the local culture.

The HSNA adopted a constitution, which defined it's goals in working with Spanish-speaking residents. A partial copy follows.

CONSTITUTION

OF

THE HOUSE OF NEIGHBORLY SERVICE
ASSOCIATION OF GREELEY

******

ARTICLE I.
Name

The name of this organization shall be The House of Neighborly
Service Association of Greeley.

ARTICLE II.
Objects

Ex Self recommended

Section 1. To cooperate with the worker, furnished by the National
Board of Missions of the Presbyterian Church under the Interdenominational
Plan for Religious Education, which is allocated to the work of the Spanish
speaking people in this community.

Section 2. To afford these people a chance to adjust themselves to their
environment, to know the real meaning of American Citizenship and the
proper use of its privileges as well as its duties; to instil the idea of
thrift.

Section 3. To effect a more sympathetic understanding on the part of
the American Public so that it can interpret the environment from which
the Mexicans and Spanish-Americans come, and therefore appreciate the
value of Americanization.

Section 4. To unite the efforts of Christian and other welfare organizations interested in this project.

III. Sponsorship

Courtesy of City of Greeley Museums.

HNSA sponsored programs and classes in the Colony's
Salon. Activities included the following:

Health: Clinics, first-aid, women's home health classes.

Social: Casework and advice, Colony meetings, clubs for
young men and women, programs, plays, folk dancing,
excursions.

Education: Kindergarten, library, story hour, drama, music,
vacation schools.

Arts and Crafts: Pastel classes, tin raffia, egg dyeing at
Easter time, sewing, embroidery, rug making, carpentry,
additional craft classes.

156

Recreation: Game rooms, table games, ping-pong, shuffleboard, baseball, basketball, football, picnics.[4]

The Greeley Tribune, November 1, 1937.

The House of Neighborly Service Association signs at both the Spanish Colony and its headquarters in a brick house at 14th Avenue and 2nd Street were printed in English and the familiar Spanish, *La Casa de Amistad.* The comfortably furnished house was also the residence of Miss Wilson who was in charge of social work at the Spanish Colony. Miss Wilson, a trained social worker from West Virginia, answered the call to serve the people of the Spanish Colony.

Her program at *La Casa de Amistad* included a kindergarten held on Monday, Wednesday, and Friday mornings at 9:30 a.m. *The Greeley Tribune,* February 18, 1931, article, "La Casa de Amistad Serves Spanish in Variety of Ways," noted, "A kindergarten was organized with 29 enrolled the first day." There was also a story hour for older children held on Saturday mornings and afternoon classes for girls and women in cooking, sewing, and subjects such as English, spelling, arithmetic, and geography. Music was taught on Friday afternoon. In addition to the younger students, attendance of older students averaged 25 to 30 or about one third of the adult population.

The Greeley Tribune, October 28, 1937, p.8.

Miss Wilson quickly gained the confidence, respect, and friendship of the Spanish Colony people. She understood their concerns, needs, and problems and learned that most were good, earnest, and conscientious citizens.

Criselda "Kate" Espinosa Cassel said, "I remembered going next door to Dad's house [on Lot 58] to attend a kindergarten. We played and did crafts like coloring, pasting, and sometimes sang old children's songs." Miss Wilson frequently opened her classes with music.

Mary Darling, who visited a kindergarten held in the Salon in January 1932, reported in her Masters Thesis that,

At about ten o'clock, thirty eager little faces and voices greeted their teacher as she entered. All the children were seated on little green benches and were in charge of Mrs. Rumero and her brother, Mr. Rodriquez, who were helpers. For more than half an hour the little people sang and had finger plays and action songs. The singing was delightful and showed real skill and excellent leadership. The group sang one stanza of "America." Then two little girls three years old sang it together with no help or accompaniment. Later, one of them sang "Springtime In The Rockies," in a way that would have been creditable to a child of twice her age. Time and sir were true, and the words were very plain... Miss Wilson is teaching them English words and speaks to them in English but the helpers interpret to the children. They respond quickly as soon as they know what they are asked to do. Tables were placed and moulding clay was passed. Soon balls, baskets, birds and tables of clay were shaped by rapid fingers. After the clay was taken away, each received a glass of milk and a graham cracker. When all were served, the lunch began. In a few minutes after the children had finished, they left, and the helpers quickly arranged everything ready for the afternoon class. Surely, this is a worthy piece of work. Comradeship, co-operation, respect for authority, the joy of doing things, and skill in doing, each has a place. The Community House (Salon) is number 311. It is adobe, as are all the other houses. Fresh curtains were at the windows, some flowers and a growing plant were on the piano, and the floor was covered with linoleum and rugs. A few good pictures were on the walls. At that time, Miss. Wilson was carrying on the work alone except for the help of the two Spanish people mentioned above. Since then, she has received the help of different persons. Some of the college girls have given their time to aid in conducting classes. [5]

Miss Wilson's duties were many and varied. Publicity was a part of her work. She gave lectures about her work to local organizations and made personal calls among the people of Greeley to promote HNSA.

Many well-known and respected Greeley citizens volunteered for the Social Service programs sponsored by the HNSA, Greeley Woman's Club, and WPA.[6]

Mrs. Warwick's kindergarten class. Photo courtesy of Robert Duran.

Nearly 200 people lived in the colony. Most were American citizens by birth. There were 76 children of school age enrolled in Gipson School who received instruction in English. For the convenience of the adult population, the Americanization school was established in the Spanish Colony under the direction of Miss Wilson.

Spanish Pre-School Children Learn American Ways

This photograph by Robert E. Hanna shows pre-school children at the Spanish colony northwest of Greeley learning American ways under the auspices of the House of the Neighborly Service.

The Greeley Tribune, November 5, 1937.

Mrs. Warwick, a volunteer for House of Neighborly Services, was fondly remembered for her contributions to the Colony. She treated young people as individuals and took them on field trips. Early childhood education was her forte.

Tito "Butter" Garcia Jr. remembered, "Mrs. Warwick took the kids on picnics and also to Denver to visit City Park, the zoo, and the Museum of Natural History. She loaded the older kids in the back of a pick up truck and took them to these places. She invited a few to spend the night at her home and do crafts or baking. She showed a lot of concern for the kids and their needs."

Josie Garcia remembered, "Mrs. Warwick interacted with the community on behalf of the Spanish Colony people. If anybody had trouble with anything, Mrs. Warwick helped out in any way she could."

Mrs. Warwick provided milk and graham crackers for the children's craft classes. Kate Cassel remembered, "After I ate my graham crackers and drank my milk, I would ask for more, but Mrs. Warwick would say very politely, 'No, we have to save some for

161

others.' I still wanted more crackers. Even today when I eat graham crackers, I sure remember Mrs. Warwick."

An article in *The Greeley Tribune*, November 19, 1937, "House of Neighborly Services Will Call at Homes for Donations" stated, "Information has come to directors of the House of Neighborly Service that there are persons in Greeley and Weld County wishing to make contributions who have not been solicited."

Another charitable organization involved with the

House of Neighborly Service Will Call at Homes for Donations

Information has come to directors of the House of Neighborly Service that there are persons in Greeley and Weld county wishing to make contributions who have not been solicited. Some were not at home when the worker called or were missed in another way.

Anyone wishing to contribute may call either Mrs. T. C. Stillwell at 1623 or Mrs. M. B. Rosenbaum at 2178, and a worker will be sent to collect the donation.

The Greeley Tribune, November 19, 1937.

Colony was the Greeley Woman's Club. This club provided milk, clothing, gifts, and money directly to the Colony residents or to the House of Neighborly Service. Many residents were more comfortable working with the House of Neighborly Service. The Greeley Woman's Club was founded in March, 1920, and disbanded in 1999. Detailed information about the club's work is contained in its records and scrapbooks.

The 1925 record noted, "Another sacred obligation placed upon us, and one which we would not if we could evade, was the furnishing of hot lunches and milk for the under privileged children in our schools."[7]

Repeatedly throughout their records, it is noted that The Greeley Woman's Club, with the assistance of other generous organizations, tirelessly raised money for their many programs of which the residents of the Spanish Colony were recipients. Clothing and material were also provided for the children of the "Mexican Colony".

162

Deborah Mumper, 1927 President, wrote,

The Child Welfare Committee furnished milk to the poor malnourished school children of the north ward, the west ward, and the Gibson district. Much good has resulted in gain in weight and in general health improvement. The Americanization Committee has done a good deal for the Spanish speaking people of our community by cooperating with and contributing to the House of Friendly (Neighborly) Service which exists for the use of these people.[8]

Franklin Children Share Benefits of G. W. C. Milk Fund

Underweight children of four local schools are attempting to build up their weight with the assistance of the Greeley Woman's club, which daily has delivered at the buildings 69 half-pint bottles of milk. They are sent to Gibson, Franklin, Washington and Lincoln schools, the latter three formerly known as West, North and East Ward schools. Not all of the underweight children, but those whose homes do not provide money for the extra milk at school, are given the added nourishment. This cheerful group of youngsters is from Franklin school, where the milk is delivered at noon.—Photo by Gardner.

The Greeley Tribune, February 17, 1931. Courtesy of City of Greeley Museums

Woman's Club Milk Service Aids Pupils

(Continued from Page 1)

and about 50 from the homes, while North Ward has 15 free and nearly 30 from the homes.

Gipson school began to be served milk in 1926, and, at first had 10 bottles daily. The teachers found it hard to make that number serve among so many Spanish-American children, so this year and last they receive 20 bottles daily. As their enrollment has increased rapidly until they now number nearly 80 children, the Girl's Association of Greeley high school is helping this year with 20 more bottles at that school.

During all these years of splendid service, it is estimated that at least 200 families have been strengthened and helped by free service, while it has reached into at least 500 more homes to build up those who bore their own financial burden.

During all this time every effort has been made to let no child feel that he is ostracized because he doesn't pay for his milk. In fact, none know that others do not pay.

The dairymen have been helpful in all this work, being usually on time, even when last winter's vigorous days made it very difficult, giving unfailing courtesy in every way and donating by providing milk at fair price. The whole community

The Greeley Tribune, February 17, 1931. Courtesy of City of Greeley Museums

164

It was noted how The Woman's Club worked along with the HNSA. The 1932 President wrote, "We have tried to cooperate with the Board of the House of Neighborly Service, and have sent twenty dollars for the milk for the Kindergartners in the Mexican Colony." [9]

Mrs. Ralph S. Baird

Spanish American Colony
Donated Material
and
Supervised Dressmaking

The Woman's Club, Volume 1. Courtesy of City of Greeley Museums.

In 1936, Agnes C. Baird, President, wrote, "The Americanization work under the direction of Mrs. Armentrout is worthy of mention. We have assisted in the work of the Spanish American Colony by furnishing milk to the Kindergarten children and giving material to the older children for dresses which they made for themselves under supervision." [10]

In 1937-1938, Aimee W. O'Byrne, President, wrote, "Mrs. M. B. Rosenbaum and her committee also did a fine piece of work in raising $126.50 for carrying on the work of the House of Neighborly Service, which aided the Spanish people of our community." [11]

In 1942, "Clothing was collected and given to the House of Neighborly Service for distribution at the Spanish Colony. Thirty gifts and $3.15 in cash were given at Christmas time for a party for the Colony children." [12]

In addition to programs which supported the social and educational needs of the Spanish-speaking people, the Greeley community was also concerned with health issues, e.g., that smallpox, tuberculosis, diphtheria, and other diseases would result when Mexicans moved into the area. Doctor J.W. Fuqua or Doctor Clayton and a nurse held a clinic once or twice a week. Hazel

Maddux noted in her Masters Thesis, "The physical records did not show the Mexican children below the American children; it also showed many of the children to be bright or superior. Evidence of common defects, normal."

—Photo by Gardner.
Mrs. Frances Marquez, nurse and leader at Social Service center, only licensed midwife among the Spanish speaking people here.

The Greeley Tribune, February 18, 1931.

Mrs. Frances Marquez, a.k.a. Dona Kika, a nurse and licensed midwife, lived in the Colony and was a leader at the Social Services Center. *The Greeley Tribune* article, February 18, 1931, p. 9, "La Casa De Amistad Serves Spanish in Variety of Ways," stated,

"Mrs. Frances Marquez is one of the outstanding women at the Colony. Through the efforts of Miss Wilson she took a course of study and became a licensed mid-wife. One of the physicians in Denver remarked as he finished examining her before granting the mid-wife license, -- "I believe this to be a step in the right direction." Her work has proved to be a real service to her own people.'"

Gene Maese commented, "I remember sitting in school and looking out the windows. We would see Dona Kika Marquez walking with her briefcase down the road and say, 'Oh, so and so is having her baby now.' We all knew who was pregnant in the colony, and who was about to give birth."

The Greeley Tribune article of February 18, 1931, continued, "Sue Beattie has opened a First Aid course of study in the school room on Wednesday afternoon from 3 to 4 o'clock, and 18 were enrolled the opening day. She is teaching them to read a

166

thermometer, bathe a sick patient, and properly make a bed, also the care and diet of infants."

An article in *The Greeley Tribune*, of March 24, 1939, "Spanish Colony Clinic Mothers Guest at Tea," noted,

> Wednesday's meeting concerned the proper feeding of babies from the time of their birth to two years of age. Bathing, weighing and other demonstrations were also taken up during the afternoon... On Thursday afternoon, the party was repeated for 42 little girls of the colony, who came with their dolls. Each doll was taken thru the baby clinic, and later orange juice and cookies were served.

Spanish Colony Clinic Mothers Guests at Tea

In connection with the regular clinic on the care of babies, conducted at the Spanish colony each week, the board of directors of the House of Neighborly Service entertained mothers attending the clinic at a tea on Wednesday.

Mrs. Vesta Bowden, public health nurse, and Mrs. Juliet G. Warrick, House of Neighborly Service worker, are in charge of the clinic. Wednesday's meeting concerned the proper feeding of babies from the time of their birth to two years of age. Bathing, weighing and other demonstrations were also taken up during the afternoon.

Approximately 39 Spanish-American women attended the clinic session and remained for the tea. Mrs. Nelson Reynolds, Mrs. S. W. Armentrout, Mrs. Theodore E. Heinz, and Miss Iva Newman presided over the prettily appointed refreshment table. Spring flowers and lighted tapers, in pastel shades, formed the centerpiece.

Charles Clay, also a member of the board, was present for the afternoon. Interpreting was done by Mrs. Sweitzer and Cora Marquez.

On Thursday afternoon, the party was repeated for 42 little girls of the colony, who came with their dolls. Each doll was taken thru the baby clinic, and later orange juice and cookies were served.

The Greeley Tribune, March 24, 1939.

167

House of Neighborly Service Thru Worker and Clinic Vital Force in Local District Health

Physicians and health authorities have felt the Spanish colony here a strategic center for the control of contagious disease, for the prevention of epidemics, for the advancement of pre-natal and infant care, thus lowering mortality rates.

Dr. Donn Barber, who for five years has sponsored the clinic at the colony center, said in a recent address:

"My interest in the health of these people has led to an understanding of other aspects of welfare work; an appreciation for the splendid work done by Miss Gladys Plekenpol, and a great admiration for the House of Neighborly Service program.

"With a population of 450 people, about 61 families living in crowded quarters, just two wells to supply water, the maintenance of good health is extremely difficult. But the people have shown a real interest, and cooperation is constantly trying to improve the unfavorable conditions which exist there.

"These people are desperately poor —they live in this type of community to be mutually helpful. The largest part of their earnings is spent for absolute necessities.

"They make every effort within their means to follow instructions. Adequate disease control is almost impossible in other districts because of lack of understanding and of fear.

"The families of this colony assume responsibility for the care of dependent children and old people. Why are all these things true in the Greeley Spanish colony? Because of the influence and cooperation of the House of the Neighborly Service which thru its active worker, Miss Plekenpol, has developed a sense of responsibility, a sense of loyalty to each other, an appreciation of the value of citizenship, and a willingness to cooperate and do all within their physical and mental means to become good citizens."

Significant in the health record of the colony is that there has never been a positive Wasserman report for any of the 30 colony mothers examined in the clinic. In the matter of tuberculosis control, the requests for examination have been unusually numerous from the colony. Only one patient is securing sanitorium treatment—all contacts have been examined.

The Greeley Tribune, October 4, 1940.

The Greeley Tribune, October 4, 1940, article, "House of Neighborly Service Thru Worker and Clinic Vital Force in Local District Health," related,

> With a population of 450 people, about 61 families living in crowded quarters, just two wells to supply water, the maintenance of good health is extremely difficult. But the people have shown a real interest, and cooperation is constantly trying to improve the unfavorable conditions which exist there. These people are desperately poor... Their largest part of their earnings is spent for absolute necessities. They make every effort within their means to follow instructions... Significant in the health records in the Colony is that there has never been a positive Wasserman report... In the matter of Tuberculosis control, the requests for examination have been unusually numerous from the Colony. Only one patient is securing sanatorium treatment—all contacts have been examined.

To date, 2004, however, there has been no record or evidence of any such epidemic, just infrequent or isolated cases as in any community.

Prominent among Mexican-American folk healers is the *curandero*. The term *curandero* comes from the Spanish verb *curar* which means "to heal". The three most common types of *curanderos* are: *Yerbero* (Herbalist), *Partera* (Midwife), *Sabador* (Masseur). The *curandero* works on three levels: the material, the spiritual, and the mental.

Dorothy Rodman was raised in the Colony and contracted polio at age 5. She remembered how Dona Kika, who also practiced *curanderismo* of massage, gave her relief from the pain of polio in her legs. Dorothy attributes much of the success of her recovery to *curandero* folk healing.

As a young woman, Dorothy, under the direction of Dona Kika, developed the gift of massage therapy and pursued a medical education to become a licensed nurse. Dorothy made a personal commitment to help Greeley's medical profession understand Hispanic folk medicine or *curanderoism.* [14]

According to Dorothy, there are six traditional health practitioners of Hispanic folk medicine:

1. *Curandero* (Folk healer) - performs rituals, offers prayers, and prescribes herbs, teas, and poultices. The *curandero* can be male or female; often the elderly *curandero* heals by virtue of a gift from God (*Don*); the common religious faith is Catholicism. Healing also occurs through dreams, unusual traits, or magical experiences.

2. *Yerbero* (Herbalist) - prescribes herbs and spices.

3. *Sobador* (Masseuse) - uses body massages.

4. *Espiritualista* (Spiritualist) - analyzes dreams, fears, and foretells future.

5. *Brujo* (Witch) - uses magic and witchcraft.

6. *Partera* (Midwife) - delivery without formal training.

Various origins of illness include hot and cold in balance, dislocation of internal organs, magical origin, emotional origin, folk-defined disease, and standard scientific disease.

Dorothy Rodman identified some specific illnesses and conditions treated with Hispanic folk medicine:

❖ *Caida de la fontanel* (fallen fontanel), a skull depression which is most common in very young children, often caused by a fall. The symptoms are skull depression, restlessness, diarrhea, high temperature, and blocked throat. The cure for *caida de la fontanel* is thumb pressure against the upper palate, egg applied to the skull depression without breaking the yolk, and prayers.

❖ *Empacho* (gastritis) can affect people of all ages and is often caused by the stress of forced eating. One symptom is sharp pain, due to food being blocked from entering the intestinal tract. The cure is spinal massage, plus herbs given to restore the patient's balance of "hot" and "cold" qualities - related to the humoral theory of medicine.

❖ *Mal Ojo* (evil eye) occurs most frequently in women and children; men are susceptible to a lesser degree. The evil eye is caused by strong glances, covetous expressions, and excessive attention. Symptoms are headache, inconsolable weeping (children only),

170

fretfulness, and high temperature. It is cured by an egg rub and an egg-water mixture placed under the patient's bed to drain away the stronger individual's power.

❖ *Susto* (spirit loss) occurs in all ages. Caused by a sudden fright or a buildup of everyday life's vexations. The symptoms are loss of appetite, and/or listlessness due to one's *espiritu* (spirit, soul) having left the body. The cure is prayers, sweeping the body with herb branches, plus a talk about the patient's personal life.

❖ *Aire* (theory of hot and cold) occurs in both the young and old. It is caused by hot or cold foods, and hot or cold temperatures. Symptoms are ear pain, headaches, and abdominal pain. The cure is herb teas, prayer ritual, and a change in diet.[14]

Both traditional medicine and Hispanic folk medicine were used to address the health issues of the Spanish-speaking residents of Greeley.

The Spanish Colony levels of health and education were improved because of the involvement of Greeley's community services and charitable organizations, such as House of Neighborly Service and The Woman's Club.

References

1. Darling, M. (1932). *Americanization of Foreign-Born in Greeley, Colorado*. (Master Degree thesis, Colorado State College). pp.132, 133.

2. Schillinger, Esther K. (1929, August). *Social Contacts of the Migrant Mexicans of Weld County*. (Master Degree thesis Colorado State College). pp.33, 35.
Darling, M. (1932). *Americanization of Foreign-Born in Greeley, Colorado*. (Master Degree thesis, Colorado State College). Pp. 86, 87.

3. Darling M. (1932). *Americanization of Foreign-Born in Greeley, Colorado* (Master Degree thesis Colorado State College). p.104.

4. *The Northern Colorado Conference on Minority Problems of Spanish Speaking People* (Sunday May 10, 1942) House of Neighborly Collections, City of Greeley Museums.

5. Darling M. (1932). *Americanization of Foreign-Born in Greeley, Colorado*. (Master Degree thesis, Colorado State College). pp.105 106.

6. *The Northern Colorado Conference on Minority Problems of Spanish Speaking People* (Sunday May 10, 1942) House of Neighborly Collections, City of Greeley Museums.

7. *The Greeley Woman's Club Volume 1*. (1942 –1938).

8. *The Greeley Woman's Club Volume 1*. (1927-1928).

9. Gonzales, Pacheco Ida and Guerrero, Jacquie L. *La Famillia Genealogy Society Newsletter*. Volume 1, Issue 2. (2002, November).

10. *The Greeley Woman's Club Volume 1*. (1936-1937).

11. *The Greeley Woman's Club Volume 1*. (1937-1938).

12. *The Greeley Woman's Club Volume 1.* (1942-1943).

13. Maddux, Hazel C. (1932 June). *Social Conditions Which Influence the Mexican Children In Greeley, Colorado, and it's Vicinity* (Master Degree thesis Colorado State College). p. iv.

14. Rodman, Dorothy. *Traditional Health Practitioners.* (2004, February 11).

Chapter 12

Help During the Depression

L to R: Domingo Duran, Arthur Lopez, Alvin Garcia, unknown man. Photo courtesy of Robert Duran.

During the Great Depression of the 1930s, the Seventy-third Congress passed Public Act No. 5, March 1933, authorizing the Emergency Conservation Work program. Another Congressional Act passed in June 1937, changed the name to the Civilian Conservation Corps. The Civilian Conservation Corp (CCC) was instituted to alleviate distress caused by unemployment in the 1930s. Young men worked on forest and conservation projects across the country. Colorado had numerous CCC camps throughout its undeveloped and forested lands.[1]

Courtesy of the Colorado State Archives.

Frank Lopez Jr. remembered, "The County or somebody tried to put a park just west of the Colony by the Cache la Poudre River. There were a couple of bridges with picnic tables and camp stoves nearby. It would have been a pretty park if they had finished it."

Criselda "Kate" Espinosa Cassel also recalled, "We walked down to the river west of the Colony about 200 feet. This park had benches and fireplaces and a bridge to cross the river. I walked with *abuelita* (grandma), which is what we called her. Her name was Dominica Ortiz. She wore a fluffy dress; it looked like she had two or three dresses on, that is how fluffy it was! She sat on the ground by the trees and watched us swim. *Abuelita* looked out for us and let us swim for a while. Then she would say, 'That is enough. We should go home.' We walked from the park back to the Colony. Dominica walked with a cane. We swam with bloomers (panties); these bloomers were made from the 20 or 50-pound flour sacks. They were white heavy cotton with the name or brand of wheat on them. My stepmother tried to remove the brand by frequently washing the sacks with bleach. After several washings, the brand name became lighter. It also made the bloomers softer, so we could wear them."

Portner Files Quiet Title Suit On CCC Project Land for Park West of Greeley Spanish Colony

Roy A. Portner of Fort Collins, Friday started in district court here in the name of the Larimer and Weld Investment company, of which he is the president, a suit to force the board of county commissioners to reconvey to him title to a strip of land along the Poudre river west of the Greeley Spanish colony which Portner says he quit claim deeded to the county in 1934 on the agreement that it would be deeded back to him six months after the CCC camp, which was to make a park of the premises, abandoned it.

Portner asks that the land be deeded back to him and also that his title be quited against any claims the county may have.

In a letter from William A. Bryans III, Portner's attorney, to the county commissioners, it is stated that Portner must remove this cloud to the title to his farm west of Greeley, else he faces danger of foreclosure of a mortgage which the mortgage holder refuses to renew unless the cloud is removed. Portner had stated the same in recent conferences with the board of commissioners here in which he asked that the property orginally deed to another board be reconveyed. The present board refused on advice of County Attorney Clay R. Apple, holding that it has no right to reconvey without a court order.

Narrow Strip Along River

The land in question is a narrow strip along the Poudre running west of the Greeley Spanish colony which the CCC camp started to work on and then abandoned when objections were raised to the title which had been obtained by the old board of commissioners and then moved to the Scout Island location below Greeley at the junction of the Platte and Poudre rivers.

Within a few months this later site was abandoned. The improvement was never popularly used by residents of Greeley and vicinity and what improvements were made in either site have long since fallen into disuse and decay.

In his complaint Portner states that on Dec. 20, 1934, he entered into an agreement with the county board which then consisted of William A. Carlson, James S. Ogilvie, and S. K. Clark, for conveying the property west of Greeley by quit claim deed.

The agreement of that date states in part that Portner has executed his quit claim deed to the property to the county, that the county has acquired the title "for the purpose of the development of river improvement by the CCC located at Greeley" . . . "that it is represented that the title to said lands so conveyed is not required to remain permanently in Weld county and the road thru said lands is being constructed for purposes other than a county highway" . . .

The county "agrees that at the expiration of six months after the abandonment of the CCC camp at Greeley, it will reconvey the lands shown in cross hatch on exhibit A and B" (which is a map of the conveyed premises.)

Agreed Never To Designate Road

The commissioners further agreed on "divers and sundry" occasions he has asked the present board of commissioners, consisting of Charles O. Plumb, Fred Arena and A. R. Riggs to recovery and has been met with refusal or neglect.

Commissioners Will Not Refuse

Commissioners said here that the part of the road Portner was to get across the Poudre near the C. & S. tracks which the county was to construct, was built, but that the bridge and some fill which was to be done by the CCC camp was never constructed.

Commissioners said that there is no fight on their part in the case, but they merely want any action of reconveyance legalized by the court. They will not resist the claim, they said.

Portner hopes to have an early decision in order to refinance his mortgage.

The Greeley Tribune, November 5, 1937.

177

An article in *The Greeley Tribune*, November 5, 1937, "Portner Files Quiet

Title Suit On CCC Project Land for Park West of Greeley Spanish Colony," noted,

> The land in question is a narrow strip along the Poudre running west of the Greeley Spanish Colony which the CCC camp started to work on and then abandoned when objections were raised to the title which had been obtained by the old board of commissioners and then moved to the Scout Island location below Greeley at the Junction of the Platte and Poudre rivers. Within a few months this later site was abandoned. The improvement was never popularly used by residents of Greeley and vicinity and what improvements were made in either site have long since fallen into disuse and decay.

During the years 1935-1942, 48 young men from the Colony, ages 17 to 22, joined the CCC. Some of their work assignments in Colorado and Wyoming included building roads in the national parks and making barbeque pits and picnic tables. Clothing was issued to the workers by the government and consisted of tall leather boots or canvas-topped boots, riding pants, and a leather coat to wear in the mountains. Pay was $25 a month. The men kept $5 and the government sent the remaining $20 to each man's family. Crew leaders earned more money, but they were allowed to keep only $5 for themselves.

Augustine "Gus" Lopez in the Spanish Colony wearing pants and boots issued by CCC. Photo courtesy of Ricardo "Rico" Lopez.

CCC Will Enroll
Here on Oct. 7th

Civilian Conservation Corps enrollment will be held at the State Ar-
mory, Greeley, Oct. 7, beginning at 9
a. m.

Any boy single and unemployed between the ages of 17 and 28 inclusive
is urged to come to the W.P.A. office,
fourth floor Court House, Greeley,
Colo., on or before Oct. 7, to make formal application for enrollment. Enrollment in these camps affords an excellent opportunity for wholesome outdoor employment in national and state
forests and parks.

Each enrollee receives food, clothing, shelter, and medical care during
his term of service and a cash allowance of $30 per month—$25 of which
is sent to relatives who are in need
of assistance. The quota for Weld
county is 90 boys and we are especially anxious to fill this quota.

The Greeley Tribune, September 30, 1936. Courtesy of
City of Greeley Museums

Some of the men served two terms in the CCC. The CCC
was open to young men whose families qualified for assistance.
Enrollment was for a six-month term, with a maximum term of two
years. The enrollees agreed to forfeit the majority of their pay to
their families.

Following is a copy of Augustine Lopez's CCC enrollment application, January 2, 1937.

UNITED STATES DEPARTMENT OF LABOR
EMERGENCY CONSERVATION WORK
GR

APPLICATION FOR ENROLLMENT

Applicant's Name LOPEZ, Augustine
Last name   First   Middle initial
Date Jan. 2, 1937

Address Spanish Colony, Greeley, Colo.
Application Received By—
Local Agency Dept. of Public Welfare

Post Office Greeley
Address Court House

State Colorado   County Weld
City or Town Greeley

Age 17   Place and date of birth New Mexico   Sept. 8,   1919
City and State   Month   Day   Year
If not born in the United States, Single
have you been naturalized?   First papers   Final papers
Date   Place   Date

Education: [Circle highest grade completed] Grammar or grade school 1 2 3 4 5 X 7 8 High school 1 2 3 4 College 1 2 3 4
Other education None
State experience in club or community activities such as:
Red Cross, Boy Scouts, 4-H Clubs, etc. None
How long unemployed   Are you registered for work with the nearest public employment office?
Months
Last job held Beet work
Work best qualified for Farming
Amount and kind of outdoor work experience
What kind of job do you hope to find after completion of C.C.C. enrollment? Beet work & farming

Previously enrolled in   If so, state former
Civilian Conservation Corps? No.   company location
Yes or no   HONORABLE
Former Company   Former individual   Type of discharge Check ADMINISTRATIVE
number   serial number   DISHONORABLE
Length of previous service   Date Enrolled   Date discharged
Months

Allotment of Pay From Monthly Cash Allowance to be Made to Dependent Relatives as Follows:
Name Frank Lopez   Relationship Father
Address Spanish Colony, Greeley, Colo Amount $25.
Name   Relationship
Address   Amount

The foregoing statements are true, to the best of my knowledge. If I am accepted and enrolled, I agree to abide faithfully by the rules and regulations governing the work and the camps in which I may be employed.

APPLICANT'S SIGNATURE Augustine Lopez

THE UNITED STATES DEPARTMENT OF LABOR

Certifies that Augustine Lopez
Name
residing at Spanish Colony, Greeley, Colorado
Address
has been properly selected for enrollment in Emergency Conservation Work (Civilian Conservation Corps) and for the completion of his
enrollment has been directed to report to U. S. Army authorities at SP — 8 — C — Boulder, Colorado
COLORADO STATE WELFARE DEPARTMENT
COLORADO WORKS PROGRESS ADMINISTRATION

NOTE: This form to be used only for "Juniors," 18-26 years of age.   339 State Capitol Bldg
ROUTING OF COPIES: Original to Army Official, Duplicate to County File, Triplicate to State File.   Denver, Colorado
By Frank A. Long
Selecting agent

CASE WORK SUPERVISOR
Official designation

Courtesy of Colorado State Archives.

The copy of the letter below is the CCC acceptance letter for Frank Lopez's son, Dave P. Lopez, to work at camp F-17-W in Laramie, Wyoming.

HEADQUARTERS COMPANY 832 CCC
Camp F-17-W
P.O. Box 718
Laramie, Wyoming

October 7, 1938

Mr. Frank Lopez,

We have been pleased to welcome to our camp Dave P. Lopez on October 5, 1938 and we hope you will give us your sincere cooperation in making this new enrollee contented in his new environment by writing frequent and cheerful letters, avoiding references to anything that might cause him to become homesick, and in general helping us to make this his second home.

Camp F-17-W is located 37 miles south-west of Laramie, Wyoming in the Medicine Bow National Forest. The camp is at an elevation of about 8,500 feet above sea level and set among pines in beautiful surroundings. A complete educational and recreational program is conducted for the benefit of the enrollees along with technical training under the supervision of the Forestry Service. Enrollees spend 40 hours per week on various Forestry projects and the remainder of the time may be spent in camp improving themselves in academic or technical studies or in recreation. Strict discipline is required for the health and comfort of the enrollees and every effort is made to stress qualities and provide each enrollee with better equipment to live a more useful and bigger life and to be a better and more useful citizen for having been in the CCC.

Very truly yours,

Frank L. Dougherty
1st Lt. Fa-Res.
Commanding Co. 832 CCC

Courtesy of Jerry Lopez.

DG = Division of Grazing (Public Domain)	NP = National Park Service
DF = U.S. Forest Service	P = Private Forest
DNP = National Park Service	PE = National Park Service
DPE = U.S. Forest Service (Private Land)	SCS = Soil Conservation
DSP = National Park Service (Municipal Park)	Service (Private Land)
F = U.S. Forest Service	SP = National Park Service
CCC Camp Designation are:	(State Park)
Designation = Agency (Land Ownership if not Agency)	G = Grazing Service
BR = Bureau of Reclamation	GLO = General Land Office
BS = Biological Survey	MA = National Park Service
CP = County Park	(Metropolitan Area Municipal
	Park
	NA = National Arboretum
	NM = National Park Service
	(National Monument)

CCC camp designations and abbreviations:

The CCC operated under the direction of the U. S. Military. Service in the CCC could be applied toward military service. Young men were Honorably Discharged when farming season began. A parent had to submit a written request for a CCC enrollee to be released and allowed to return home to work in the fields.

Below is the letter requesting the release of Augustine Lopez from the CCC to return to fieldwork.

Weld County Department of Public Welfare

COURT HOUSE
GREELEY. COLORADO

DWIGHT O. CLINE
ACTING DIRECTOR

CHAS. O. PLUMB, CHRM.
A. R. RIGGS
FRED ARENS

May 15, 1937

Miss Genevieve Affolter
CCC Representative
Colo State Dep't of Public Welfare
339 State Capitol Building
Denver, Colorado

RE: LOPEZ, Augustine
CCC Enrollee

Dear Miss Affolter:

Will you make the recommendation to the Commanding Officer at N-4-C, Estes Park, that the above named enrollee be discharged for other employment? His father, Frank Lopez, has a thirty-seven-acre beet contract with Chas. Johnson, who lives one mile north and one-half miles west of the Spanish Colony in Greeley. Mr. Lopez needs his son's help in caring for this contract and would like to have him discharged as soon as possible as they are ready to work in the fields now.

Thanking you for your kind cooperation in this matter,

Very truly yours,

Rita Koll
(Miss) Rita Koll
Case Worker

Approved: D. O. Cline
D. O. Cline
Acting Director

RK:rk

Courtesy of the Colorado State Archives.

After approval of the request, Augustine Lopez received an Honorable Discharge from the CCC.

Co. 388 , Camp -4-C
stes ark, Colorado

State Department of Public Welfare
341 State Capitol Building
Denver, Colorado

Dear Sir:

CCC Enrollee __Augustine Lopez, CC8-3884137 ___ __ ___ CCC
Co. 3884, Camp N?-4-C, Estes Park, Colorado, was discharged from
the Civilian Conservation Corps on __May 22, 1937_____.

The monthly allotment of $_25.00____ in favor of __Frank____
Lopez, Spanish Colony, Greeley, Colorado ___ _____ is
therefore terminated.

he services of this enrollee were terminated by a(n)
Honorable_____ discharge by reason of _To accept___
employment.

LEO A. NOBLE
Capt., Inf-Res.
Commanding

Courtesy of Colorado State Archives.

The CCC promoted literacy, kept enrollees busy and out of trouble, and helped ensure their well-rounded development. In 1936, academic, vocational, and handcraft classes were held, as well as English, mathematics, history, radio and telegraphy, woodwork, leather work, first aid, political science, surveying, auto mechanics, and music.[2]

No job was too big for the men in Colorado's CCC camps. Many of the long-term projects were ended in haste when the CCC was disbanded immediately after Pearl Harbor

A CCC article, "Historic Morrison" noted,

Trading their picks and shovels... many enlisted in branches of the Armed Services and served their country in an endeavor that was grander yet... It became clear that the program had trained enrollees well for America's next big challenge: winning World War II. The "boys" had become men well equipped for the war effort in which many of them immediately enlisted. Their skills and experience, their adaptability to hard work and difficult living conditions, their pride in getting the job done, all served them well in the European and Pacific theatres as the war progressed.[3]

Of the Colony's 23 men who fought in World War II, there are twelve known CCC enrollees; Joe Benavides, Ernest Espinosa, Moses Espinosa, Tito "Butter" Garcia Jr., Manuel Jojola, Augustine "Gus" Lopez, Edward "Lalo" Lopez, Ernest Marquez, Arthur Martinez, Ray Martinez, Tony Martinez, and Max Tellez.

Works Progress Administration

The Work(s) Progress Administration was created by Franklin D. Roosevelt on May 6, 1935, as a reaction to the great Depression, to provide relief work for the unemployed persons through public work projects. The WPA provided jobs to unemployed workers on public projects sponsored by federal, state, or local agencies; and on defense and war-related projects... The Work(s) Progress Administration was abolished by an executive order on December 4, 1942.[4]

186

The organization operated for seven years out of Denver, Colorado. Many of the residents of the Spanish Colony, along with others from Weld County, were among the WPA enrollees.

Five Million dollars have been spent by the Federal Government and local sponsors spent during the seven year's existence of the WPA. Regulations required local sponsors to furnish at least 25 percent of the total money spent for labor and material; Weld County provided 42 per cent, a record to be envied throughout the nation.[5]

WPA workers were employed to build and replace twenty-six local bridges that were washed out due to flooding from heavy rains in Eastern Colorado on May 30,1935. Flood control was given considerable attention. The Cache la Poudre River was cleared of debris, and "McGrew" Reservoir east of Nunn, Colorado was repaired.[6]

WPA workers were used to build and repair streets, alleys, curbs, and gutters in Greeley, La Salle, Erie, Eaton, and Johnstown. One of the biggest achievements of the WPA was to improve the Greeley water system. When completed, it was considered one of the finest systems in the State of Colorado.

Island Grove Park received spacious livestock barns and stables for its Spud Rodeo and Weld County Fair.[7]

Housing Project for Horses competing in the Fourth of July Greeley Spud Rodeo is being used for the first time this year. The extensive barns will house also the fine animals exhibited annually at the Weld County Junior Fair. The City of Greeley, the Rodeo committee and the WPA cooperated in the $8,425 project. The picture here is the fifth of a series showing the varied activities of the municipal government for the benefit of the people.—Photo by Gardner, Engraving by the Tribune.

Photo of an NYA project: new stables for horses at Island Grove Park. *The Greeley Tribune,* July 1, 1938 page 2.

187

The WPA also had many humanitarian and professional services to offer. Moses Espinosa remembered, "My dad, Otavio Espinosa, worked for the WPA in Kersey, Colorado. Kersey was located in the desert and the rattlesnakes were plentiful. Kersey had wooden sidewalks. The rattlesnakes hid under the sidewalks. As people walked over the boards, the rattlesnakes came slithering out. The residents were scared. The WPA brought several men, and my dad was one of them, to kill the rattlesnakes in Kersey."

Schools benefited from the labor of the WPA workers. They did much needed repairs to buildings and school grounds. The WPA also instituted the school hot lunch program. Nursery schools, adult education, classes in English, writing, and sewing were held in the Spanish Colony. A day nursery was started to care for the children after school until their parents were able to return home from work in the Colony.[8]

Hispanic women learn to sew. This photo was taken from "Your Children At School: A Pictorial Progress Report of the Greeley Public Schools" from May 1938.

COURTESY CITY OF GREELEY MUSEUMS

Top center facing forward L to R: Ponposa Madrid and Eugina Gonzales. Bottom right corner: Santitos Lopez Garcia. Photo courtesy of City of Greeley Museums.

National Youth Administration

The National Youth Administration (NYA) was launched by President Franklin D. Roosevelt at the urging of the First Lady, Eleanor Roosevelt, in 1935. Its objective was to provide part-time employment for boys and girls between the ages of 16 and 25 to help them remain in school. Those who had dropped out or had already finished their education were also offered jobs by the NYA in order to reduce the unemployment of young people and keep them out of the labor market.[9]

Worth To City Cannot Be Measured In Dollars

In 1932 America faced the greatest crisis in its history. In addition to a large per cent of the adult population being thrown out of work, tens or thousands of this country's youth were sent out onto the roads of the nation, destitute and homeless. The youth side of the question, we believe, was the greatest problem which at that time faced the country.

Since that time, through the aid of the United States government, the youth of America have taken a new lease on life and are once more being turned towards an opportunity for good citizenship. This change has been brought about through a New Deal agency known as the National Youth Administration or NYA. Following is a brief survey of what NYA has meant to Greeley and Weld county.

One of the greatest public institutions in any community is the public library. Through government funds which supplied youth workers and materials seven Weld county communities have obtained library facilities that they would not otherwise have had. These communities are Gill, Keenesburg, Grover, Frederick, Erie, Pierce and Nunn.

Courtesy of City of Greeley Museums.

A November 15, 1940, *The Greeley Tribune* article, "NYA
Here Will Make Furniture for C. S. School," noted,

> Construction work and cutting up wood for the new NYA
> national defense training school being started at Colorado
> springs will be made by NYA youth in Weld County at the
> NYA shops at Island Grove Park, it was announced
> Thursday. Boys who will work on the projects are out-of-
> school youths in this area.

Below is a copy of the card giving Augustine Lopez
permission to work at Island Grove Park in the NYA workshop.

Courtesy of Jerry Lopez.

NYA projects included making furniture for the Weld
County Library such as card catalog cases, cabinets, shelves, a book
mobile, and bookbinding and clerical projects. Other projects of the
NYA included constructing four tennis courts, helping out in nursery
schools, and building furniture for other public needs.

NYA Workshop at Island Grove has built much equipment for government shops and offices. It is well equipped with woodworking machinery, some of which is shown here. In the background is the nearly finished Weld county library bookmobile, and at various jobs are some of the NYA boys who worked on it. John Sauer, at the left of the door, is in charge of the shop. The bookmobile will be available for regular service sometime next week. Tribune photo and engraving.

The Greeley Tribune, April 15, 1941.

Federal programs were offered across the United States to help alleviate the economic hardships felt by its citizens during the Great Depression. Like the rest of America, the young men of the Spanish Colony took great pride in helping their families through the Depression by enlisting and serving in the various government programs.

References

1. *Civilian Conservation Corps in Colorado/Workers in Progress Association Projects.*
   (www.archives.state.co.us/ccc/cccscope.htm).
   Viewed March 2003.

2. *Historic Morrison the Civilian Conservation Corp.*
   (www.town.morrison.co.us/historical/CCC.htm).
   Viewed March 2003.

3. Ibid.

4. *Work(s) Progress Administration Photograph Collection at the Colorado State Archives.*
   (www.newdeal.feri.org/library/i39.htm.). Viewed June 2003.

5. WPA Left Many Permanent Improvements in Weld, Besides Supplying Jobs for Thousands at Total Cost of Approximately 5 Million. *The Greeley Tribune.* February 23, 1943.

6. Ibid.

7. Spacious Livestock Barns Ready for Rodeo and Junior Fair. *The Greeley Tribune.* June 1938.

8. WPA in Weld County. *The Greeley Tribune.* March 4, 1943.

9. *National Youth Administration*
   (http://www.austin.cc.tx.us/lpatrick/his234/new.html).
   Viewed May 2004.

Chapter 13

Spanish American Patriots

World War II photo in Germany. L to R: Lopez, Neddie Lopez, Baca, Beward. Photo Courtesy of Palmer Lopez..

Hispanic Americans have served in all branches of the U. S. Military. The residents of the Spanish Colony likewise responded to the call to serve their country, and have served during peace time and war time.

Spanish Colony residents known to have served in World War I were Elias Espinosa, Epiphamo Garcia, Don Gonzales, Julian Marquez, Luis Ortega, Sylvan Talmadge, and Frank Sanchez.

World War II

During World War II the following residents were known to have enlisted: Frank Beltran, Pinon Benavidez, Franscualo Duran, Arthur Espaline, Ernest Espinosa, Moses Espinosa, Fred Garcia, Paul Garcia, Tito "Butter" Garcia Jr., Manuel Jojola, Augustine "Gus" Lopez, Edward "Lalo" Lopez, Ynez "Neddie" Lopez Jr., Emilo Lozano, Johnny Lozano, Ernest Marquez, Arthur Martinez, Ray Martinez Jr., Tony Martinez, Sam Rios, Charley Sanchez, Ray Talmadge, Enrique Tellez, Henry Tellez, and Max Tellez.

Before the men left for training camp, the parents and family observed a few traditions; for example, the parents gave a blessing, a *bendicion,* and prayed for their son's safe return. The son kneeled, and the parents with other family members made the sign of the cross on his forehead while saying the blessing. A priest presented a medallion, a *comulgar,* on a cord to each man, and this was worn around the neck.

Example of a Medallion Courtesy of Ricardo "Rico" Lopez

Traditionally, the song "*Ha La Guerra, Ha Me Llevan*" (They Are Taking Me To War, I Must Go) was sung by the parents, especially the mothers for their sons who were leaving for the war. When Augustine "Gus" Lopez left in 1942, Tito "Butter" Garcia Jr. remembered Gus's parents, Martina and Francisco, along with friends and family (Arthur Lopez, Jenny Rios, Mary Rios, Jess Gonzales) singing this song for him.

Butter recalled the Spanish words to *Ha La Guerra*, which were translated into English by Ricardo "Rico" Lopez.

Ha La Guerra Ha Me Llevan	**THEY ARE TAKING ME TO WAR, I MUST GO**

<table>
<tr>
<td>

*Ha la guerre ha me llevan
madrecita mía.
Me agarron de la lleva del dia
ayer
Hay te quedas sin tu hijo muy
solitaria
Solo Diós sabe si no nos
volveranos a ver.*

*En el pecho llevo siempre la
medalla
Que mi madre me la dió
con tanta fe
Y si acaso no me mata la metralla
A tus brazos madrecita volver.*

*So lo quiero que le digas a mi
chata
Que hay le dejo mi rendido
corazon
Que lo trate con cariño
Y no sea ingrata
Que lo trate con cariño y con
amor*

*Ya con esto me despido mardecita
Que se está haciendo tarde
y tengo que tomar el tren
Solo quiero que le rueges al santo
nino
Que ha tus brazos algún día
volver.*

</td>
<td>

They are taking me to war my
dear mother
They have grabbed me by the coat
since yesterday
You will be left all alone without
your son
God only knows if we will see
each other again

On my chest I will always wear
this holy medal
That my mother gave to me in
good faith
And if the weapons of war don't
kill me
To your arms I will return.

So I want you to tell my
girlfriend
That I will leave her my
devoted heart
Tell her to treat it with affection
and gratefulness
To treat it with affection and
love.

It is time to say goodbye now
mother
It is getting late and I have to
catch the train
All I ask you mother is to pray to
baby Jesus
That to your arms some day I will
return.

</td>
</tr>
</table>

Augustine and Francisco "Pancho" Lopez Sr., circa 1941, in Arizona before Augustine was sent overseas during World War II. Photo courtesy of Gabriel Lopez.

"*Soldado Raso*", a song about a buck private, was also popular among the Colony residents.

Augustine Lopez in France in World War II. Photo courtesy of Gabriel Lopez.

Augustine "Gus" Lopez served in the European Theater. Jerry Lopez remembered, "Dad said he landed on Omaha Beach the second day, and bodies were still floating in the ocean and laying on the beach. Dad said, 'I will never forget those bodies or what the war was like.' Dad never spoke of the war again after that."

Gus reminisced about being in an infantry unit which followed General Patton's troops in Europe. Towns were devastated. Gus said, "It was terrible and so was the war." Gus Lopez received awards and medals from the army including one for excellent marksmanship.

Six months after Gus's father, Francisco Lopez, died on December 15, 1944, he received a letter about his father's death just prior to his coming home. Gus was discharged in November 9, 1945.

Joe P. Martinez's photo which appeared in the dedication pamphlet for Our Lady of Peace Catholic Church Dedication.[1] Courtesy of City Greeley Museum

Many of the World War II enlistees from the Colony knew Joe P. Martinez of Ault, Colorado, who was the first Coloradan to receive the Congressional Medal of Honor during World War II for his heroic efforts in defending Attu in the Aleutian Islands, from the Japanese in May 1943.

Colonists saved World War II mementos including letters from soldiers, ration books, government-issued war bonds, V-mail, and coupons. These items illustrate the colonists' involvement in defending their country.

V-Mail or Victory Mail was a valuable tool for the military during World War II. The process, which originated in England, allowed letters to be microfilmed. Instead of using valuable cargo space to ship original letters overseas, microfilmed copies were sent instead and then enlarged at an overseas destination before being delivered to military personnel. The system of microfilming letters was based on the use of special V-mail letter-sheets which were a combination of letter and envelope. The letter-sheets were constructed and gummed so as to fold into a uniform and distinctively marked envelope. The user wrote the message in the limited space provided, added the name and address of the recipient, folded the form, affixed postage, if necessary, and mailed the letter. V-mail correspondence was then reduced to thumbnail size on microfilm. The rolls of film were sent to prescribed destinations for developing at a receiving station near the addressee. Finally, individual facsimiles of the letter-sheets were reproduced at about one-quarter of the original size and the miniature V-mail was then delivered to the addressee.[2]

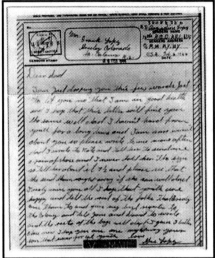

Augustine "Gus" Lopez V-Mail to his dad Francisco Lopez December 25, 1943. Photos Courtesy of Gabriel Lopez.

Each family member or family head was issued ration books. Coupons in the ration books were exchanged for items such as coffee, sugar, butter, bacon, sweets, petrol, clothing, and soap. Black marketeers tried to take advantage of the short supply of food and material; rationed goods were sold without proper coupons, and food could be sold at very inflated prices.

Ration book No. 1 was issued for sugar. Before receiving coupons, the recipient was asked, "How much sugar do you have?" Based on the answer, the required amount of coupons would be removed from the book. Each person was allowed 8 oz. of sugar per week.

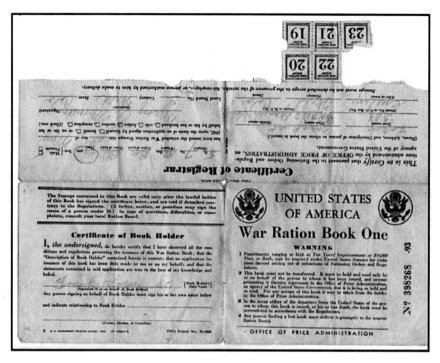

Francisco Lopez's ration book. Courtesy of Palmer Lopez.

Ration book No. 2 contained coupons for food, clothing, and petrol.

Ricardo Lopez ration book. Courtesy of Palmer Lopez.

Ration Book 3
Is Due Shortly

(Associated Press)

Washington, April 15.—OPA officials disclosed today that Ration Book No. 3 will be issued soon, probably late in July, but will be used primarily for shoes, sugar and coffee as soon as Book No. 1 runs out of stamps.

The No. 3 volume issue also may be used to provide a couple more months of canned goods and meat stamps, since it was designed to handle both point and unit system of rationing.

Officials said they had no intention of using the No. 3 book to ration any new commodities, but could make no promises because of the theoretical possibilities of special emergencies. Books 4, 5 and 6 are in the design stage, so No. 3 probably would not be needed for new rationing if any did become necessary.

On April 15, 1943 *The Greeley Tribune* announced the issue of Ration Book 3. Coupons in this book were for shoes, sugar and coffee.

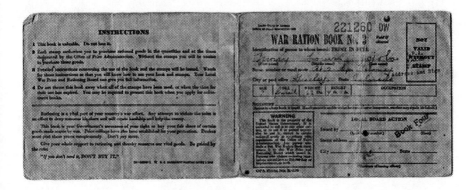

Ration book No. 3 had pictures of military planes, canons and ships.

Mary Jojola ration book. Courtesy of Gus and Mary Martinez.

Ration summaries and updates appeared in regular Associated Press columns in *The Greeley Tribune* as seen below.

from Axis government

Ration Summary For This Week

By The Associated Press

Meat, Cheese, Fats, Canned Fish

Red coupons A, B, C and D in ration book No. 2 valid now and through April 30. Coupon E becomes valid April 25.

Processed Fruits & Vegetables

Blue, D, E and F coupons in book 2 valid through April 30.

Sugar

Stamp 12 in book 1 good for 5 pounds through May 31. Extra canning sugar available from local ration boards.

Coffee

Stamp 26 in book 1 good for one pound through April 25. Stamp 23 good for one pound April 26 to May 30, inclusive.

Shoes

Stamp 17 in book 1 good for one pair through June 15.

Gasoline

No. 5 coupons worth 3 gallons in East, 4 gallons elsewhere. In East, A coupons must last through July 21; elsewhere through May 21.

Fuel Oil

Period 5 coupons valid until fall. Worth 10 gallons each on household type and 100 gallons each on institutional type throughout the East and also in Washington, Oregon, Kentucky, rationed counties in Idaho, and southern counties of Ohio, Indiana, Illinois, Missouri and Kansas. Worth 11 and 110 gallons in remainder of rationed midwest states.

The Greeley Tribune, April 19, 1943, page 7.

Wartime and postwar rations allowed people limited quantities of rationed food and goods. Every member of the family had their own ration book, which gave precise details of the amounts of certain types of food allowed during one week:

Bacon and ham: 4oz (100g)

    Meat: Meat was given to the value of 1s.2d (6p today). Sausages were not rationed but difficult   to get: offal (liver, kidneys, tripe) was originally not rationed but sometimes formed part   of the meat ration.

    Cheese: 2oz (50g) sometimes it went up to 4oz (100g) and even up to 8oz (225g).

    Margarine: 4oz (100g)

    Butter: 2oz (50g)

    Milk: 3 pints (1800ml) occasionally they would drop to 2 pints (1200ml). Household milk   (skimmed or dried) was available: 1 packet per four weeks.

    Sugar: 8oz (225g). There were one or two ways we could make this go further. One way was   using beetroot as pudding.

    Jam: 1lb (450g) every two months.

    Tea: 2oz (50g).

    Eggs: 1 fresh egg a week if available, but often only one every two weeks.

    Dried eggs: 1 packet every four weeks.

    Sweets: 12oz (350g) every four weeks.

All school children had to have a weekly dose of VIROL, a sweet and sticky extract of malt, in order to make sure they got their proper ration of vitamins.[3]

The Korean War

    The Korean War began June 25, 1950, and ended July 27, 1953. Many men from the Colony, following in the footsteps of their fathers and brothers, joined the military; for example, after graduating from Greeley High School in 1954, ten young men, including four from the Spanish Colony, joined the military together. Some of them joined the Army Paratroopers and others the Air Force. They were; Rico Lopez, Gilbert "Gil" Carbajal, Victor Torrez, John Torrez, Frank Gonzales, Manuel Alcaraz, Henry Ciddo, Theodus Holland, Don Gonzales, and Pete Magdaleno.

    Seven went to training camp immediately, but three (Rico Lopez, Gil Carbajal, and Victor Torrez) went later. During the summer of 1954, Rico and Gil played for the Greeley Grays Semi-Pro baseball team, and Victor waited for them to finish the season.

Three young friends just before leaving for Japan and Korea in June 1955 standing next to their mothers. L to R: Ricardo and Martina Lopez, Gil and Sara Carbajal, and Victor and Rose Torrez. Photo courtesy of Gil Carbajal.

These three childhood friends from the Colony enlisted in the Army on October 11, 1954, in Greeley and were inducted at Denver. They were sent to Camp Fordorf, California. Upon completing basic training, the three got together and decided to sign up for Airborne training. Army paratroopers were sent to Fort Campbell, Kentucky, for jump school. On completion of jump school, they were assigned to the 508th Battalion Paratroopers.

Rico Lopez recalled, "The 508 Airborne Regimental Combat Team was called the "Bastard Outfit" as it did not belong to any division. It replaced the 187th Airborne Regimental Combat Team in Korea and was put on alert due to the Koreans becoming more aggressive. The war had already ended. Upon completion of jump school, we were sent to Japan via San Francisco, California, then to Honolulu, Hawaii, to Wake Island, then to Tokyo, Japan. We were then transported by train to the southern-most island called Kyushu. We were stationed at Camp Chimauga near Beppu, Kyushu."

Rico was discharged from the Army at Fort Bragg, North Carolina, on October 26, 1956, with a total of 17 jumps; Gil Carbajal and Victor Torrez each had 30 jumps. Gil and Victor were assigned to the reactivated 101st Airborne in August of 1956.

All ten friends completed their military service, nine returned to Greeley. Six of them attended their 40th High School class reunion as pictured below.

Six of the ten young friends are pictured at their 40th class reunion in 1994. L to R: Gil Carbajal, Rico Lopez, John Torrez, Frank Gonzales, Manuel Alcaraz, and Pete Magdaleno. Photo courtesy of Gil Carbajal.

The Viet Nam Conflict

U.S. involvement in Viet Nam began with the training of South Vietnamese soldiers in 1956. By 1965, 200,000 Marines arrived in Da Nang. The War ended in 1973 when a cease-fire aggreement was signed in Paris, and the last Americans left Viet Nam.[4] Young men from the Colony were among those who served in Viet Nam.

Palmer Lopez joined the Army on June 2, 1965. In July, he reported for basic training at Fort Leonard Wood, Missouri. Palmer remembered, "They held a competition with all the brigades to see who was the Top Gun soldier. I was the Top Gun that year. I won the high proficiency on August 12, 1965. I competed against four brigades; a brigade contained about two thousand men. I competed against eight thousand men!" Palmer scored the highest in the 1st Battalion's Proficiency Test during his basic training with a score of 459. He received a meritorious promotion and award for his accomplishment in basic training camp.

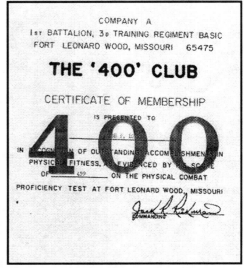

Trophy and Certificate of the award given to Palmer Lopez. Courtesy of Palmer Lopez.

Palmer mentioned, "Several other men won awards, so, at the end of basic training and during the parade, I got to stand with the Generals and others, and we saluted as soldiers marched by. We were honored for what we did as individuals."

Palmer Lopez. Photo courtesy of Palmer Lopez.

Palmer continued, "The Army kept us there for advanced training in the field we were in. I received orders to go to Frankfurt, Germany, but before going, they cut our orders, and we were put on alert for Viet Nam. Sure enough, that is where we went. Our company arrived in Oakland, California. We boarded a troop ship headed to Hawaii. In Hawaii, we received more advanced training in preparation for Viet Nam. We were there two and half months. I remember being awakened at 3:00 a.m. They were screaming at us, 'WAKE UP! WE ARE GOING TO NAM!!" I got up, and they sent us to supplies, and we were issued our M-14s and ammo. We were sent to Schofield, an airport in Hawaii. We drove up to a C1-33

Cargomaster airplane when its tail was opening up. I thought, 'This thing is going to swallow me.' We drove in, and inside the plane there was another bigger truck with ammo already in it. We took off to Wake Island to refuel, and stopped in the Philippines because of engine trouble. We left there and landed at Pleiku, Viet Nam. We were five miles from the DMZ and close to the Ho Chi Minh trail. I remember coming in at night. We started to receive small arms fire. I couldn't believe they were shooting at the plane. We had to go to another base until the next day, so we could land in daylight. They were bringing troops in by the thousands, and there was no airtime. We had to start our engines and keep them running. The minute the plane landed and slowed down to about 5 to 20 mph, the tail opened up, and we had to back out on the runway while it was still moving. When the last truck was unloaded, the tail of the plane lifted up, and the plane took off to get another load. We then traveled about a mile before meeting up with the convoy that was taking us to the camp. I remember seeing Vietnamese standing along the road waving at us as we drove by. We finally arrived at Camp Holloway on the Annam highlands of the Kon Tum Province. In my unit, there were four divisions in the 25th Infantry Division. It had a 4,000-man task force. We were called the Tropic Lightning Division. There were no front lines; it was open season on us no matter what we did. We were in God's hands while we were in Viet Nam. I returned to the States in March 1967."

For the first known time, women of the Spanish Colony joined the ranks of military service. Lorraine "Lori" Garcia Sadler, raised in the Colony, advanced the status of women in the military during her career with the U.S. Marine Corps Lori became the first female Hispanic Colonel in the Marine Corps. She attended the Basic Intelligence Course at the Intelligence School, Ft. Holabird, MD, one of the first two female Marines to attend this course. Lori was the first woman Marine to attend the Defense Intelligence Course at the Defense Intelligence School, Anacostia, MD, 1974-1975. Her other accomplishments before retiring in 1992 included:

- Assignment to the Defense Intelligence Agency, Pentagon.
- Promotion to Major, then to Lt. Colonel, then to Colonel

- Recipient of the Defense Meritorious Service Medal
- First Woman Marine assigned as the Assistant Chief of Staff for Intelligence, 2nd Force Service Support Group, Camp Lejeune, NC., 1979-1982
- First Woman Marine assigned as the Assistant Chief of Staff for Intelligence, 1st Marine Amphibious Force, Camp Pendleton, CA 1987-1990
- Only Woman Marine assigned as the Director of Intelligence, C4I Division, HQMC, 1990-1992
- Recipient of the Legion of Merit

ARMED FORCES

Colonel Lorraine M. Sadler daughter of Alvin and Jenny Garcia of Greeley, will retire from the U,S Marine Corps July 10 after serving for 25 years. She will be awarded the Legion of Merit award t a cer emony in Washington, D.C. She is a 1963 graduate of Greeley High School and also attended the University of Northern Colorado. She is the senior woman in the Marine Corps Intellengence community  Lorraine Sadler and the first and currently the only Hispanic woman to hold the rank of colonel in the Marine Corps. She was asked earlier this year to head a commission to study "Women" Issues in the Marine Corps." She and her family will reside in Lex ington, Virginia.

Armed Forces article in *The Greeley Tribune,* July 1992.

The Greeley Tribune August 1, 1992, article, "Playground to Honor Hispanic Colonel," reported, "She was recognized as being the first Hispanic Colonel, as a pioneering, top-ranking woman officer."

As with young men and women across the United States, the youth of the Spanish Colony felt it their patriotic duty to enlist for military service. They fought and died with their fellow Americans while serving their country.

References

1. *Our Lady of Peach Pamphlet.* 1949.

2. *V-Mail - World War II.*
   (www.timewitnesses.org/exhibits/2d2avmail.html).
   Viewed June 2004.

3. Wartime (and Postwar) Rations.
   (www.timewitnesses.org/english/food/ration.html).
   Viewed June 2004.

4. *The Viet Nam War.* (www.vietnampix.com/intro.htm).
   Viewed July 2004.

Chapter 14

Misunderstanding, Racial Prejudice, and Baseball

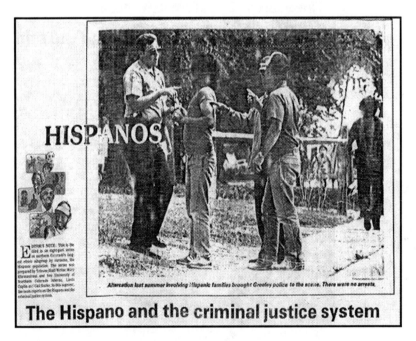

HISPANOS

Alteration last summer involving Hispanic families brought Greeley police to the scene. There were no arrests.

The Hispano and the criminal justice system

The Greeley Tribune, September 21, 1980.

Any group of people may become victims of prejudice through malice or misunderstanding; the residents of the Spanish Colony were no exception. One reason for locating the Spanish Colony five miles northwest of Greeley was to keep the *Mexicans* out of the city. The stoop laborers endured ongoing prejudicial treatment from the community, including not being paid for work in the fields.

Prejudice and discrimination were evident in Greeley from the 1920s to the 1960s. In response to the newcomers, many of them Hispanic-Americans recruited as field laborers by the Great Western Sugar Company, merchants in Greeley's main business district prominently displayed NO MEXICANS signs in their store windows. These discriminatory signs caused resentment and hard feelings. The Mexican Consul visited with Greeley's Chamber of Commerce in November 1926 and requested these signs be removed. As recently as the 1960s, people recalled seeing signs, NO DOGS AND NO MEXICANS in some downtown Greeley businesses.

"NO MEXICANS" SIGNS REMOVED

By friendly discussions with the business men, the chamber of commerce has secured the removal of "No Mexicans" signs from practically all of the small group of local business places which displayed them. The Spanish speaking people are very resentful of such discriminatory signs. Recently the Mexican consul came here and asked cooperation in securing the removal of the signs.

The business people generally do not desire to see a Spanish American, or Mexican business district established in the city. Most of them welcome the Spanish-American trade, it was said at the chamber of commerce meeting Friday. The Great Western Sugar company is attempting to colonize the highest class Mexicans in the district and is asking the cooperation of the city and business men in its efforts.

The Greeley Tribune, November 1, 1926.

215

Alvin Garcia remembered prejudicial treatment in some of Greeley's eating establishments. He said, "Some boys and I went to Greeley to eat. The restaurant gave us our hamburgers, and we ate them. When we got the bill, it was double the price. The other two boys wanted to argue the price, but I said all that would do was put us in jail for disturbing the peace."

There were Anglos who considered Mexicans as being a necessary evil. To illustrate such derogatory thinking, the *Through the Leaves* article, "Mexican Invaders Relieving Our Farm Labor Shortage", September 1920, p.522, quoted Mr. John Carrington.

> We couldn't do it if we didn't have the labor. Yes, sir, we are dependent on the Mexican farm-labor supply, and we know it... They are sentimental and romantic. No Mexican peon trekking up into the Southwest to *hunt work* would dream of coming without his "old woman." The latter seldom has any claim to good looks, but, surrounded by a numerous brood of offspring, is either corpulent as a medieval friar or stringy and lean, yet her man would not dream of moving without her. Perhaps the fact that she can be counted on to find food for him when all his own efforts fail has something to do with that. Nevertheless, the fact remains that family ties are strongly knit.

To care for the laborers, one had to care for the families, and then the laborers could perform their duties to the fullest.

The November 1923 *Through the Leaves* article, "Regarding Mexican Beet Workers", p.464, reported,

> Jose Queralt-Mir, A Consul for Mexico, Denver, said, I desire to make a few suggestions to the farmers who give them employment. I do it with the sole object of helping the farmers to understand the character of the Mexican worker, who will render much better service if the farmer handles him in an understanding way. In general, the Mexican character is courteous, kind and extremely sensitive. When he is treated fairly the Mexican worker does not try to get the

best of anybody. He is grateful and lives up to his promises. Living in a strange country, lacking knowledge of the English language, the Mexican worker is likely to be timid, and many times he cannot express his claims to his rights. Also, he is apt to fear everyone or to feel uneasy because he has heard "no one likes a Mexican in this country." When your Mexican worker comes to your farm he judges the way he is going to be treated by the way he is received. If the farmer is kind to him and shows interest in himself and the members of his family, if the farmer talks in a kind way and gives them fairly decent place in which to live, it is certain that the Mexican is going to do his best to satisfy the farmer. The worker will try to repay in that manner, the kindness that the farmer has shown him. But if on the contrary he is received in a rough manner, without kindness, the Mexican worker feels unwelcome. That is just the beginning of work done without interest on the side of the worker, but of vital interest to the farmer. There are some nationalities that one cannot commend without making them think they are doing more than they should to earn their money. However, that does not apply to the average Mexican. When you see him doing his work well, tell him so, and you will stimulate him to do even better. If he does poor work of course you must correct him and I realize that this is necessary in some cases. When you promise to do a certain thing at a certain time, keep your promise or if unable to do so, explain why in advance, if possible. Otherwise you will lose the Mexican worker's confidence and you must keep his confidence to get the best work done. It is said of some foreigners that "the more you do for them the more they expect you to do." For Mexican workers, however, I think this should be stated thusly: "the more you do for them, the more they will do for you." The little favors you do for your Mexican help will be greatly appreciated by them. For example, you may know of an opportunity for the Mexican worker to obtain employment during the summer on a road gang, possibly at some distance from your home. Inform him of the chance. Or if you plan to go to town on Saturday on your own business, why not ask the Mexican worker if there is something in town that you

217

can do for him, like bringing back some groceries. Or if you observe that some auto salesman is trying to sell your Mexican a car that will prove to be a liability instead of an asset, why not advise him. Just now the Mexicans are thinking of moving to the city, to Denver or Pueblo, Fort Worth or Kansas City. In a great many cases this is an unwise move for them to make. Railroad tickets are expensive. The cost of living in the City is higher than in a small town in the beet district or on the beet farm. Even though work may be scarce around the farm, he may be able to live in better fashion than unemployed in a large city. It is to the farmer's own interest to help them solve this winter's problem, because next summer the farmers who do help their beet workers over winter will have hands that will work to the utmost for the farmer's interest.

Esther Schillinger wrote, "Some people would solve the Mexican problem by sending the Mexicans back to Mexico...Who would tend the beets? Would the white man take the Mexican's place? No, the white man will not do much of the work the Mexican does unless he is absolutely forced to do it." [1]

Clearly, some prejudice experienced by members of the Spanish Colony and other Greeley Hispanics was lack of understanding of their culture. Many did not distinguish between the Mexican Nationals and the Spanish Americans. The Spanish Americans, by the Treaty of Guadalupe Hidalgo of 1848, were American citizens. In 1938, Spanish Americans met with the City Council to clarify this issue as seen in the article below.

Spanish Americans in Protest To City Council on Confusing Them with Socalled Mexicans

Delegation of Spanish Americans, led by Herman De Herrera of Greeley as spokesman, appeared before the city council here Tuesday night seeking to make it clear that there is a difference between "Spanish Americans" and Mexicans.

De Herrera told the council that only three of the 16 persons run thru police court last week and who were lumped by Mayor E. M. Colpitts under the name of "Spanish Americans," were actually Spanish Americans. The rest, he said, were Mexicans.

De Herrera explained that there is a differnece, defining Spanish Americans as being generally native born American citizens of Spanish descent, while Mexicans are from Mexico.

The spokesman admitted that it is sometimes hard to tell the difference. Mayor Colpitts reiterated that there is a problem here and asked De Herrera and other Spanish Americans to help control the situation here.

The Greeley Tribune, October 5, 1938.

Even in 2004, the dilemma remained. Laborers willing to do the work that no one else wanted to do were needed, but there were still many complaints about "these people". Laborers were too often not accepted into everyday society, and some people suggested that they go back to where they came from, as they did in the 1920s and 1930s.

Esther Schillinger wrote about this attitude.

Many American people regard the Mexicans as unquestionably inferior. Because of language and color he is foreign and always will be until Americans are cured of assuming that persons of another color are different from them, and because they are different are therefore inferior. To the Mexican this attitude is a constant irritation. One Mexican when asked whether he intended to become naturalized said, "I have been here and all family too, twenty three years. I am a citizen of Mexico, not from United States. They treat you just the same anyway. Germans, Italians here, get naturalized, are treated like Americans. Mexicans are always treated like Mexicans. That's bad. There's just one sky for everybody.[2]

Esther Schillinger noted that in Colorado forty percent of the Germans had become naturalized, while only two and a half percent of the Mexicans were naturalized citizens.

The Mexican is not treated any differently if he does become an American citizen. In fact, some Mexicans feel that they are worse off. Before they become American citizens, if mistreated they can go to the Mexican Consul for help. When they become naturalized they lose this last friend. We native Americans should realize what a step naturalization means to the Mexican and should do all we can to make him feel that he has profited by becoming naturalized.[3]

Schillinger also noted the proportion of crime committed by Mexicans was no greater than among other ethnic groups. Causes of crime which were compared included misunderstanding or no knowledge of the laws, prohibition, petty larceny, and disturbing the peace during quarrels with fellow Mexicans. From December 1, 1928, to July 15, 1929, of the 185 entries in the county jail register, 85 were Mexicans. Very few crimes were committed by Mexicans during their seasonal employment. It was only during the winter months when they were out of work and in need that these crimes were committed.[4]

In *The Greeley Tribune,* May 4, 1996, article, "Segregation of Confusion: Hispanics World Change," Tito "Butter" Garcia Jr., was reported as saying,

> There was a highly decorated army officer by the name of Jess Ugalde, who went to a barbershop here in town and told the man who owned it: 'Why don't you hang that sign up on the front lines?' ("White Trade Only") It came out in the paper the next day and that's when the signs started coming down.

The Greeley Tribune, May 4, 1996, page 8.
Courtesy of Tito "Butter" Garcia Jr.

Later, Butter commented, "If these same Hispanic individuals fought for that man's freedom, then he should be respected more for doing so."

Tito "Butter" Garcia's generation are those who worked the fields, were raised speaking Spanish, and held on to family values their parents brought from New Mexico. Butter said, "It was not the cultural differences that set apart the Mexican people from the Anglo population, it was the language barrier. The Anglos didn't like us because we couldn't communicate well with them. People would think we were stupid, because our English was bad and broken."

Merchants capitalized on this language barrier and charged double the interest rates, sometimes up to eight percent on items purchased on credit by Hispanics. When they ran out of food before the winter was over, they would again purchase many of their necessities on credit. The combination of low pay and inflationary charges kept Spanish-speaking people in perpetual poverty. In interviews with the Colony residents, many commented, "We were poor, but we didn't know it. We were happy."

Because of prejudice and ignorance, a few bad examples could quickly and erroneously be generalized as the norm for a particular race or community. An example is an article in *The Greeley Tribune,* September 19, 1924, "Counties May Balk at Winter Mexican Relief" which stated,

> Colonization of Mexicans in northern Colorado is raising many serious new problems. Besides the problem of support during the winter months is an equally grave question of the desirability of segregation of the Mexican children in the schools. Physicians have reported to the commissioners that so large a percentage of Mexican children are afflicted with highly malignant and communicable diseases that their presence in the schools is a grave menace.

Former Colony residents were asked in interviews if there were any diseases or outbreaks of disease in the Colony. Their common answer was that they could not remember any such cases. Alvin Garcia's emphatic response was, "No, if there was a family that was not clean, the trustees would take care of the problem, either by making sure they cleaned up or by tossing them out of the Colony. I am so proud of the constitution those trustees made for the Colony."

Educating the Hispanic child received much opposition from farmers and citizens as noted by Hazel Maddux, in her 1932 Master thesis,

> Educational difficulties arise from the strong opposition of farmers and citizens. They think efforts to educate the Mexican children is a waste of time and money. They resent the Mexican children's association with their children, and say they are dirty and repulsive.[5]

As noted in the June 9, 1954, District 6 School Board meeting minutes, however, "Superintendent Grimes read a petition signed by residents of the east side, requesting the Spanish Colony children not be placed in the Lincoln-Jefferson schools next year. No action was taken."

In *The Greeley Tribune,* May 16, 2004, article, "Language of Change," it was noted,

> The Supreme Court's historic ruling making segregation unconstitutional was barely felt in Weld. Then, there was little tolerance of other cultures ... The May 17, 1954 decision changed little, if anything, in Greeley and Weld County. Stories in *The Greeley Tribune* were written by wire services in Washington, D. C., and nothing was written about the local impact. The ruling was only indirectly discussed once at a Greeley-Evans School District 6 school board meeting: Parents petitioned the board not to bus elementary students from the Spanish Colony in north Greeley into the city schools. The board took no action on the petition and never discussed it again, according to board minutes.

Concerning the Hispanic children who lived in the city and went to the city's schools, Hazel Maddux, in her 1932 Master Thesis, wrote,

> In many towns children are segregated in separate buildings and rooms in school... The teaching seems to be of good quality though handicapped in many ways. Often the rooms are located in the basements with bad lighting and poor ventilation...Lack of equipment is noticeable everywhere. In Kersey the small children have to sit on cigar boxes brought from home, during socialized recitations.[6]

Carmen Solis said, "I remember, when we ate our lunches, that if a bean fell from our lunch, the Anglo kids would pick it up with two toothpicks and carry it to the trash. They would talk about the Mexicans, telling others that the Mexican food was poison. Sometimes they would chase others with that bean, saying if it touched you, you would be poisoned and die."

Butter Garcia remembered, "When it was time for classes for our first communion, we went to St. Peter's in Greeley. They put all of us Chicano kids on one side and the Anglos on the other. When they served us cereal after the class, the Anglos got bananas and we didn't. One of the teachers who taught us at the Colony asked, 'How come they are not getting a banana?' They [St. Peter's] said, 'We ran out.' The teacher walked in the kitchen and saw a paper sack full of bananas. The teacher said, 'That is not fair!' So they gave us each a banana."

Josie Garcia commented, "There are things that bring Hispanics and Anglos together, a common love for the same kinds of foods, a common desire for our children to be successful, and a common concern for our city's future. But some things still keep us apart. We worship in different churches. We shop in different stores. We stay within the invisible boundaries of 'our sides' of town."

Recognizing the division of cultures in the area, *The Greeley Tribune* compiled a series of articles called, "Worlds Apart." [7]

Eddie Guerrero, a Chicano activist who has lived in Weld County most of his life, said, "People who have moved here say they've never seen the divide between Anglos and Hispanics so blatant, so black and white as it is here. You know, though, it's blatant and it's subtle at the same time. It's blatant because the Hispanics feel it every day. But it's subtle because the Anglos can't see it." [8]

One event that bridged the gap between Hispanics and Anglos was the Semi-Pro baseball teams of the National Semi-Pro Congress, of which the Greeley Grays from the Spanish Colony were members.

Today many Hispanics are raised with English, not Spanish as their first language. As more people become interested in their Hispanic heritage and culture, they are separated from a deeper knowledge and appreciation of their "roots" by the language (Spanish) they were never taught. Language is the culture glue that creates strength and identity. Hispanics are steeped in, yet divided by the traditions of both cultures, and can suffer discrimination from Anglos because of their color, or discrimination from Hispanics who are bi-lingual and resent those unable to speak the language of "la gente."

The Grays would gradually become integrated. Tito "Butter" Garcia said, "It helped the Spanish Colony to become integrated into the Greeley community. We had these Anglos coming to play with us, and they found out that we lived just as clean a life as they did, and that we were on their same level in baseball."

Some of the Greeley Grays players would go on to pro baseball careers or become teachers of the game, e.g. Frank Carbajal, coached at Hartnel College in Salinas, California, and he was inducted into the University Of Northern Colorado's Hall of Fame; Greg Riddoch coached for the San Diego Padres and scouted for the Texas Rangers baseball organization; and Tom Wheeler is with the Colorado Rockies baseball organization.

The residents of the Spanish Colony endured and rose above the racial prejudice of the larger community around them. Baseball, the American national pastime, was one way they were able to bridge the gap between their culture and other cultures.

References

1. Schillinger, Esther K. (1929 August). *Social Contacts of the Immigrant Mexicans of Weld County.* (Master Degree thesis,Colorado State College). p. 3.

2. Ibid. pp. 9, 10.

3. Ibid. p. 12.

4. Ibid. p. 30.

5. Maddux, Hazel C. (1932 June). *Some Conditions Which Influence the Mexican Children in Greeley, Colorado, and its Vicinity.* (Master Degree thesis, Colorado State College). p. 29.

6. Ibid. pp.5, 34, 45.

7. Weld's Untold Story. (2001, April 1). *The Greeley Tribune.* p. A2.

8. Ibid. p. A9.

Chapter 15

The Love and Need for Baseball

Alvin Garcia (left, standing) and Gabriel Lopez (front left) at a Greeley Grays game, 1957 or 1958.
Photo courtesy of Alvin Garcia.

After a week of hard work, the young men of the Colony relaxed on weekends by playing baseball and socializing. Many were strong, coordinated, and athletic men, and baseball honed these skills.

In 1925, Dimas Salazar organized a Hispanic baseball team in the Colony. He was the owner and manager and had played organized baseball in Walsenburg, Colorado. His players were: Charles Benavidez, Joe Borrego, Lojio Contreras, Elias Espinosa, Otavio "Toby" Espinosa, Alvin Garcia, Don Gonzales, Espiridion Gonzales, Francisco "Poncho" Lopez Sr., Paul Maese, Julian Marquez, and "Lalo" Villa.

The name of the team was Spanish Colony of Greeley, fondly called *La Colonia*. It began as a softball team and was played with the same enthusiasm as hardball. The team's uniforms were black and the socks were black with white stripes.

In 1938, Dimas Salazar left the Colony, and Alvin Garcia became the team's manager, coach, and catcher. At this time, baseball teams in Greeley consisted of talented and mostly Anglo players.

When the Spanish Colony team had a softball game at Greeley's Island Grove Park, the opponent did not show. As they were packing up their equipment, the Greeley American Legion coach asked them to play a practice game of hardball. The Colony team said, "Why not. We have nothing to lose." When the game ended, the Colony team had lost by only one point. The players reasoned, if they did that well against a good Legion team, then perhaps they could play hardball instead of softball. In 1939, the Spanish Colony team played hardball, and Alvin Garcia changed its name to the Greeley Grays. The team was referred to as The Grays in honor of Alvin's favorite Negro League team, The Homestead Grays.

The players at that time were Charlie Benavidez, Jose Borrego, Lucindo Cordova, Alvin Garcia, Henry Garcia, Willie Garcia, Asiano Gonzales, Espiridion Gonzales, Octavio Espinosa, Art Lopez, Dan Martinez, Hologio Renteria, Ladis Tellez, Tacho Tellez, and "Lalo" Villa.

From 1938 to 1942, some players left and new players filling the roster were Jess Gonzales, Joe Hernandez, Art Jojola, Augustine "Gus" Lopez, David Lopez, Frank Lopez Jr., Mario Lopez, Pete

"Junior" Rocobo, Paul Smith, and George Villa. The first black player for the Greeley Grays was Paul Smith, but the majority of the men who played on the team were from the Colony.

The weekend baseball games provided community entertainment. Families loaded children and food into their cars and caravanned to the games. Alvin and Jenny Garcia brought soft drinks, candy, and food to sell. In later years, Alvin built a portable "snack shack" to sell hotdogs, sodas, and candy.

Frank Lopez Jr. said, "When there was a baseball game, there was no one to be found in the Colony. All the Colony people traveled wherever the Grays played, even when the baseball games were played in a field near the Colony."

After the game, both players and fans shared their food and drinks in a picnic-type atmosphere. They talked and laughed with one another about game highlights which triggered memories of highlights of previous games. They all looked forward to the camaraderie and picnics. The children played tag, chase, and, sometimes, baseball. The post-game festivities built friendships among teammates and opponents which often lasted a lifetime.

In interviews with players and their wives, many commented, "I remember the old days when baseball was fun to play and watch, and the excitement it would bring for the spectators." The games were eagerly anticipated, and rivalries were common. The Grays' opponent was "the enemy." Spectators sounded the horns on their cars if there was a homerun or if a player made a good play or sometimes just to irritate the other team. The women yelled to distract the other team and draw their attention away from the game.

Sally Quezada Lopez remembered a story about a family on opposite teams. She said, "My sister, Ruth, was the scorekeeper for the Greeley Charros team. My dad managed the team at that time. I was the scorekeeper for the Grays, because my husband, David, played for them. As we kept score, we hollered at each other. It was Josie Garcia and I for the Grays versus my sisters who were for the Charros. To hear us, people didn't think we were sisters and friends, but after the game, David and I would go to my parents' house where mom would have a picnic for the Charros team. My sister and I laughed about our antics. My sister would say, 'You said this and that to me,' then we would really start laughing. But during the game, NO SIR, WE WERE ENEMIES!!"

Alvin Garcia at a Grays game 1957 or 1958.   Photo courtesy of Alvin Garcia.

Children lined up along the side of the field and behind the backstop. As "ball shaggers" they retrieved foul balls. The team managers paid a nickel or dime for every ball they brought back. The team only had a few balls or as many as they could afford. Every ball not returned left the team short. The ball shaggers played an important role.

Equipment was expensive and hard to come by. Ricardo "Rico" Lopez recalled, "The guys, if they got hold of a glove, kept it for life. We could not afford to buy another. Taking care of it was important. It would have been oiled almost every day to keep the leather soft and durable. I remember Paul "Paulie" Villa's glove looked like a taco, but he could really glove the ball."

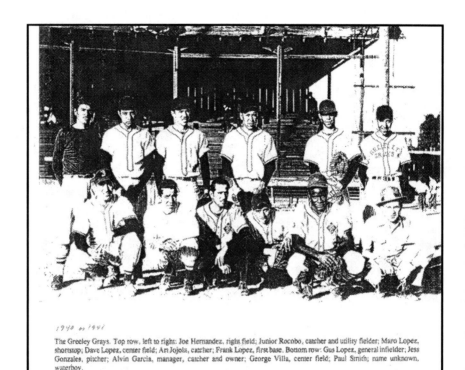

The Greeley Grays. Top row, left to right: Joe Hernandez, right field; Junior Rocobo, catcher and utility fielder; Maro Lopez, shortstop; Dave Lopez, center field; Art Jojola, catcher; Frank Lopez, first base. Bottom row: Gus Lopez, general infielder; Jess Gonzales, pitcher; Alvin Garcia, manager, catcher and owner; George Villa, center field; Paul Smith; name unknown, waterboy.

Believed to be 1940 or 1941 Greeley Grays game played in Cheyenne, Wyoming. Photo courtesy of David and Sally Lopez.

In 1942, Johnny Lopez and Alvin Garcia helped organize the Northern Colorado Semi-Pro Baseball League. Teams included The Ault Tigers, Cheyenne (Wyoming) Lobos, Fort Collins Legionnaires, Fort Lupton Eagles, Gilcrest Aztecs, Greeley Charros (later renamed The Bears), Greeley Grays, Hillrose, and Wattenburg.

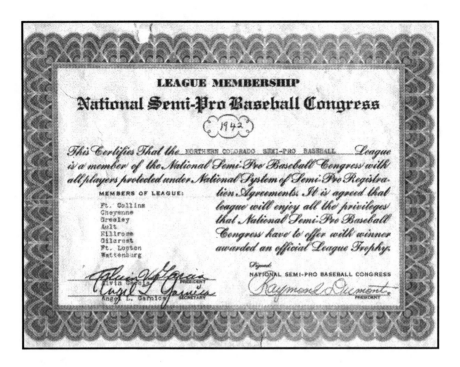

A 1942 league membership certificate for the National Semi-Pro Baseball Congress. Courtesy of Tito "Butter" Garcia.

From 1942 to 1951, the Grays added the following players: Pat Chagola, Robert Hernandez, Edward "Lalo" Lopez, Arnulfo "Nudy" Lopez, Richard "Rico" Lopez, Jimmy Mock, Johnny Tellez, Tony Tellez, Paul Villa, and Richard Villa.

In 1942, many Grays' players enlisted in the military. Returning from WWII, they resumed playing baseball. During the war, the young men left behind stepped up to the plate and kept the game alive for their older siblings and friends. The Greeley Grays had enough players to play through WWII, the Korean War, and the Vietnam Conflict.

Alvin Garcia had a stroke in 1952, and Tito "Butter" Garcia, Augustine "Gus" Lopez, and Ray Talmadge stepped in as coaches and managers until Alvin was able to resume his duties. During his recovery, he insisted on being present at the games. Butter recalled, "We pushed Alvin in a wheelchair to the games so he could watch the team win the tournament that year." In 1952, three Greeley

Grays players, Gus Lopez, Dave Lopez, and Johnny Torrez, made the all-star team.

The Greeley Grays became one of the premiere teams in the Northern Colorado Baseball League. Rubin Moore, speaking at a reunion of the Rocky Mountain League in Fort Collins, Colorado, in March 2002, said, "The Grays were the hallmark of the league and beating them was like winning the World Series." Mr. Lee Zuniga said, "When the babies of the Greeley Spanish Colony got off their knees and walked, they were playing baseball. It was the children's dream to play for the Greeley Grays. Playing from a young age is what made them good."

Both the boys and girls of the Carbajal family getting ready to play baseball. Back row standing: Maggie, Middle row L to R: Connie holding bat, Josie, Gilbert "Gil" with his glove. Front row sitting on the porch: Lupe with his glove. Photo courtesy of Gilbert "Gil" Carbajal.

Below is a photo of the Spanish Colony little league team.

Back row L to R: Henry Martinez, Sunny Nuanez, Leo Solis, Danny Tellez, Steve Garcia, Jerry Tellez.
Front row L to R: Frank Carbajal, Adolph Duran, Claudie Garcia, Abraham "Abe" Garcia, Robert
Duran, Sam Lopez, Johnny Martinez. Photo courtesy of Robert Duran.

Tito "Butter" Garcia, Jr. had a passion for baseball at a very young age. He started by playing with a sandlot team from the Colony. When asked why the Grays were a premier team, he said, "The umpires of the early days were so bad they couldn't tell if a pitch was a strike or a ball. The players were taught to hit anything near home plate. This allowed them to hit any ball anywhere in the playing field. That is why they were so tough to beat. In 1944, when I was going to Meeker Jr. High school, the school team wanted to play the kids from the Colony. "Neddie" Lopez pitched and I caught. We played them on a weekend; they were our age and from town. We beat them really bad. The next time we were asked to play, they put a team against us from town and they were high school kids. We beat them 10 to 4. We were so far ahead, because we played baseball from morning to night in the Colony."

Butter Garcia Jr., had vivid memories of their games. He coached and played for the Greeley Grays from 1952 to 1969 when the league ended. Butter recalled, "We won the tournament in 1952 when I started and in 1969 when the league disbanded."

Butter continued, "In the early years, there was no coaching the pitchers. They were taught by players who said, 'I was told if you turn your hand one-way the ball would do this (curve ball, slider ball, drop ball, etc.).' The only one at that time who could teach the basics of the game was Lalo Villa, because he was more familiar with the game. He came from a place that played more organized baseball. I can't remember where he came from though."

In the 1950s, one family in the Spanish Colony had seven boys who played for the Greeley Grays. They were known as the Lopez boys. Other teams throughout the league also had a few brothers who played on the same team. Instead of saying the Greeley Grays verses Fort Collins, they would say, the Lopez boys against the Moores or Pachecos and from Gilcrest it was the Penaflors.

L to R: Nudy Lopez, Frank Lopez, Mario Lopez, Rico Lopez, David Lopez,, Gus Lopez. Greeley Grays 1952 or 1953. Photo courtesy of Gabriel Lopez.

The Northern Baseball League participated in the annual Labor Day tournament sponsored by Our Lady of Peace Catholic Church in Greeley. Butter said, "It was the World Series of the Northern League."

The 1952 Our Lady of Peace tournament was played in Cheyenne, Wyoming. Butter recalled that, "The Greeley Grays won that one, and it was the first time in the history of the *Colonia* (Colony), that I remember they won."

In the late 1950s, the Greeley Grays started recruiting from Colorado Teachers College and Greeley American Legion teams and, in some cases, from the local high schools. The Greeley Grays were no longer Spanish Colony players only. Many players wanted to play for the Grays because of their reputation. Another team, the Greeley Rocky Grays was established in 1959. Both teams played for the Semi-Pro League.

Frank Carbajal played for Greeley Central High School, Greeley Legion A, and the Greeley Grays. He recalled he once spent the night at the "Greeley Grays Hotel." With a huge smile and twinkle in his eyes he recalled his favorite story about the Grays

Hotel. "George Villa was very unique, and I was 15 yrs old. We were playing - and it was late in the summer - in a league tournament in Fort Collins. We won the tournament. I was ready to get into somebody's car and say, 'Let's go home'. George Villa put his arm around me and said, 'Just relax. We are staying at the Greeley Grays Hotel tonight. I thought 'MAN, THIS IS FIRST CLASS!' We were going to stay in a hotel instead of going home. After the game, we walked to the park. The women were making great food, everybody pitched in and brought stuff, and we were eating. Of course, there was always the perfunctory beer, the drink of choice. It was getting later and later, and I said, 'Hey, George, when do we go to the hotel?' He said, 'Come here.' He took me over to a tree, leaned up against it, and said, 'This is the Greeley Grays Hotel,' and fell asleep. I was shocked, but I slept under the tree and woke up the next morning to the women cooking a good breakfast. I wasn't prepared for that. It hit me unexpectedly, but I found my tree, and we pretty much all slept in the park, without blankets. It was hot enough; the nights were not so cold." He also said with pride, "These are great memories and what a great initiation into the team. It didn't matter to them [Grays players] if you were just a youngster. You had to go through the rites of passage if you wanted to be a part of it [baseball]."

Frank started laughing again and said, "I have another one for you. One time Butter Garcia was coaching third base. I had just come on the team. We had a guy on first base. I was watching Butter to see what his signal was, because I was used to pretty well-organized baseball. Butter was going through his signals - hands and arms flying around his upper body, touching the bill of his cap, like he was doing some sort of a dance. Then he rolled his hands and pointed to second base. I bumped the guy next to me and said, 'What was that signal?' He said to me, 'That is the "steal" sign. 'I said. 'I am afraid to ask this, but what is the bunt signal?' The guy held his two hands up like holding a bat in a bunting position and said, 'This is the bunt signal.' Laughing hard, Frank continued, "We beat teams letting them know what we were going to do to them. It was so ridiculous that our opponents didn't think we were going to actually do that."

In 1965, the Greeley Rocky Grays and the Greeley Grays played each other in a tournament. The Greeley Rocky Grays defeated the Greeley (Senior) Grays 4-1 and were the regular season champions.

RML SEASON CHAMPIONS — The Greeley Rocky Grays defeated the Senior Grays 4-1 for the regular season championship then the Senior Grays defeated the Rocky Grays 19-2 in the finals for the RML tournament championship. The Rocky Gray players are,. front row, left, Sonny Naurez, Frank Villa, Char Rucobo, Bob French, Junior Marez, George Martinez and Danny Grimes. Back row, Jerry Tellez, Abie Garcia, Art Armijo, Adolph Belo, Neil Foreman, George Tellez and Sonny Gonzales. Not pictured, Jack Steele. (Tribune photo by Wylie Smith)

1965 Greeley Rocky Grays, season Champs. Courtesy of Tito "Butter" Garcia Jr.

The Greeley Grays played the following teams in Greeley and the surrounding area including Wyoming, and Nebraska:

Greeley:
Greeley Charros 1952-1956
Greeley V.F.W. 1953-1954
Greeley Bears 1956-1960
Greeley Rocky Grays 1959-1969

Colorado:
Ault Tigers 1935
Brighton Rams (unknown date)
The Rock Busters (Colorado State Penitentiary team, Canon City) 1962-1969.
Eaton Bears (unknown date)
Fort Collins Spanish American Baseball Team 1932
Fort Collins Legionnaires 1956-1970's
Fort Collins Merchants 1954
Fort Collins Rebels 1949-1950
Fort Lupton Eagles 1950-1965
Gill Indians 1930-1937
Gilcrest Aztecs 1933-1969

239

Kersey Primos 1946-1976
Los Caballeros 1946-1960
Wattenberg Blue Jays 1953-1970

Wyoming:
Cheyenne Lobos 1943
Cheyenne M.A.C. (Mexican Athletic Club) 1935-1950
Cheyenne Merchants 1958-1960s
Cheyenne Todds Jewelry 1950s
Laramie Merchants (unknown date)

Nebraska:
Scottsbluff Nebraska (unknown date)

Throughout the years, the Greeley Grays played their home games on several baseball diamonds. Four diamonds were made by the Colony residents and team on land owned by neighboring farmers. The Grays were allowed to use their fields when they were fallow. The first one was built in 1925 at the southwest corner of the Colony. The second was built in 1938 in a field on the southeast side of the Cache la Poudre River. The third and fourth were built in 1939, in the field behind the Gipson School and in the field east of the Colony.

Many games were played at both diamonds in Island Grove Park and at the Kuner Canning Company's baseball field. The Kuner field was nicknamed "the Home of the Brave." It had a lot of big rocks, which made it hard to field balls and slide into the bases.

Forbes field was located at 23rd Avenue and 8th Street in Greeley. It was formerly a garbage dump. Home runs were hit into the Union Colony Ditch Number 3 which formed the boundary of the outfield. The ditch had a steep embankment and in order to catch a fly ball one might have to race up the embankment. The last one was the Butch Butler Field located at 23rd Avenue and Reservoir Road in Greeley.

Butter said, "The 1960 Greeley Grays was the best Grays team that ever played. We had Frank Carbajal, a left-handed pitcher; Julie Yearling, a catcher from UNC; Ernie Andrade; and Ron English. That year the Grays won 14 games by shutouts."

240

1960 Greeley Grays Back row: Julie Yearling, Joe Garcia, Rico Lopez, Frank Carbajal, Nudy Lopez, Jounior Mares. Middle row: John Blatnick, George Villa, Ernie Andrade, Paul Villa. Front row: Butter Garcia, Jerry Tellez, George Tellez, Gil Carbajal. Photo courtesy of Tito "Butter" Garcia Jr.

John Blatnick remembered, "It was challenging. You didn't have a position made, because there was always someone there just as good or better than you. You had to be ready to move around and could not have just one position. I tried to move around in positions. We were there to play ball. That was the thing to do back then. I enjoyed it, because there weren't really a lot of other things to do. Everybody strived to be the better ball player and to be a better team."

Richard "Rick" Sullivan, who lived in Cheyenne, Wyoming, and played for the Grays from 1962 to 1968, said, " Butter called me in early May or early June and said, 'I want to remind you to come on down, we have a game today.' I said; 'Butter, you have to be kidding about this!' I was on the telephone talking to him and looking out the window - there was a blizzard outside. The snow was drifting and coming down horizontally across the front yard. You couldn't even see across the street. Again I said, 'Butter, you have got to be kidding! There is a blizzard out here. I can't possibly get down there!' Butter said, 'We are playing 9 innings. It is 85 degrees here in Greeley. You had better get down here! So I put my uniform on and plowed my way through, and as soon as I got to the state line, 10 miles south of Cheyenne, the weather started to turn decent. I got to Greeley, and it was 75 to 80 degrees. We played a 9-inning game, and I drove back into the blizzard. School was canceled the next day. I don't remember the outcome of the game, but it was a wonderful experience for me."

Rick was asked, "Why did you keep coming to Greeley? That is a 50 mile drive; what was the draw?" He said, "My teammates, the friendship, the acceptance, the uniqueness of the experience. It had to do with family, because it was beyond the baseball fields. Families were there, sons, daughters, grandparents, friends and relatives. They were all there and took me in. Somebody had to take care of me."

Butter and Rico Lopez, who played for the Greeley Grays from 1952 to 1965, also had a lot of Grays stories.

Butter said with a chuckle, "I was asked to umpire one of Uncle Alvin's games. I gathered the managers together and told them that it was all right to say, 'The ump needs glasses or things like that, but I will not allow cursing at me.' The game started, and the other team's players were cursing at me and saying how I couldn't call the game. I called time out and walked over to the dugout and asked those players, 'How long have you been involved with baseball?' They said 'About 10 to 15 years'. I said, 'When they invented this game of baseball, if they thought the umpire could call the game from the dugout, that is where they would have put him. Everything looks good from the dugout, so be quiet and play the game.' They left me alone the rest of the game."

Rico Lopez laughed and said, "I remember one night game played at Forbes Field. We played Cheyenne, Wyoming, and, Man, was it cold! I had my jacket on, and it was my turn to bat. I don't remember which pitch it was, the first, second, or third, but it was tight and close inside about belly high. I moved my arms high in the air to avoid being hit by the ball. The ball swooshed by, and I thought it missed me. The catcher and ump turned to see if it went to the backstop and so did I. They couldn't find it, and I felt something in my pocket. There was the ball! It had landed in my coat pocket and I didn't even feel it."

Wildly gesturing with his arms and hands while laughing hard, Butter said, "One time I was batting, and the pitcher struck me out. I started walking back to the dugout not knowing that the catcher had dropped the ball. You see, you can still run for first base, if the catcher drops the ball, and no one is on first base. If you made it, you were safe. Anyway, he tried to tag me out, and when I noticed this, I took off running around the bench where the team sat. The catcher was chasing after me to tag me out, when someone said, 'Look at that stupid Butter running around the bench.' Paulie Villa said, 'Well, look at the stupid catcher chasing him.'"

Rico Lopez recalled, "One game a ball was hit, a hard fly ball, into the outfield, and Tacho Tellez was chasing after it to try and catch it. When the ball was close, Tacho couldn't get his glove around to catch it, so he stuck out his bare hand and the ball fell right into it. I thought that was something else, catching it bare-handed."

Butter said, "Remember the bee-liner that Georgie Villa caught? Georgie was playing third base when a player hit a ball hard and straight at Georgie. He couldn't catch it with his glove, so he stuck his bare hand up and caught the ball. They asked him how his hand was, and if it hurt. Georgie said, 'No, it was like catching an apple, just like catching an apple.'"

Butter started laughing. "I remember one of the players said, 'Mr. Baggot told the boys [Doug Smith, John Blatnick] not to play with the Grays. They were going to pick up bad habits from their style of baseball.' I said, just after Gus Lopez jacked (baseball lingo meaning for "hitting a homerun") out of the park - three homeruns that game, 'I would like to have Gus's bad habits.' I remember how other teams nit-picked everything the Grays did. One game we played against Brighton, Colorado, and a young man came up to me and asked if he could play. His last name was Gomer. He was eligible to play for us the following week but not this one. I said, 'Go ahead and play.' The Brighton coach came over and complained, "That ain't no Romero." I said, 'That is his name, just ask him.' The coach said, 'What is your name?' Gomer said, 'Romero.' I said, 'See, I told you.' The coach said, 'O.K. he can play.'" Butter reached over and in a whisper continued, "His name is Gomer; we just dropped the G, added an R, and just put an O at the end," he started laughing hard.

Rico then said, "I remember a game we played in Milliken, Colorado. The field we played on had no fence in the outfield. Gilbert (Gil) Carbajal was on first, and I came to bat. I hit a hard shot into the gap, and it was rolling beyond the outfield. Gilbert was not too fast. I was thin and could run fast. As I was running around second, I looked to see where the ball was. I said, 'This is an easy homerun.' As I ran around third base, I saw Gilbert and he was running as hard as he could. I looked to see where the ball was, and they were throwing it into the infield. I told Gilbert to hurry up. As we got closer to home plate, I was a couple of feet away from Gilbert. He started to slide into home plate and so did I. I slid under Gilbert and our feet simultaneously touched home plate before the ball got there and we were both safe."

Rico continued, "Remember Robert Lind? He was a farmer who lived just northwest of the Colony. He played ball with us and did such a good job. He pitched and was a very good hitter, a really sweet guy."

Butter said, "Yeh, I remember Georgie Villa and Frank Lopez Jr. took him [Robert] to Ragtown [Eaton, Colorado] and got him toasted [drunk]. He was a proper man and very nice, and didn't do anything bad."

Gil Carbajal, who played for the Grays from 1953 to 1965, remembered, "I think the Grays won 90 percent of the ball games. What I remember more are the relationships, fun, and the wonderful experiences we had. When we sit and visit, we now talk about the Grays. It is hardly ever about the games we won or how good we were. We talk about the relationships we had and how it was a family affair. The wives, mothers, and cousins, everybody went to the games. We played Fort Collins, Cheyenne, Brighton, Gill, and Galeton. There was always a parade of cars with hundreds of people who came and watched the game. It was a weekly activity or respite for those who worked the beet fields. The older ball players, if they had the proper training and professional coaching, could all have been professional ball players. I don't remember any jealousy among the players or any major arguments. If anyone got upset, they remembered that only nine could play the game. Everyone wanted to play for the Grays, so they did what they could." Gil Carbajal retired from the Grays in 1965, and, in 1966, he played for the Fort Collins Legionnaires, and his last game was against the Greeley Grays.

Greg Riddoch, who played for the Grays in 1965, remembered, "I tried out for the Grays and afterwards I asked Butter if I had made the team. Butter said, 'Kid, you are the team.'"

"I remember one time Frank Carbajal was pitching for us. I didn't know him well. The first game he pitched, he told me what to do at shortstop. He would turn around and say, 'I am going to throw this on the inside, so get ready for the ball in the hole.' So I would backhand it and throw the guy out. Then he turned around and said, 'Move over. I am going to throw one up the middle.' He threw it up the middle and the guy hit it to the middle. I started thinking, is there magic in the air? What is going on? How does he do it? I thought, at 17, this is the smartest pitcher I have ever seen."

In the 1950s, Colorado State Penitentiary allowed their prisoners to play baseball. Many teams in the Northern Colorado Semi-Pro Baseball League (NBL) traveled to Canon City to play these prisoners. They were called the Rock Busters.

Grays player, Rico Lopez, said, "I remember my first trip to the prison. I was scared, as I passed through the big gates and heard them slam shut behind us. After we were inside the prison, I looked around and said, 'Whooooo!' I was so scared. The prison team was friendly, and the prisoners told lots of jokes, probably because they didn't have time for anything else. It was a great experience. They had players who were pro material. They just made mistakes in life and were imprisoned for these mistakes. There were players from triple A and double A teams. They had a good team, and we had to hone our skills in an unusual way. We would "beat up on them", because we had a good team too!"

Don Foster pitched for the Grays in 1950 and then for the Gilcrest Aztecas. He remembered a game at the penitentiary. He said, "There was a fella who was the umpire, and every time we played them he would always umpire behind home plate. First pitch I threw one down the middle, pretty close from my viewpoint. Of course, from my viewpoint, everything I threw was a strike. The pitch was in the strike zone, and he called it a ball. I thought, 'Well, you know, I don't think so!' So I threw another one right down the pipe [middle of the strike zone]. He called it a ball, and I thought, 'Wait a minute, this isn't right!' I pitched another one right down the pipe, no doubt about it, waist high and down the middle. He said, 'Ball!' and I remarked about his ancestry, accused him of cheating,

245

because it appeared to me he was. He called 'Time out', and walked half way to the mound, leaned forward and said, 'I'm not in here, cause I am honest,' and walked back. What else could I do?"

John Blatnick, who played for the Grays from 1960 to 1962, remembered, "We played the prisoners in Canon City. Once in a while, team members would run into somebody they knew there. We were not looking for them, but they would say, 'Hey, I know you.' Ron Lyle was the catcher for the prisoners. He was well known in Colorado as a professional boxer who fought against George Forman in the title match and lost. The guards checked all of our equipment to make sure we didn't have anything for the prisoners to use. The guards told us, when we ate together in the cafeteria or toured the prison, not to give the prisoners chewing gum. The prisoners would use the gum to mess up the locks."

Char Rucobo remembered a 1964 game at the penitentiary. "We had to check in everything and go through metal detectors. We dressed in a big room and then walked across the open field to the ballpark. We walked across the yard where the inmates exercised and then proceeded to the baseball field. Inmates always asked for gum. Somehow a player would sneak gum. George Villa dropped sticks of gum as he was walking. The prisoners gave us baseballs, bats, and gloves for gum. One of the guards told us that they would make impressions of the gate keys with the gum. When we played at the prison, we were fed well and ate in the cafeteria with the guards. It was a daylong event. Inmates cheered for us and served as umpires. They got into some good arguments. Their favorite cheer was, 'Hit it over the wall. I will go get it.'"

Three articles were found in *The Greeley Tribune* that reported on the prison games as noted below.

Combined Grays Team Set for State Tournament

Greeleys combined Grays team tuned up for the State semi-professional baseball tournament last Saturday with an exhibition game at the Colorado State Prison.

The Prison team won, 6-3, scoring four runs in the fifth inning to clinch the victory.

The Grays will begin quest of the State semi-pro title at 9 p.m. Saturday at Hugo. It is the final game of the first round of the tournament that starts Wednesday.

The Grays lost this 1963 exhibition game at the Colorado State Prison 6-3. *The GreeleyTribune,* July 24, 1963, page 15.

Rocky Grays Play Lupton Team Sunday

The Greeley Rocky Grays resume Rocky Mountain League play at 2 p.m. Sunday against Fort Lupton at Island Grove Park.

The Rocky Grays Wednesday lost a 6-5 exhibition game to Fort Collins Legion. Last Saturday, the Rocky Grays defeated the Colorado Penitentiary Rock Busters, 9-7, scoring all of their runs in the last four innings.

The Greeley Tribune, July 23, 1966, page 10.

Grays Schedule Game at Prison

The Greeley Grays combined baseball team will play an exhibition game Saturday at the Colorado State Prison at Canon City.

The Grays (combined Rocky Grays and Senior Grays) will also be entered in the 1963 State semi-pro tournament July 24-August 7 at Hugo.

The Greeley Tribune, July 17, 1963 page 15.

247

During their 44 years of play, the Grays competed against more than 88 teams.

There were about 251 individuals who played for the Greeley Grays and/or the Greeley Rocky Grays from 1925 to 1969.

Baseball came to be lifeblood to the residents of the Spanish Colony. The legacy of the Greeley Grays to work hard, play hard, and respect your fellow man has survived for decades. Through the years, various softball teams have named themselves the Greeley Grays, and a little league team also adopted the name. In 2005, a collegiate team of the Rocky Mountain Collegiate League took the name Greeley Grays to honor all the Grays stood for.

Chapter 16

The Spanish Colony Today

Spanish Colony, September 7, 2005, North 26th Avenue, looking south. Photo courtesy of Gabriel Lopez.

Those whose roots were in the Spanish Colony have realized many of their dreams through perseverance and hard work. They availed themselves of educational opportunities and improved their status in life. Most of the early residents have left the Colony, and their children have pursued a wide range of careers and professions. Today, Hispanics work as professors, farm laborers, realtors, custodians, technicians, teachers, day care providers, nurses, and homemakers, and are owners of farms and businesses.

A *The Greeley Tribune* article, "Untold Story," April 1, 2001, p. A9, noted,

> Today's Hispanic population in Weld County is a reflection of those who came in the early 1900s. Their families started out as farm workers, settled in Greeley and other towns, struggled to learn English and assimilate to Anglo ways and sent their children to public schools. They are the second and third generations of their families to live in Weld County... But there's also a new generation of Hispanics: Central Americans, South Americans, and Mexicans. They flee similar circumstances - political upheaval, natural disasters, low paying jobs. And they seek the same thing - better lives for themselves and their children. The promise of a better life drew them to Weld County 100 years ago. And it continues to draw them today.

In 1973 two years before it became law, Greeley started a bilingual education program.[1] Today, thirty percent of Greeley's population is Hispanic, and in the Greeley-Evans School District Six, Hispanic enrollment was 49.8 percent in 2003.[2] It was noted in the December 27, 2004, *The Greeley Tribune* article, "Latinos Outnumber Anglos in District 6," that more English teachers had been hired to provide English language instruction for the District's Spanish-speaking students.

Although Greeley has a visible and significant Hispanic population, in 2004 the 80th anniversary of the founding of the Spanish Colony, few in Greeley were aware of its existence and history. Geographically, the Colony is still isolated from Greeley, surrounded by gravel companies and farms.

There have been many changes in the Colony since it's founding. Some of these developments are:

Roads have been paved.

Most of the adobe homes have been torn down and new homes built. Only nine original homes remain and only a few original colonists or their descendents live there now. Today there are 49 homes, 1 church, and a homeless shelter named the Guadalupe Center.

The Garcia Store, opened in 1924, closed its doors in 1999. It was sold and reopened as *La Tienda*, serving take-out Mexican food.

The Greeley Grays stopped playing after the 1969 season. The spirit of the Greeley Grays has lived on in softball teams and little league teams. In 2005, the Rocky Mountain Collegiate Baseball League named one of its team the Greeley Grays in honor of the original 1938-69 team. Inspired by the Grays' dedication to baseball and spirit of good sportsmanship, the 2005 Greeley Grays opened its inaugural season at the University of Northern Colorado Jackson Field in Greeley.[3]

Until 1979, the Salon, or Community Center, was used for wedding receptions, dances, small gatherings, and meetings. In 1980-81, the homeless began to sleep there, and, in 1987, the Salon was converted into a homeless shelter called the Guadalupe Center, the first homeless shelter in Greeley. Although many residents of Greeley know of the Guadalupe Center, few realize it is in the Spanish Colony.

The Pentecostal Church still holds services in the Colony, but the Catholic Church is no longer there. In 2005, the Pentecostal Church in the Spanish Colony, Betel Spanish Assembly of God, celebrated its 72 year anniversary. *The Greeley Tribune* article, September 17, 2005, p. B3, article "Betel Spanish Assembly marks 72 years" noted, There were many Spanish-speaking members during the first 10 years. Attendance at the service was about 100 whereas attendance averages around 50 parishioners today. One of Colorado's first Spanish-speaking Assembly of God churches it was founded by the Rev. Augustin López and his wife, Maria.

By the late 1950s Great Western Sugar Company began closing its "white gold" factories. The sugar industry lagged by 1985 but made a come back early in the 1990s. The Great Western Sugar Company went bankrupt in 1986 and Tate & Lyle of London

251

purchased the company.[4] In 2002 a farmer-owned co-op purchased Western Sugar Co. from Tate & Lyle, operating as the Western Sugar Cooperative. Twice in its 100-year history, the Greeley sugar beet factory sat idle.[5] Greeley's sugar factory was closed in 2002 and in 2006 was put up for sale, leaving the Fort Morgan facility as the only one in the state.[6] By the late 20th century, sugar beets were being used to produce ethanol to meet the rising global demand for alternative fuels.[7] Sugar beets have made a steady comeback. Weld County produced about 40 percent of Colorado's beets. Colorado ranked 9th in the U.S. in beet production in 2004.[8]

Photo *The Greeley Tribune*, February 18, 2006, p. A5. With today's technological advancements this 12- row harvester, harvests 33 acres of beets, and has nearly eliminated the need for *white gold laborers.*

Today, technological innovations are prevalent in all aspects of agriculture. There will always be a need for hand laborers. Today, the field worker is considered a migrant or seasonal worker. Field workers are no longer recruited to come and live and work as permanent residents, but many of the migrant workers have chosen to make Greeley their home. Weld County remains an agricultural giant, and is consistently among the nation's top ten ag-producing counties and the only one that is a non-citrus producing contender. The county is ranked 19th in the U.S. for pinto beans; 15th for corn (for livestock feed); 21st for dairy; 23rd for hay; (Livestock e.g. turkey, poultry, pig, cattle, goat, sheep, and related products ratings unknown). Weld also produces vegetables and wheat. In almost all crop and livestock categories, Weld is ranked #1 in Colorado.[9]

The demographics and attitudes of the Colony have changed. It no longer feels like one large homogenous family. With a few exceptions, their senses of pride for the community and its overall appearance have diminished. Current residents are from Mexico and Central America and speak a variety of Spanish dialects.

The history of the Spanish Colony is preserved in the memories of those who lived there, and whose stories are told to their children and grandchildren. *White Gold Laborers* preserves the collective memories and stories, honoring the spirit of Greeley's Spanish Colony, a community within a community. This book is dedicated to all who struggled and survived in order to find safety and security for their families in an unfamiliar environment.

We extend our heartfelt respect and gratitude to them for our heritage.

Gabriel and Jody Lopez standing in doorway of the adobe Colony House at Centennial Village Museum, Greeley, Colorado. A replica, this house was built (from the plan reproduced n page 19 in this book) in the summer of 1993 by the Weld County Youth Conservation Corps. Photo courtesy *La Tribuna,* January 26, 2006. Photographer James Gregg.

It has been a privilege and an honor to document a part of American history that is rapidly disappearing as former residents move or die. The hardships, struggles, sadness, laughter, and success became the legacy of the Spanish Colonists at Greeley. Their accomplishments and spirit are shared and reflected in all those who seek better opportunities for themselves and their families. It is the story of courage, hard work, and perseverance ultimately triumphing over poverty and prejudice.

Authors of the White Gold Laborers,
Gabriel A. and Jody L. Lopez
With Peggy A. Ford

References

1. Dist. 6 program preceded state law. (1980, September 28). *The Greeley Tribune.* p. C-3.

2. Weld's Hispanic Numbers Jump. (2003, September 18). *The Greeley Tribune.*

3. Going Gray. (2004, November 18). *The Greeley Tribune.*

4. Sugar Beets becoming a sweet success in Weld. (1990, October 7). *The Greeley Tribune.*

5. Factory closes for season. (2003, May 24). *The Greeley Tribune.*

6. This season, more beets. (2006, April 1). *The Greeley Tribune.*

7. Farmers to increase sugar beet crop. (2006, February 18 p. A5). *The Greeley Tribune.*

8. Raised in Weld a Look at Agriculture in the County. (2004, October 10 p.16,). *The Greeley Tribune.*

9. Ibid. pp. 4, 5, 7, 8, 10, 12, 14, 17, 18.

Appendix A

What is a Mexican?

In the 1920s, the term *Mexican* was applied to two groups of peoples indiscriminately, those born in the United States and those who immigrated to the U.S. Both groups were Spanish-speaking.

Many who emigrated from Mexico fled their country during revolutionary war and from mistreatment by their own countrymen. The term Mexican is correctly applied to these people.

Another kind of migrant laborer was the Spanish-American, born and reared in America. They were citizens in every respect. Their ancestors had settled in Colorado, New Mexico, Texas, and Arizona long before the United States acquired the land from Mexico through Guadalupe-Hildago treaty in 1848. They were Americans.

In 1960, President Johnson formed an office called Mexican-American Affairs. When President Nixon was elected, he had the votes of the Cubans in Florida who were Republicans; Mexican-Americans were Democrats. President Nixon changed the Mexican-American Affairs Office to Hispanic Affairs to satisfy the Cubans who voted for him. He combined all the nationalities of Spanish or Portuguese descent under one term Hispanic. By doing so the individual heritages were ignored. The use of terms applied to Spanish-speaking people varied greatly due, to in part, to time and location.

Appendix B

Spanish Colony Constitution and Rules

APPENDIX B

Constitution and Rules of the Spanish Colony
Neighbors to Greeley, Colo.
Estab. in the County of Weld, Nov. 1924

First Chapter

Rules for the Corporation. Section 1:

The object of this corporation is the best social improvement of its habitants. In effect to it, is accorded to
follow it under the rules of the civil law. It is accorded
to elect a commission of five members to rule as civil
law to habitants of the colony.

Section II: The said commission will rule for the
time not less than one year nor more than two. Understanding that none of the members who have given service in
said period of time can be re-elected unless the town may
vote them.

Section III: The same commission has the right to
elect out of five members one President, one Secretary,
and one Treasurer and two

Section IV: No person of the habitants of this
locality will have the right to collect from the same any
money for any use, unless an order may be extended by the
Secretary of the Commission signed by him and the President
of the same.

Second Chapter

Duties of all property owners and every one of the habitants
of this town.   Section I:

That all the habitants of this town that are owners or renters: shall have the best cleaners possible so as to save
the honor of the town.

Section II: That each owner of property or residents
of the colony is prohibited to dump rubbish in private property or in others property unless he may have the permission.

Section III: That each property owner shall have a
regular sized box to deposit said rubbish, which shall be
made in line with the others so the same owner may be able
to clean it when necessary and throw it to a place where
the Commission may say.

Section IV: That each property owner may be obliged
to maintain the costs in benefit of the town for which they
should pay a due of $1.00 a year each one being ₡.50 the
15th day of July and $.50 the 15th day of November of each
year.

Section V: That said dues shall be paid for sure and
they shall be paid to no other person but the Secretary of
this Commission, said Secretary shall give said money to
the Treasurer of the same Commission.

Section VI: The said Treasurer, will have to deposit

the money in a bank in name of colony, and no checks shall be drawn out unless signed by the Secretary and the President of said Commission.

Section VII: That the same property owners shall obey said Commission and shall have the right to enforce their authority always being in the best improvement for the habitants of this locality; and in good benefit of the same.

Section VIII: That this Commission vote by the town, will always be on the right way to justice if any trouble comes in inhabitants of same town.

Section IX: That the members of this commission will have at least three regular meetings in the year to let the town know how business is going, and in addition all meetings extra that the town may think are necessary.

THIRD CHAPTER

Duties of the Parents: Section I: That the fathers of families that have sons of daughters seven years old or more shall send them to school unless in case of sickness they can keep them out of school.

Section II: That all parents that may have sons under eighteen years of age shall tell them that in the winter at eight o'clock P.M. and in summer at nine o'clock at that time they should not be out of their homes.

All persons driving inside the Colony must not exceed the Speed Limit of 15 miles an hour.

The Commission shall elect one man to give the hour of silent with the bell of this town. Said man has the right to prosecute all the boys that may be out after said hours, and notify their parents.

Section III: Said person elected by the Commission will have the right to prosecute the boys if they should play ball games, and at the streets of this town, and in all things that may bring trouble to them and to the parents, and at the same time not let them crowd in or by cars or trucks going through the streets of this town, and in all things that may bring trouble to them and the parents of said boys.

In meeting had the 10th day of April 1927, were approved the rules that read above here by a number of 26 votes of property owners of the colony.

> Yenez Lopez, Sr.   Pres.
> Dimas Salasar   Sec.
> Daniel Martinez   Treas.
> Rufino Ortez
> Espiridion Gonzalis

Appendix C

Colony Leases

COLONY LEASE

AGREEMENT, Made this **first** day of **August**, 19 24, by and between The Great Western Sugar Company, a corporation of the State of New Jersey (hereinafter called the "Lessor"), party of the first part, and _____ Porfirio Candelaria of _____ Greeley _____, State of _Colorado_, (hereinafter called the "Lessee"), party of the second part, WITNESSETH,

That the Lessor for and in consideration of the covenants and agreements hereinafter set forth to be kept and performed by the Lessee, has leased, and does hereby lease unto the Lessee the following described property, situate in the County of _Weld_ and State of _Colorado_, more particularly described as follows, to-wit:

Lot No. 29 in Colony located near Greeley. See attached plat.

TO HAVE AND TO HOLD the above described premises unto the said Lessee for the full period xxxxxxx[Six]xxxxx, commencing on the _first_ day of _August_, 1924, and ending on the _first_ day of _November_, 19 28, unless the term of this lease is sooner terminated as hereinafter provided. And the Lessee in consideration of the leasing of said premises by the Lessor does hereby covenant and agree to and with the Lessor, its successors and assigns, as follows, to-wit:

1. The Lessee will at his sole cost and expense build, construct and complete, in a good and workmanlike manner, prior to November 1, 1924, a dwelling house of _2_ rooms upon said leased premises, which said dwelling house shall be constructed of adobe bricks and shall be of the dimensions of _18_ by _25_ feet, or larger. For the purpose of constructing said dwelling house as aforesaid, said Lessee may enter upon said leased premises at any time or times between _August 1_, 19 24, and _November 1_, 1924. The Lessor agrees that it will furnish, at its sole cost and expense, all straw, lime and gravel reasonably necessary for the construction of said dwelling house and will deliver the same on said leased premises, and said Lessor further agrees that it will advance to the Lessee during the construction of said dwelling house, on account of the cost of such lumber, doors, windows and cement as may be used in the construction thereof, a sum of money, not to exceed in the aggregate the sum of approximately _268.42_ Dollars - Provided, that the said Lessor may at its sole option pay said sum of money directly to the person or persons from whom said material is purchased by the Lessee, in payment therefor, or on account thereof. The Lessee covenants and agrees to repay to the Lessor one-third of any amount so advanced by the Lessor to the Lessee or on his account, on or before the _first_ day of _November_, 19 25, and to pay a like amount on or before the _first_ day of _November_, in each of the years 19 26 and 1927, without interest.

2. That the Lessee will occupy said dwelling house as his place of residence during the entire term of this agreement and will at his sole cost and expense at all times during the life hereof maintain said dwelling and other improvements and the grounds and fences upon said leased premises in good order and repair and in a clean and sanitary condition, to the satisfaction of the Manager at Lessor's _Greeley_ factory, and will keep said grounds and premises free from weeds, rubbish and other inflammable and objectionable material and will remove such weeds, rubbish and material therefrom, as and when requested so to do by said Manager - and the Lessee agrees that he will not permit or suffer the commission of any waste upon said leased premises, and further agrees not to use said premises for any purpose prohibited by law, or for any improper or questionable purpose whatsoever, and agrees to permit the agents of the Lessor to enter into or upon, and go through and inspect said premises at any reasonable

Courtesy of City of Greeley Museums

261

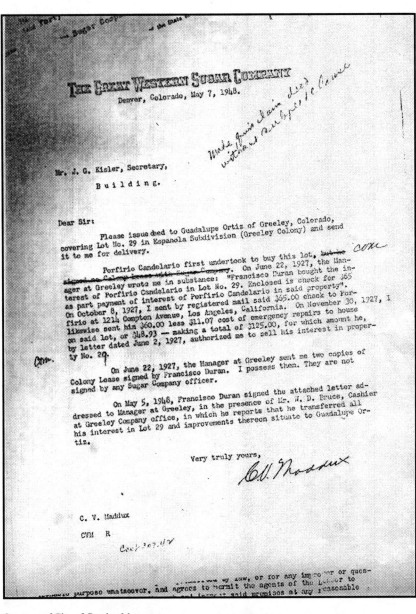

THE GREAT WESTERN SUGAR COMPANY

Denver, Colorado, May 7, 1948.

Mr. J. G. Kisler, Secretary,

    B u i l d i n g.

Dear Sir:

Please issue deed to Guadalupe Ortiz of Greeley, Colorado, covering Lot No. 29 in Espanola Subdivision (Greeley Colony) and send it to me for delivery.

Porfirio Candelario first undertook to buy this lot, ~~as he now~~ COXE ~~signed a Colony Lease with Sugar Company~~. On June 22, 1927, the Manager at Greeley wrote me in substance: "Francisco Duran bought the interest of Porfirio Candelario in Lot No. 29. Enclosed is check for $65 as part payment of interest of Porfirio Candelario in said property". On October 8, 1927, I sent by registered mail said $65.00 check to Porfirio at 1214 Compton Avenue, Los Angeles, California. On November 30, 1927, I likewise sent him $60.00 less $11.07 cost of emergency repairs to house on said lot, or $48.93 — making a total of $125.00, for which amount he, by letter dated June 2, 1927, authorized me to sell his interest in property No. 29.

On June 22, 1927, the Manager at Greeley sent me two copies of Colony Lease signed by Francisco Duran. I possess them. They are not signed by any Sugar Company officer.

On May 5, 1948, Francisco Duran signed the attached letter addressed to Manager at Greeley, in the presence of Mr. W. D. Bruce, Cashier at Greeley Company office, in which he reports that he transferred all his interest in Lot 29 and improvements thereon situate to Guadalupe Ortiz.

              Very truly yours,

              C. V. Maddux

C. V. Maddux

CVM R

Courtesy of City of Greeley Museums

262

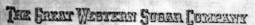

THE GREAT WESTERN SUGAR COMPANY

Greeley, Colorado, May 5, 1948

Mr. R. L. Simmons, Manager
Greeley, Colorado

Dear Sir:

This is written for the purpose of advising you that I have transferred all my interest in property located on Lot No. 29 in the Greeley Colony to Guadalupe Ortiz on this date.

Very truly yours,

Francisco Duran

Witness:

W. D. Bruce

Guadalupe Ortiz
Rr Bx 53 Spanish Colony
Greeley Colo

able purpose whatsoever, and agrees to permit the agents of the _____ to
r into or upon, and go through and inspect said premises at any reasonable

Courtesy of City of Greeley Museums

KNOW ALL MEN BY THESE PRESENTS, That the undersigned Jesus Jojala is the same man who on August 1, 1924 made and executed a written contract with The Great Western Sugar Company, a New Jersey Corporation, for the purchase of property known as Lot 8 in Espanola Subdivision hereinafter mentioned and further defined; and that the undersigned Jesus Jojala for and in consideration of the sum of One Dollar ($1.00) and other good and valuable considerations to the undersigned in hand paid by Benito Archuleta, the receipt whereof is hereby acknowledged, does hereby sell, assign, transfer and set over unto said Benito Archuleta all of the right, title and interest, both legal and equitable, of the undersigned in the undersigned's contract of purchase from The Great Western Sugar Company, a New Jersey corporation, for lot numbered eight (8) in Espanola Subdivision, according to the plat thereof recorded in Book 6, page 73, of the records in the office of the Recorder of Weld County, Colorado, together with all improvements thereon situate; together also with all of the right, title and interest, both legal and equitable, of the undersigned in and to said property and improvements thereon situate.

Dated this _17th_ day of _____, 1929.

Jesus Jojola

Witness to Execution:

_____

STATE OF NEW MEXICO)
COUNTY OF _____) ss.

The foregoing instrument was acknowledged before me this _17th_ day of _____, 1929, by Jesus Jojala.

Witness my hand and official seal.

My commission expires _____

NOTARY PUBLIC
My Commission Expires Dec. 21, 1930

_____
Notary Public

Courtesy of City of Greeley Museums

H 23

C O L O N Y   L E A S E

AGREEMENT, Made this **first** day of **August** , 19**24**, by and between The Great Western Sugar Company, a corporation of the State of New Jersey (hereinafter called the "Lessor"), party of the first part, and _____ **Dioese Gr nillo** , of **Greeley** , State of **Colorado** , (hereinafter called the "Lessee"), party of the second part, WITNESSETH,

That the Lessor for and in consideration of the covenants and agreements hereinafter set forth to be kept and performed by the Lessee, has leased, and does hereby lease unto the Lessee the following described property, situate in the County of **"eld** and State of **Colorado** , more particularly described as follows, to-wit:

Lot No. 43 in Colony located near Greeley. See attached list.

_____

_____

TO HAVE AND TO HOLD the above described premises unto the said Lessee for the full period xxxxxxxxxxxxxx, commencing on the **first** day of **August** , 19**24**, and ending on the **first** day of **November** , 19**25**, unless the term of this lease is sooner terminated as hereinafter provided. And the Lessee in consideration of the loasing of said premises by the Lessor does hereby covenant and agree to and with the Lessor, its successors and assigns, as follows, to-wit:

1. The Lessee will at his sole cost and expense build, construct and complete, in a good and workmanlike manner, prior to **November 1** , 19**24**, a dwelling house of _____ **3**rooms upon said leased premises, which said dwelling house shall be constructed of adobe bricks and shall be of the dimensions of **15** by **25** feet, or larger. For the purpose of constructing said dwelling house as aforesaid, said Lessee may enter upon said leased premises at any time or times between **August 1, 1924** , and **November 1** , 19**24**. The Lessor agrees that it will furnish, at its sole cost and expense, all straw, lime and gravel reasonably necessary for the construction of said dwelling house and will deliver the same on said leased premises, and said Lessor further agrees that it will advance to the Lessee during the construction of said dwelling house, on account of the cost of such lumber, doors, windows and cement as may be used in the construction thereof, a sum of money, not to exceed in the aggregate the sum of approximately **161.93** Dollars - Provided, that the said Lessor may at its sole option pay said sum of money directly to the person or persons from whom said material is purchased by the Lessee, in payment therefor, or on account thereof. The Lessee covenants and agrees to repay to the Lessor one-third of any amount so advanced by the Lessor to the Lessee or on his account, on or before the **first** day of **November** , 19**25**, and to pay a like amount on or before the **first** day of **November** , in each of the years 19**26** and 19**27**, without interest.

2. That the Lessee will occupy said dwelling house as his place of residence during the entire term of this agreement and will at his sole cost and expense at all times during the life hereof maintain said dwelling and other improvements and the grounds and fences upon said leased premises in good order and repair and in a clean and sanitary condition, to the satisfaction of the Manager at Lessor's **Greeley** factory, and will keep said grounds and premises free from weeds, rubbish and other inflammable and objectionable material and will remove such weeds, rubbish and material therefrom, as and when requested so to do by said Manager - and the Lessee agrees that he will not permit or suffer the commission of any waste upon said leased premises, and further agrees not to use said premises for any purpose prohibited by law, or for any improper or questionable purpose whatsoever, and agrees to permit the agents of the Lessor to enter into or upon, and go through and inspect said premises at any reasonable

Courtesy of City of Greeley Museums

265

hour of the day..

3. It is expressly agreed between the parties that this lease and agreement may at the option of the Lessor be terminated and cancelled by the Lessor at any time, by the Lessor giving the Lessee 30 days written notice of such cancellation, and from and after the date of any such cancellation hereof this lease and agreement shall be of no further force or effect. Upon any such cancellation of this agreement, the Lessor shall pay to the Lessee the reasonable value at the time of the cancellation of this lease and agreement of all improvements placed upon said premises by the Lessee, less any amount or amounts then due or thereafter to become due from the Lessee to the Lessor and then unpaid; and in the event of a disagreement between the parties hereto as to the reasonable value of said improvements, the amount thereof shall be determined by three arbitrators, one of whom shall be selected by the Manager of the Lessor's said factory, another shall be selected by the Lessee, and the third shall be a person selected by the other two arbitrators. In case of the failure of the Lessee to select an arbitrator, an arbitrator for and on behalf of said Lessee shall be named and appointed by the County Assessor of said County. If in any case, the first two arbitrators so chosen shall fail to agree upon the selection of an additional arbitrator, such third arbitrator shall be designated by the County Assessor of said County. The written decision of said arbitrators, signed by any two of them, shall be binding and conclusive as to both parties.

Notice of any such cancellation of this lease and agreement may be made by letter duly addressed and mailed to the Lessee at the leased premises or by posting said notice upon the dwelling house or other building thereon.

4. It is further agreed between the parties hereto that if the Lessee shall faithfully keep and perform all the covenants and agreements by him to be kept and performed hereunder and this lease shall continue in force and effect until _____ November 1_, 19 28 and shall not have been terminated by the Lessor at any time prior thereto, the Lessor shall sell and convey said lot to the Lessee, and the Lessee shall purchase the same at and for the price of $ 30.00 , which sum shall be paid to the Lessor by the Lessee on said _____ first _____ day of _____ November _____ 19 28, and upon payment thereof on said date the Lessor shall convey said lot to the Lessee by special warranty deed in the usual form, free of all liens and encumbrances, excepting those, if any, incurred by the Lessee subsequent to the date hereof, and excepting all general and special taxes and assessments, and installments thereof, if any, due or payable subsequent to said _____ first day of _____ November _____, 19 28 and excepting also all building and other restrictions, reservations, conditions, rights of way and easements, if any, now of record affecting said property hereby leased, as to which such conveyance shall be made subject. Time is of the essence of this agreement and in case of the failure of the Lessee to pay said purchase price in full on the date last aforesaid, the agreement in this paragraph contained for the sale and conveyance of said property shall become null and void. It is further understood and agreed that in case of any termination of this lease and agreement by the Lessor prior to the date last aforesaid, the provisions of this paragraph shall thereupon be of no further force or effect.

5. The Lessee further agrees that he will not make or incur any mechanic's or other lien or encumbrance upon said described premises, and that he will not suffer, allow or permit any lien or encumbrance of any kind or character to be placed thereon.

6. The Lessee agrees that upon any termination of this lease and agreement, the Lessee will yield up possession of said land and premises and of all improvements erected thereon, unto the Lessor, in good order and repair, ordinary wear and tear only excepted.

7. The Lessee agrees that in case he shall fail for any reason to occupy said dwelling as his place of residence or shall for any reason fail to

-2-

Courtesy of City of Greeley Museums

.... therein for or during a period of nine consecutive months during the term hereof, then and in any such event, this agreement and all rights of the Lessee hereunder shall at the option of the Lessor and without notice at once expire and terminate, and that the leased premises, with all fixtures and improvements thereon, shall forthwith be and become forfeited to the Lessor, and in any such case, and/or on any cancellation of this lease as in Paragraph 3 provided, ██████████ agrees to surrender up and deliver to the Lessor the quiet and peaceful ████████ ████ ██████, ██ ██ ██████ of an ███████████ ████ ███ ███ ████ with be evicted from said premises forcibly or otherwise, with or without due process of law, and the Lessor may enter into and upon the same and take possession thereof as of its former estate.

8. It is understood that this lease and agreement is personal to the Lessee, and the Lessee agrees that he will not assign the same or any interest therein or sublet said premises or any part thereof, without the written consent of the Lessor first had and obtained.

9. The Lessee may, with the consent in writing of the Manager of said _____Greeley_____ factory, at any time during the life of this agreement, sell the said dwelling and other improvements placed upon said leased premises by the Lessee to any purchaser satisfactory to said Manager of the Lessor's said factory, provided all amounts then due or thereafter to become due from the Lessee to the Lessor shall be paid, and on the further condition that such purchaser shall at the option of the Lessor enter into an agreement running five years from its date, similar to this agreement, in which event this agreement shall concurrently therewith be mutually cancelled and terminated.

10. This agreement shall inure to and be binding upon the heirs and personal representatives of the Lessee and the successors and assigns of the Lessor.

_____

_____

_____

IN WITNESS WHEREOF, the parties hereto have executed this agreement in duplicate the day and year first above written.

THE GREAT WESTERN SUGAR COMPANY

By _____

Lessor.

Bianta granillo

Lessee.

Courtesy of City of Greeley Museums

KNOW ALL MEN BY THESE PRESENTS, That the undersigned, Bicente Granillo, for and in consideration of the sum of One Dollar ($1.00) and other good and valuable considerations to the undersigned in hand paid by Ynez Lopez, Sr., the receipt whereof is hereby acknowledged, does hereby sell, assign, transfer and set over unto said Ynez Lopez, Sr. all of the right, title and interest, both legal and equitable, of the undersigned in the undersigned's contract of purchase from The Great Western Sugar Company, a New Jersey corporation, for lot numbered forty-three (43) in Espanola Subdivision, according to the plat thereof recorded in Book 6, page 73, of the records in the office of the Recorder of Weld County, Colorado, together with all improvements thereon situate; together also with all of the right, title and interest, both legal and equitable, of the undersigned in and to said property and improvements thereon situate.

Dated this ___17"___ day of August, 1929.

Bicente granillo

Witness to Execution:

Berrell

STATE OF NEBRASKA, }
COUNTY OF _Garden_ } ss.

The foregoing instrument was acknowledged before me this ___17"___ day of August, 1929, by Bicente Granillo.

Witness my hand and official seal.

My commission expires ___Sept 18" 1934___

Berrell
Notary Public

Courtesy of City of Greeley Museums

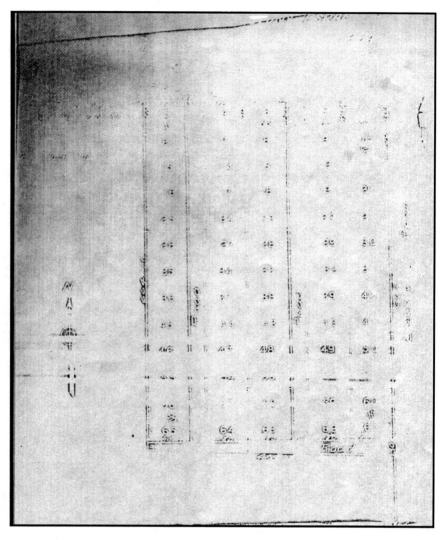

Courtesy of City of Greeley Museums

STATE OF COLORADO,
City and County of Denver. } ss.

The foregoing instrument was acknowledged before me this
_20_ day of January, 1931, by W. D. LIPPITT and S. P. SAUNDERS,
as the Vice-President and Secretary, respectively, of said The Great
Western Sugar Company, a corporation.

Witness my hand and official seal.

My commission expires _June 13, 1933_

_____ Notary Public.

Courtesy of City of Greeley Museums

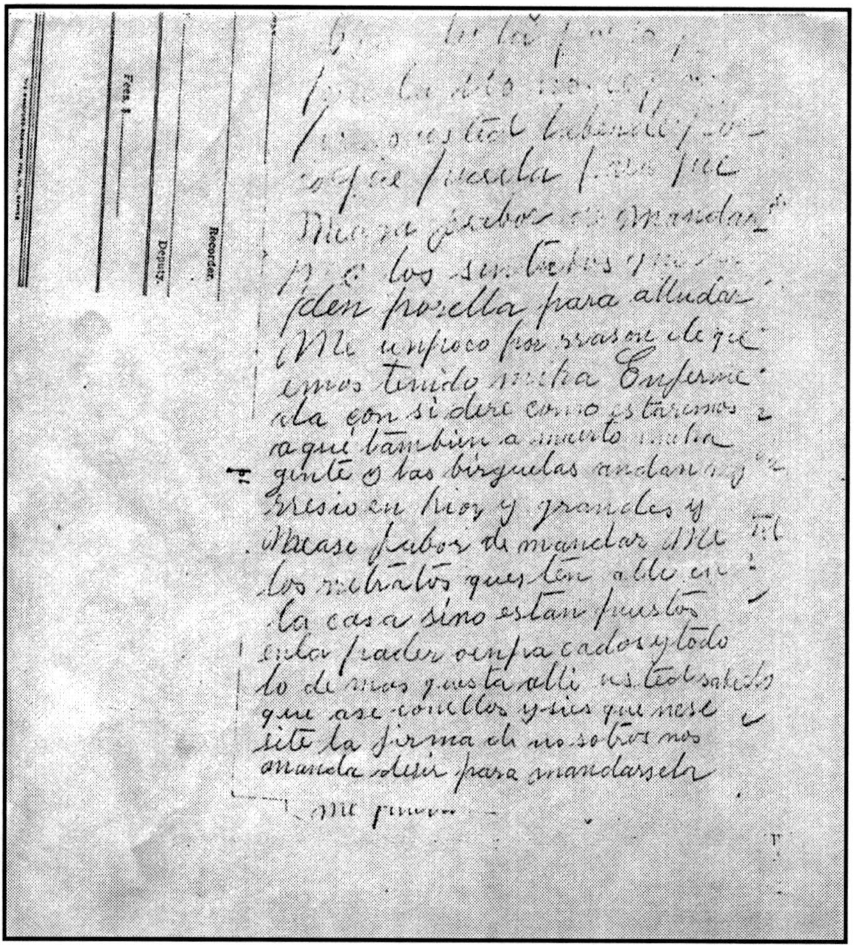

Courtesy of City of Greeley Museums

Me un y... me a todc y
Saludar me a todc y
su familia Engene
ral y me saluda a mi
compadre Crepin y a todc
la familia y me saludi
a todos los que demi
a yan buena rrecuerdos
y usted rresita los mas
gratos rrecuerdos de
Mi y toda Mi
familia JJ
Bisente Granillo
me contesta con esta division
Oshkoh, Nebea,
Bisente Granillo

... regard the ... of the payment
... up to you to see the ...
...
regard the ...
the ... to sell it for ... ever
...
send me the money you ... for
it

H. Terrell
Notary Public

Courtesy of City of Greeley Museums

272

Courtesy of City of Greeley Museums

Courtesy of City of Greeley Museums

Notary Public

Courtesy of City of Greeley Museums

Appendix D
Vato and Hood Talk

Gilbert "Gil" Carbajal, Contributor
Translated By Tito "Butter" Garcia Jr.

Vamos a refinar - vamos al refín
Lets go Eat   Lets go Eat

El jale or jalar – vamos al jale
Job   Lets go to Work

Vamos a tirar chancla
Lets go Dancing

Vamos al borlote
Go to some Doings or Dance

La ficha, el jando
Money   Money

Echar un pitaso… te hecho un pitaso
Honk Horn   Honk horn

La ranfla
Car

La huisa
Girl Friend

El chante
House

Trampar oreja
Sleep

Un frajo
A Cigarette

La mota, la yerba, la grifa… un toque
Pot (Marijuana)

El pisto… vamos a pistiar
To Booze

El tacuche
Suit (Dress Up)

A todo dar, a toda madre, que padre
That's Real Fine

Me puse pedo
Got Drunk

Hubo pedo
There was a Fight

El vacil, andaba vacilando
Go on a Date or Taking out a Girl

La fila
Knife

El cuete
Gun

Orale cuate
What's Happening Buddy

El jefe, la jefa
Dad   Mom

Me vaciló
He made a Dummy out of Me or Jived Me

Torció
Turn or Passed Away

Que gacho
Really Bad

Tirar la mesa
Go to the Bathroom (Bowl Movement)

La chamba
Job

Pura Madera… es maderista
Over Complimenting oneself, **Bragging**

La teórica… le gusta teoricar
Talk

De volada
Instantly

Pachuco Talk
Tito "Butter" Garcia Jr., Contributor

This portion is about the *Pachuco* talk he learned in San Francisco, California. Butter said, "This way of talking originated in El Paso, Texas. It was then taken to California in 1941 during World War II.

Butter explained, "The migration from El Paso to California was due to the jobs at defense plants. San Francisco was not as tough or bad as Los Angeles. Mary Lopez and I went to a dance at the Suites Ball Room in San Francisco. On Sunday, they had Rumba, and Mambo dances there. It was strictly Chicanos or Hispanics or Latinos.

Because of the Zoot Suit riot in L.A., anyone wearing that type of clothing was searched at the doors. I was wearing a Semi Pant Suit; it was just like the Zoot Suit but not as tight at the ankle. The Zoot Suit was banned in California. But anyone wearing the suit was considered to be in a gang."

Following are some Pachuco expressions:
"Me acabé de refinar un salva vidas con escante de chanate y estaba bute y ha madre.

I just finished a cup of coffee and a doughnut, and it was really good or it hit the spot."

"Nel ese carnal, ha mi me la filipe en Juarez, para la catorse venida de la cachetona, sin per huisio de una pinche rosa flaca.

You can play with my (wahoo), you don't scare me. If you have a weapon (knife) we can go outside and settle this."

"Se me hace que si lo mandaba por aqua.
Ni las cantinas me mojaba ese.

*You don't even hold water, (I don't sweat you).
You can't even wet my canteens."*

"Y si trai to lolochi, pa jualires donde se poninas ese.

And if you have a knife, then lets go outside, where we can settle this."

"Le heche una dima al estrambouca y me le lleva hasta Wilma's.

Put a dime in the streetcar and it will take you to Wilma's, you can get a transfer to another streetcar from there."

"Y lleger a Los (Los Angeles) con cual feriecita de cuatro cientos grandes.

I got to Los Angeles with some change about $400.00 in my pockets."

"Me apanie un tachuchi a toda madre y me fui a tirar chancla.

I put on my suit and I look really good (or look fine)."

"Y me puse de pipa y guante.

I got all decked out (upper class like, with a pipe and gloves)."

"Toda madre *(mother)*.

Real fine."

Appendix E

Zoot Suit

This is the author's son, Mario Lopez (left) and Mario's Great Uncle, Palmer Lopez (right) modeling Zoot Suits.

Picture taken in summer of 2002 in Denver and Greeley, Colorado. Courtesy of Gabriel Lopez

Notice how the pant cuff is tight at the ankle, causing the pants to "balloon" from the ankle to the waist. Notice the difference between the pants seen here and the Semi-Zoot Suit pants shown on page 41.

280

Gilbert "Gil" Carbajal, Contributor
These are the sayings remembered from childhood.

Aphorism se puede traducir figurado, literalmente o conceptual.
Aphorisms can be translated/stated figuratively, literally or
conceptually.

1. A buen hambre no hay pan duro.
When you're really hungry, no such thing as bad food (beggars can't
be choosers).

2. A camino largo, paso corto.
When you have a long road to walk, short steps will keep you from
tiring.

3. A donde el corazón se inclina el pie camina.
Wherever the heart goes, the feet will follow.

4. A mal tiempo buena cara.
When things are bad, fake a smile.

5. Amor con amor se paga.
Wrong love repays itself.

6. Antes de decir de otro-cojo es mirate los pies.
Before you criticize another, have a look at yourself.

7. Antes de hablar es bueno pensar.
Think before you speak.

8. Antes que te cases mira lo que haces.
Before you marry, think it through.

9. A su tiempo maduran las uvas.
Good things take time.

10. Caballo que vuela no quiere espuela.
A wild horse doesn't want to be tamed.

11. Cada día que amanece el número de tontos crece.
With each new day, another fool is born.

12. Cada oveja con su pareja.
To each his own.(We each have different tastes).

13. Casa sin mujer pobre ha de ser.
A home without a woman is an incomplete home.

14. *Cien refranes, cien verdades*.
A hundred proverbs, a hundred truths.
15. *Comprar barata es gran riqueza.*
Frugal buying brings great riches.
16. *Con un buen traje se cubre mal linaje.*
A good façade hides a bad past.
17. *Cortesia de boca, mucho vale y poco cuesta.*
Kind work is worth a lot and cost little.
18. *Cuando está abierto el cajón el más honrado es ladrón.*
When money lies unguarded, even an honorable person becomes a thief.
19. *Cuando estamos buenos damos consejos a los enfermos.*
When we're healthy, then we can counsel the sick.
20. *Cuando la vieja tiene dinero no tiene carne el carnero.*
When we have money to shop, we can't find what we want.
21. *Cuando la zorra predica, no están seguros los pollos.*
When a fox is present, the chickens are not safe.
22. *De la mano a la boca se pierde la sopa.*
We shouldn't make a living "hand to mouth."
23. *De médico, poeta y loco todos tenemos un poco.*
We each have a little talent of doctor, poet, and fool.
24. *Diez mujeres, cien pareceres.*
Ten women, one hundred opinions.
25. *Dijo el muerto al dinero – Para nada te quiero.*
Said the dead man to money, "I don't need you any more."
26. *Discreción es saber disimular lo que no se puede remediar.*
Discretion is knowing what we can solve and that which we can't.
27. *Donde hay amor hay dolor.*
Where there is love, there is pain.
28. *Mejor lo proprio que lo bueno.*
Better to do what's right than to do what's good.
29. *Mejor respetado que aceptado.*
Better to be respected than accepted.
30. *El Reino de Diós es recibido no Ganado.*
Salvation is received not achieved.
31. *Donde menos se piensa salta la liebre.*
Challenges in life surface when least expected.
32. *El acusar es fácil, lo difícil es probar.*
To accuse is easy, to prove is difficult.

33. El amor es dulce carga, pero al fin amarga (cuidalo y no se amarga).

To love is a sweet burden however, it can turn bitter.

34. El amor y los cellos son hermanos gemelos.

Love and jealousy are twins.

35. El bien no es conocido hasta que es perdido.

The good in life isn't recognized until it's lost.

36. El bien que se hace hoy constituye la felicidad de manana.

Doing good today brings joy tomorrow.

37. El consejo de la mujer es poco, y el que no lo toma es loco.

A women's counsel is little and the one who doesn't take it is a fool.

38. El día de placer vispera es de pesar.

A new day brings joy after an evening of stress.

39. El día que me casé, Buena cadena me eché.

The day I married, I was linked to a good chain.

40. El día que no me afeité vino a mi casa quien no se.

The day I didn't dress up was the day a stranger visited.

41. El dolor de viudo cortito y agudo.

A widower's pain is sharp but short.

42. El ejercicio hace maestro.

Exercise makes you healthy.

43. El oro es rey del mundo.

Gold is king. (Gold rules).

44. El que adelante no mira, atrás se queda.

He who doesn't plan will be left behind in life.

45. El que bien te quiera te hará llorar.

The one who really loves you will also bring tears.

46. El que oye y se calla un tesoro se halla.

He who keeps his mouth shut will learn a lot.

47. El que larga vida vive, mucho mal ha de pasar.

The longer one lives, the more challenges there will be.

48. El río pasado, el santo olvidado.

In time, all difficulty is forgotten.

49. El tiempo es oro.

Time is precious.

50. En buen día, buenas obras.

On good days, produce much.

51. En cada legua hay un pedazo de mal camino.

On every journey, there is a short period of hard times.

52. En la boca cerrada no entran moscas.
Flies don't enter a closed mouth.
53. En el hombre prudencia, y en la mujer paciencia.
Men are wise, women are patient.
54. En una mentira te cogí, y nunca más te creí.
When caught in a lie, it's difficult to be trusted again.
55. Entre dos perros amigos echa un hueso y los verás enemigos.
Feed two hungry friends only one piece of food and they'll become enemies.
56. Es cosa fácil añadir a lo ya inventado.
It's easy to add to which has already been figured out by someone else.
57. Febrero es loco y marzo otro poco.
February is bad weather, March is worse.
58. Cada quien paga las que debe.
We each pay the price for our misdeeds.
59. Dime con quien andas y te digo lo que eres.
Tell me who your friends are and I'll tell you what kind of person you are.
60. Cada quien con su papalote.
Each with his own likes and dislikes.
61. Gran amor es gran dolor.
Great love brings great pain.
62. Gran caballero es Don Dinero.
A "great friend" is Mr. Money.
63. Goza de su poco mientras busca más el loco.
Most are happy with sufficient but fools want more and more.
64. Hablar sin pensar es tirar sin apuntar.
To speak without thinking is to shoot without aiming.
65. Hay más refranes que panes.
There is more (Unwanted) advice than there is food.
66. Haz bien y no mires a quien.
Do good to all and expect nothing in return.
67. La fortuna de un loco es encontrarse con otro.
The luck of a fool is to meet another fool.
68. La gran dama debe tener tres ezas: Belleza, nobleza y riqueza.
A great lady should possess these three…beauty, nobility, prosperity.

69. La mujer sabe una palabra más que el Diablo.
A woman always knows at least one more word than satan.

70. La música y la poesía no toleran medianía (El amor, el exito, etc).
Music and poetry do not tolerate mediocrity.

71. La pereza es llave de la pobreza.
Laziness is a step toward poverty.

72. La pobreza tiene por amiga la tristeza.
The sister to poverty is sadness.

73. Larga ausencia causa olvida.
Absence makes the heart go fonder.

74. La fortuna nos da el bien y el mal.
Luck brings both good and bad.

75. Las mujeres y los jarros de barro no se pueden devolver.
Women and clay jars can't be exchanged.

76. Leer y comer, despacio los has de hacer.
Reading and eating…do them both slowly.

77. Loca es la oveja que al lobo se confiesa.
Foolish is the girl who gives her all to a playboy.

78. Los hermanos y los gatos, todos ingrates.
Siblings and cats…both unappreciative.

79. Los niños y los borrachos siempre dicen la verdad.
Children and drunks always spill the truth.

80. Los refranes te daran consejo y alivio en sus afanes.
With eagerness, proverbs provide counsel and relief.

81. Lo que de prisa se escribe, despacio se llora.
What is written carelessly and quickly, slowly brings tears.

82. Lo que has de hacer una vez, medítalo diez.
Do things right the first time around.

83. Lo que mucho vale, mucho cuesta.
That which is valuable demands a great price.

84. Llorando y riendo, va el niño aprendiendo.
As one cries and laughs, a person learns.

85. Mal amigo y mal amor olvidarlos es major.
A bad friend and bad love, best to forget both.

86. Mal va al enfermo que nombre a su médico heredero.
It is wise to name your doctor as Executor of your will.

87. Marido celoso no come ni duerme con resposo.
A jealous husband doesn't eat or sleep in peace.

88. *Amar no es pecar.*
To love is not a sin.

89. *Amor de lo lejos es para los pendejos.*
Long distance love is for fools.

90. *Cada cabeza es un mundo.*
Each mind is a world of its own.

91. *Mas ablanda el dinero que palabras de caballero.*
Money smoothes easier than a gentlemen's words.

92. *Mas cerca estan mis dientes que mis parientes.*
My teeth are closer to me than my relatives.

93. *Mas enseña la necesidad que diez años de universidad.*
Necessity is a better teacher than ten years of college.

94. *Mas sabe el necio en su casa que el cuerdo en la ajena.*
A fool knows more in his own home than a wise person in a stranger's home.

95. *Mas puede un necio negar que Aristóteles probar.*
It's easier for a fool to lie than a prophet to prove something.

96. *Mas son los amenazados que los acuchillados.*
Threats are more common than action upon those threats.

97. *Mas vale callar lo que sabe que decir lo que no se sabe.*
Better to keep quiet about what you know than to talk about what you don't know.

98. *Mas vale pájaro en mano que ciento volando.*
A bird in hand is worth more than 100 in flight.

99. *Mas vale tarde que nunca.*
Better late than never.

100. *Mas vale una onza de práctica que una libra de gramática.*
An ounce of action is worth more than a pound of talk.

101. *Mientras hay vida, la esperanza no se pérdida.*
Where there is life, there is hope.

102. *Mientras que en mí casa estoy, rey soy.*
When I'm in my home, I am king.

103. *Mejor es evitar que remediar.*
Better to avoid than to repair.

104. *Mujer celosa, leona furiosa.*
Jealous woman, furious lioness.

105. *Ninguno que beba vino llame borracho a su vecino.*
Whoever drinks wine can't call his neighbor a drunk.

106. Ni un dedo hace mano, ni una golondrina verano.
One finger does not a hand make nor does one swallow mean it's summer.

107. No es oro todo lo que reluce.
Not everything that glitters is gold.

108. No es sabio el que mucho sabe, sino el que l importante sabe.
The wise person is one who knows the important not the one who knows a lot.

109. No firmes carta que no leas; no bebas agua que no veas.
Don't sign a paper you haven't read; don't drink water you haven't seen.

110. No hay bueno que no pueda ser major, ni malo que no pueda ser peor.
There's nothing so good it can't be better or bad that can't get worse.

111. No hay espejo major que amigo Viejo.
There's no better mirror than an old friend.

112. No hay mal que dure cien anos.
A bad thing can't last long.

113. No hay mal que por bien no venga.
Every adversity has a seed of equal or better benefit.

114. No hay mayor pena que perder una mujer Buena.
There's no bigger loss than to lose a good woman.

115. No hay rosa sin espina.
Every rose has thorn.

116. No te cases con mujer que te gane el saber.
Don't marry a woman who knows more than you.

117. No te cases con viejo por la moneda; el dinero se acaba y el viejo queda.
Don't marry an old man for his money, the money is gone and he just gets older.

118. Atraes lo que eres no lo que quieres.
You attract what you are not what you want.

119. Oír, ver y callar son cosas de gran preciar.
To listen, observe and keep quiet are great attributes.

120. Palabra suelta no tiene vuelta.
You can't take back an uncalled-for word.

121. Para muestra basta un boton.
It takes very little to model the good.

122. Peso cambiado es caballo desbocado.
To relieve a burden is like unbridling a horse.
123. Poco a poco se va lejos.
Little by little, most everything is forgotten.
124. Por el dinero se mueve el mundo.
Money makes the world go around.
125. Por la boca muére el pez.
A fish gets hooked because he opens his mouth.
126. Preguntando acá y alla, a todas partes se va.
An inconsistent person is an unreliable person.
127. Quien bien te quiera te hara llorar.
The one who loves you a lot will make you cry.
128. Quien busca, halla.
Seek and you shall find.
129. Quien canta sus males espanta.
The complainer chases people away.
130. Quien compra sin poder, venda sin querer.
He who buys foolishly will sell foolishly.
131. Quien díce lo que siente se expone a sentir lo que dice.
You get what you speak, you get what you expect.
132. Quien mucho duerme poco aprende.
He who sleeps a lot learns little.
133. Quien sólo come su gallo, sólo ensilla su caballo.
The loner will always be lonely.
134. Quien supo olvidar no supo amar.
He who forgets easily doesn't know real life.
135. Quieres perder el amigo más verdadero? Prestale dinero.
Want to lose your best friend…lend him money.
136. Quiero cantar ahora que tengo gana por si acaso me toca llorar mañana.
I want to sing now in case I have to cry later.
137. Quien mucho habla, mucho yerra.
He who speaks much will error much.
138. Quien no se aventura no pasa la mar.
He who explores little learns little.
139. Quien se acuesta con perros, se levanta con pulgas.
He who sleeps with dogs awakens with lice.
140. Quien se casa por amores ha de vivir con Dolores.
When you marry for love, there will be pain.

141. Quien se viste de mal pano, dos veces se viste al ano.
A bad dresser changes clothes only twice a year.

142. Reír con exceso es señal de poco seso.
He who laughs loudly has little brain.

143. Respeta la autoridad si quieres tranquilidad.
Respect authority if you want tranquility.

144. Riendo se va aprendiendo.
As you laugh, you learn.

145. Secreto dicho a mujer, secreto deja de ser.
If you want a secret to be no more, tell a woman.

146. Gato escondido, cola de fuera.
Half-hidden truths will eventually be revealed.

147. A cada perrito, le toca su tiempesito.
Every dog has his day.

148. Si quieres saber quien eres, preguntalo a tu vecino.
If you want to know who you really are, ask the neighbor.

149. Si quieres dichoso verte, conformate con su suerte.
If you want to be happy, be satisfied with what life gives you.

150. Si te cierra una puerta, otro hallaras abierta.
If a door closes on you, open another.

151. Sin hijos y sin cellos no hay desconsuelos.
No children, no jealousies, no discontentment.

152. Sin mujeres y sin comeres, no hay placers.
No women, no food, no pleasures.

153. Sin mujeres y sin vientos, tendriamos menos tormentos.
No women, no windstorm, no difficulties.

154. Si el remedio no alcanza la dolencia, major medicina es la paciencia.
Patience is good medicine.

155. Sobre gustos no hay nada escrito.
Happiness is not a prescribed emotion.

156. Tal padre, tal hijo.
Like father, like son.

157. Tiempo pasado, major olvidado.
Forget the past.

158. Tiempo pasado traído a memoria da más pena que Gloria.
Bad memories bring pain not glory.

159. Todo se acaba y el dinero antes de todo.
Everything disappears, especially money.

160. Tío rico siempre tiene mucho sobrinos.
A rich uncle always has many nieces and nephews.

161. Tus secretos no diras, si quieres vivir en paz.
To live in peace, keep secrets to yourself.

162. Tenemos que bailar al son que se toca.
We have learned to roll with the punches of life.

163. Todo se parece a su dueño.
Everything resembles its originator.

164. Un grano no hace granero, pero ayuda a su compañero.
Every little bit helps.

165. Un diablo bien vestido por un ángel es tenido.
The devil in disguise looks like an angel.

166. Vive cien años y versa desengaños.
If you live to be a hundred, you'll finally figure out life.

167. Vaca de muchos, bien ordenada y mal alimentada.
Don't spread yourself too thin and become worthless.

168. Vale más sabre que tener.
It's better to be knowledgeable than to own.

169. Verdades y rosas tienen espinas.
The truth hurts.

170. Vivir para ver, y ver para vivir.
To live is to see, to see is to live.

171. Ya que la casa se quema icalentemonos!
Turn the bad into the good. (Make lemonade from lemons).

172. Dijo el sabio: "Ya me voy, aqui los dejo,
   que el hombre más vivo,
   viva del más pendejo."
Said the sage…I'm leaving now.
   May the wise,
   Live off the foolish!

Appendix G

1930 Federal Census

Precinct 16, Gibson, Weld County, Colorado

Spanish Colony entries with the family of Salazar, Dimas on line 22

1930 Federal Census

Precinct 16, Gibson, Weld County, Colorado

State: Colorado
County: Weld
Township or other division of county: Gibson Precinct 16

Line	Dwelling	Family	Name	Relation	Home Data	Sex	Color	Age	Marital	Age at Marriage	School	Read/Write	Birthplace	Father	Mother
51			Garcia—August	son		M	W	20	S		No	Yes	New Mexico	New Mexico	
52			Nestor	son		M	W	17	M?		Yes	Yes	New Mexico	New Mexico	
53			Dan?	son		M	W	10	S		Yes	Yes	New Mexico	New Mexico	
54			William	son		M	W	5	S				Colorado	New Mexico	
55	134	123	Badilla, John	Head	O 200	M	W	60	M		No	No	New Mexico	New Mexico	
56			Maria	wife-H		F	W	36	M	16	No	No	New Mexico	New Mexico	
57			Juanita	daughter		F	W	20	S		No	No	New Mexico	New Mexico	
58			Cornelia	son		M	W	19	S			No	New Mexico	New Mexico	
59			Jane	daughter		F	W	17	S		Yes	Yes	New Mexico	New Mexico	
60			Henry	son		M	W	16	S		Yes	Yes	New Mexico	New Mexico	
61			Bell?	daughter		F	W	14	S		Yes	Yes	New Mexico	New Mexico	
62			Joe	son		M	W	12	S		Yes	Yes	New Mexico	New Mexico	
63			Minnie	daughter		F	W	9	S				New Mexico	New Mexico	
64			Ramon	son		M	W	6	S		No		New Mexico	New Mexico	
65			Margie	daughter		F	W	4	S				New Mexico	New Mexico	
66			Alfonso	son		M	W	3	S				Colorado	New Mexico	
67						M	W	1	S				Colorado	New Mexico	
68	135	124	Sato, ...	Head	O 300	M	W	48	M	33	No	No	Old Mexico	Old Mexico	
69			Benita	wife-H		F	W	39	M	14	No	No	Texas	Old Mexico	
70			Tony	daughter		F	W	13	S		Yes	Yes	Kansas	Old Mexico	
71			Joe	son		M	W	11	S		Yes	Yes	Colorado	Old Mexico	
72			Junita	son?		M	W	9	S		Yes	Yes	Colorado	Old Mexico	
73			Castul	son		M	W	7	S		Yes	Yes	Colorado	Old Mexico	
74			Henor	son		M	W	5	S		No		Colorado	Old Mexico	
75			Louis	daughter		F	W	3	S		No		Colorado	Old Mexico	
76			Feliciano	son		M	W	1	S		No		Colorado	Old Mexico	
77	136	125	Aterica, Patricia	Head	R cash	M	W	44	M	19	No	No	New Mexico	New Mexico	
78			Jenita	wife-H		F	W	38	M	19	No	No	New Mexico	New Mexico	
79			Rose	daughter		F	W	10	S		Yes	Yes	Arizona	New Mexico	
80			Eulalia	daughter		F	W	8	S		No	No	New Mexico	New Mexico	
81			Domitilia	daughter		F	W	3	S				Colorado	New Mexico	
82	137	126	Catorga, Alfonsa	Head-H	W—	F	W	40	Wd	20	No	No	Old Mexico	Old Mexico	
83			Joe	son		M	W	16	S		Yes	Yes	Old Mexico	Old Mexico	
84			Lee	son		M	W	13	S		Yes	Yes	Texas	Old Mexico	
85			Jose	son		M	W	9	S		Yes	Yes	Nebraska	Old Mexico	
86			Manuel	son		M	W	7	S		No		Colorado	Old Mexico	
87			Petra	daughter		F	W	5	S		No		Kansas	Old Mexico	
88			Victoria	daughter		F	W	3	S		No		Colorado	Old Mexico	
89	138	127	Marquez, Querito	Head		M	W	46	M	30	No	No	New Mexico	New Mexico	
90	121		Trinidad	wife-H	O 70	F	W	44	M	11	No	No	New Mexico	New Mexico	
91			Cana	daughter		F	W	16	S		No	No	New Mexico	New Mexico	
92			Tom	son		M	W	16	S		No	Yes	New Mexico	New Mexico	
93			Familia	son		M	W	16	S		No		New Mexico	New Mexico	
94			Bonnard	son		M	W	12	S		Yes	Yes	New Mexico	New Mexico	
95			Ramos	son		M	W	13	S		Yes	Yes	New Mexico	New Mexico	
96			Augustina	daughter		F	W	11	S		Yes	Yes	New Mexico	New Mexico	
97			Effie	daughter		F	W	12	S		Yes	Yes	New Mexico	New Mexico	
98			Galinda, Grace	wife?		F	W	31	M	21	No	No	Old Mexico	Old Mexico	
99			Caroline			M	W	5	S		No		Colorado	Old Mexico	

1930 Federal Census

Precinct 16, Gibson, Weld County, Colorado

1930 Federal Census

Precinct 16, Gibson, Weld County, Colorado

1930 Federal Census

Precinct 16, Gibson, Weld County, Colorado

Spanish Colony ends with the family of Deleo, Pandaleon on lines 34 - 37

295

1930 Federal Census

Precinct 50, Pierce, Weld County, Colorado

Greeley Spanish Colony residents on lines 9 and 17

1930 Federal Census

Precinct 18, Crow Creek, Weld County, Colorado

Greeley Spanish Colony residents on lines 84 and 89

1930 Federal Census

Precinct 34, Lucerne, Weld County, Colorado

Greeley Spanish Colony resident on line 46

1930 Colorado Census   Weld County   District 54

Bibliography

Audio, Video Interviews in reference collection at City of Greeley Museums

Aragon, Edna (Sept. 1999, Nov. 2000, Feb. 2004)

Blatnick, John (April 2003)

Carbajal, Frank (Aug. 2003)

Carbajal, Gil (Feb. 2003)

Cassel, Kate (Feb. 2002)

Chavez, Lloyd (Mar. 2003)

Crosier, Bill (April 2003)

Duran, Robert (June 2003)

Espinosa, Moses (Dec. 2002)

Fiechter, Delilah (Feb. 2003)

Garcia, Alvin (numerous interviews 2002-2004)

Garcia, Claudie (July 2004)

Garcia, Josie (Jan. & Feb. 2004)

Garcia, Tito Jr. (Mar. & Aug. 2002)

Gomez, Jess (Mar. 2003)

Hinojosa, Emma (Jan. 2003)

Jojola, Art (Jan. 2003)

Leal, Carlos (June 2003)

Lind, Bob (June 2003)

Lopez, David (numerous interviews 2002-2003)

Lopez, Frank (Aug. 2002, 2003)

Lopez, Jerry (Jan. 2003)

Lopez, Nudy (Aug. 2002, Feb 2004)

Lopez, Palmer (Mar. 2002)

Lopez, Ricardo (Feb. 2002, Dec. 2002)

Lopez, Sam (Jan. 2003)

Maese, Gene (Jan. 2003)

Marquez, Jose Jr. (Mar. 2002)

Martinez, Gus & Mary, (June 2002)

Nuanez, Robert (June 2003)

Ortiz, Florence (Summer 2003)

Padilla, Joe (numerous interviews2003)

Riddoch, Greg & Linda (Aug. 2003)

Rios, Lola (Spring 2003)

Rodman, Dorothy (Feb. 2004)

Rucobo, Char (April 2003)

Sadler, Lorraine (July 2004)

Sadler, Woodson (July 2004)

Salazar, Beatrice (2003)

Salazar, Secundino (Jan. 2004)

Salazar, Selustriano (Feb. 2003)

Schultz, Bernard Reverend (2004)

Solis, Carmen & Dan (Summer 2002)

Solis, Alice (Summer 2002)

Steele, Dwight (April 2003)

Steele, Jack (June 2003)

Stewart, Catherine (Jan. 2003)

Sullivan, Rick (Aug. 2003)

Swanson, Brad (Aug. 2003)

Tellez, George (Aug. 2004)

Weekley, Carmen Lozano (numerous interviews 2004)

Newspapers, Magazines, Journals, and Scrapbooks

Coloradoan Today, 1934

Denver Mile High Magazine, June/July 2003

Hispanic Colorado: The Colorado Chronicles, Volume 4

La Familia Genealogy Society Newsletter, Nov. 2002,Volume 1, Issue 2

Raices Y Ramos Journal, "Colony Past and Present", 1991 Volume 1, #3

The Greeley Booster, 1934 - 1940 (numerous articles)

The Greeley Tribune, 1924 – 2006 (numerous articles)

The Greeley Woman's Club, 1924-1948, *Scrapbook*, Volume 1

The Weld County News, 1932 (numerous articles)

The Wyoming Tribune, July 12,1952

Through The Leaves, 1913 – 1936

Books

Anaya, Rudolfo. (1999) *My Land Sings: Stories from the Rio Grande*

Baek, Warren A. (1962) *New Mexico: A History of four centuries*

Byrne, C.E. (March, 1946) *"Imprimature"* Hymnal

Cobos, Ruben. (1983) *A Dictionary of New Mexico and Southern Colorado Spanish*

Echevarria, Evelio, and Otero, Jose. *Hispanic Colorado Four Centuries: History and Heritage,* Centennial Publication, Fort Collins, Colorado

Hugner, Henry. (1927) *A History of the Beet Sugar Industry of Northern Colorado*

Morera, Dominic Rev. (Feb. 1955) *Alabemos Los Dulces Nombres: Traditional Spanish Hymns*

Onis, Jose de. (1976) *The Hispanic Contribution to the State of Colorado*

Rolph, George M. (1917) *Something About Sugar*

Shwayder, Carol Rein. (1992) *Weld County Old and New People and Places,* Volume 3

Steinel, Alvin Theodore. (1926) *History of Agriculture in Colorado 1858-1926*

Internet Search

www.archives.state.co.us/ccc/cccscope.html, "Civilian Conservation Corps in Colorado," and "Workers in Progress Association Projects" viewed March 2003

www.austin.cc.tx.us/lpatrick/his2341/new.html National Youth Administration viewed June 2004

www.farmworkers.org/benglish.html, "Bracero Program" viewed March 2003

www.greeleytrib.com/apps/pbcs.dll/section?Category=WORLDSAPART viewed July 2004 www.leaonline.com/doi/pdfplus/10.1207 Sugar Beets, Segregation, and Schools: viewed July 20,2004

www.library.ci.co.fortcollins.co.us/local_history/Topics/Ethnic/Mex-rules.htm viewed July 20,2004

www.musicalspanish.com/flashdemo3.htm, "Las Mananitas" viewed August 2003

www.postalmuseum.si.edu/exhibits/2d2a_vmail.html, "V-Mail WWII" viewed June 2004

www.socqrl.niu.edu/forest/Moore.html, "History: An American Minority Appears," "Early History of the Mexicans: To 1900" viewed March 2003

www.timewitnesses.org/english/food/Rations.html, "Wartime (and postwar) rations" viewed June 2004

www.vietnampix.com/intro.htm, "The Viet Nam Wars" viewed July 2004

Theses

E. Andrade. (1971). *A Descriptive Analysis of Schools for Migratory Children in Northern Colorado 1969 – 1970.* (Masters Degree Thesis, University Northern Colorado)

Esther K. Schillinger. (August 1929). *Social Contacts of the Immigrant Mexicans of Weld County.* (Masters Degree Thesis, Colorado State College)

Hazel C. Maddux. (June 1932). *Some Conditions Which Influence the Mexican Children in Greeley, Colorado, and it's Vicinity.* (Masters Degree Thesis, Colorado State College)

M. Darling. (1932). *Americanization of Foreign – Born in Greeley, Colorado.* (Masters Degree Thesis, Colorado State College)

Miscellaneous

City of Greeley, Colorado, Public Works, Division – GIS maps

Colorado State Archives

Federal Census (1930). Department of Commerce- Bureau of the Census,

Fifteenth Census of The United States

Greeley - Evans (Colorado) School District Six, Board Minutes 1929-1954

Greeley Grays Reunion, August 2003, City of Greeley Museum, Greeley, Colorado. Video recording of reunion events by Richard Merrill Jr., and B. Solis.

Greeley, Colorado City Directories 1928- 1965

The Northern Colorado Conference on Minority Problems of Spanish Speaking People (Sunday May 10, 1942) House of Neighborly Collections, City of Greeley Museums.

Our Lady of Peace (Catholic Church), Greeley, Colorado.
Dedication Pamphlet (1949)

Rocky Mountain League Semi-Pro Baseball Reunion, March 2002, Fort Collins Museum, Fort Collins, Colorado. Video of proceedings, by Gabriel Lopez

Rodman, Dorothy. Manuscript, Feb. 2004, *Traditional Health Practitioners*

Weld County Clerk and Recorder, Greely, Colorado. Land Records

Weld County Public Health and Environment, Greeley, Colorado.

304

305

Fiechter, Delilah Gomez, 68, 93,
94, 103, 148
field workers, 3, 154
Fink, Miss, 147
fireflies, 92
First United Presbyterian Church
of Greeley, Colorado, 155
flowers, 16, 27, 63, 64, 67, 75, 88,
113, 159
folklore, x, 74, 89
food, 251
box lunch, 130
candy, 77, 96, 98, 102, 103,
105, 124, 149, 229
carrots, 49
green beans, 47, 48
hot lunches, 162
kelites, 123
masa, 130
onion, 4, 47, 48, 49, 123
pinto beans, 252
potatoes, 2, 4, 47, 48, 49, 98,
123, 127
ristra, 68
Forbes Field, 240
Ford, Peggy A., i, iii, iv, 44, 254
Forman, George, 246
Foreman, Neil, 239
Fort Bragg, North Carolina, 207
Fort Campbell, Kentucky, 206
Fort Collins, Colorado, 75, 128,
148, 231, 233, 236, 238, 239,
244
Fort Collins Legionnaires, 231,
239, 244
Fort Collins Merchants, 239
Fort Collins Rebels, 239
Fort Collins Spanish American
Baseball Team, 239
Fort Leonard Wood, Missouri, 207
Fort Lupton, Colorado, 13, 231,
239
Fort Lupton Eagles, 231, 239
Fort Morgan, Colorado, 13
Fort Morgan, Colorado facility,
252

Foster, Don, 245
Fountain, John, Dr., 35
Frankfurt, Germany, 209
French, 89
French, Bob, 239
Ft. Holabird, MD, 210
Fuqua, J.W., 165

Galeton, Colorado, 8, 244
Galinda, Caroline, 292
Galinda, Conca, 292
Galinda, Joe, 292
gambling, 99, 120, 121
games, x, 99, 110, 125, 157, 229,
232, 236, 240, 242, 244, 246
bolitas negro y blanca, 119
boxing, 120, 127, 129
carnivals, 118
Chinese checkers, 119
conicos, 97
crack-the-whip, 122
doll house, 146
dressed up, 69, 118
hide-'n'-seek, 119
ice skated, 122
kick-the-can, 118, 124
marbles, 118, 119, 120, 121
pinball, 103, 149
rivalote, 119
stilts, 118, 122
wrestling, 129
Garcia, Abraham "Abe", 117, 235,
239
Garcia, Abram, 98, 297
Garcia, Alfred, 157
Garcia, Alvin, 32, 35, 36, 37, 45, 46,
63, 69, 77, 78, 79, 96, 97, 98, 100,
102, 103, 104, 105, 110, 114, 117,
120, 127, 128, 129, 131, 132, 134,
174, 216, 211, 222, 227, 228, 230,
231, 232, 297
Garcia, August, 292
Garcia, Beatrice, 291
Garcia, Claudie, 117, 129, 235
Garcia, Deciderio, 291
Garcia, Dorotea, 297

308

310

311

312

313

315

317

Printed in the United States
150945LV00002B/158/A

9 781425 995621